Competitiveness and Private Sector Development

Enhancing Competitiveness in Central Asia

OECD
BETTER POLICIES FOR BETTER LIVES

This work is published under the responsibility of the Secretary-General of the OECD. The opinions expressed and arguments employed herein do not necessarily reflect the official views of OECD member countries.

This document, as well as any data and any map included herein, are without prejudice to the status of or sovereignty over any territory, to the delimitation of international frontiers and boundaries and to the name of any territory, city or area.

Please cite this publication as:
OECD (2018), *Enhancing Competitiveness in Central Asia*, Competitiveness and Private Sector Development, OECD Publishing, Paris.
http://dx.doi.org/10.1787/9789264288133-en

ISBN 978-92-64-28812-6 (print)
ISBN 978-92-64-28813-3 (PDF)

Series: Competitiveness and Private Sector Development
ISSN 2076-5754 (print)
ISSN 2076-5762 (online)

The statistical data for Israel are supplied by and under the responsibility of the relevant Israeli authorities. The use of such data by the OECD is without prejudice to the status of the Golan Heights, East Jerusalem and Israeli settlements in the West Bank under the terms of international law.

Photo credits: Cover © designed by Renaud Madigner

Corrigenda to OECD publications may be found on line at: *www.oecd.org/about/publishing/corrigenda.htm*.

Foreword

Kazakhstan, Kyrgyzstan, Mongolia, Tajikistan, Turkmenistan and Uzbekistan have recorded impressive economic growth rates since 2000, driven mainly by the export of commodities and labour. However, the end of the commodity super-cycle and the economic slowdown that followed have highlighted the risks inherent in this reliance on minerals exports and remittances, as well as the challenges to be overcome to achieve more stable and inclusive growth.

The Central Asian countries have long recognised the importance of enhancing the competitiveness of their economies, diversifying the production structures and improving resilience to external shocks. This will require ambitious reforms in the areas of governance, connectivity, and business environment.

This publication focuses mostly on aspects of the business environment and reflects several years of OECD work with Central Asian countries on access to finance, business internationalisation and skills development. Each of the country case studies presented here is the result of a country-specific project carried out by the OECD, hand-in-hand with the governments of Kazakhstan, Kyrgyzstan, Mongolia, Tajikistan, Uzbekistan.

Enhancing Competitiveness in Central Asia is the result of co-operation between the OECD and the European Commission's Directorate General for International Co-operation and Development (DG DEVCO), in partnership with the governments of the above-mentioned countries and in consultation with international experts, representatives of the private sector and other stakeholders. The work was conducted under the aegis of the European Commission's Central Asia Invest programme and as part of the OECD Eurasia Competitiveness Programme. We look forward to continuing this collaboration on policy reforms in Central Asia and to extending it to address new and broader challenges in the future. Going forward, we will also aim to work with Central Asian countries on monitoring and advancing the pace of reform.

A more stable and inclusive growth model for the region is within reach. The OECD stands ready to continue its support for Central Asia, so that it can achieve higher growth, better jobs and better development perspectives, ultimately providing "better policies for better lives".

Andreas Schaal

Director, Global Relations Secretariat, OECD

Acknowledgements

This report is the outcome of work conducted in Kazakhstan, Kyrgyzstan, Mongolia, Tajikistan and Uzbekistan, within the framework of the Central Asia Invest programme co-ordinated by the Directorate-General for International Co-operation and Development (DG DEVCO) of the European Commission, and the OECD Eurasia Competitiveness Programme under the authority of the Central Asia Initiative Steering Committee.

The report was written under the guidance of Andreas Schaal, Director of Global Relations, OECD; as well as William Tompson, Head of the Eurasia Division, OECD.

The work was led by Grégory Lecomte, Eurasia Division, OECD. The principal authors of the report are Arnault Prêtet, Marco Bianchini (lead author of the first chapter), Sebastian Kupferschmid and Olga Olson, Eurasia Division, OECD. Valuable research and drafting support was provided by Tabea Klang, Damiano Fior and Evgeniia Zherzdeva, Eurasia Division, OECD.

The report benefitted from further inputs provided by Marzena Kisielewska, Head of South East Europe Division, OECD (Chapters 2, 3, 4); Irène Hors, Head of Special Partnerships and New Initiatives Division, OECD (Chapter 2); Antonio Fanelli, Special Partnerships and New Initiatives Division, OECD (Chapter 1); Jean-Francois Lengellé, Eurasia Division, OECD (Chapter 1); Professor Richard Pomfret, University of Adelaide (Chapter 1); Chiara Monticone, OECD Directorate for Financial and Enterprise Affairs (Chapter 2); Kris Boschmans, OECD Centre for Entrepreneurship, SMEs and Local Development (Chapter 2); Clément Brenot, South East Europe Division, OECD (Chapters 2, 3); Péline Atamer, Directorate for Financial and Enterprise Affairs, OECD (Chapter 3); Jovana Pavlovic, South East Europe Division, OECD (Chapter 3); Stuart Thompson, OECD Centre for Entrepreneurship, SMEs and Local Development (Chapter 3); Jibran Punthakey, OECD Centre for Entrepreneurship, SMEs and Local Development (Chapters 2, 3); Kateryna Obvintseva, Directorate for Education and Skills, OECD (Chapter 4); and Wouter Meester, Eurasia Division, OECD (Chapter 4).

In partner countries, the following stakeholders led their countries' participation in all stages of the various country-projects: H.E. Yerbolat Dossayev, Deputy Prime Minister of Kazakhstan; Madina Abylkassimova, Vice Minister of National Economy of Kazakhstan; H.E. Tolkunbek Abdygulov, First Deputy Prime Minister of Kyrgyzstan; Daniiar Imanaliev, Deputy Minister of Economy of Kyrgyzstan; Asel Uzagalieva and Asel Albanova, GIZ, Kyrgyzstan; H.E. Sergelen Purev, Minister for Food, Agriculture and Light Industry of Mongolia; Dashdorj Luvsandash, Citizen Participation and Economic Policy Advisor to the President of Mongolia at the time of the peer review; Lakshmi Boojoo, Director of the Economic Policy and Competitiveness Research Center of Mongolia; H.E. Azim Ibrohim, Deputy Prime Minister of Tajikistan; Saidrahmon Nazrizoda, First Deputy Minister of Economic Development and Trade (MEDT) of Tajikistan (2009-2017); Muhammad Murod Asludinov, MEDT of Tajikistan; H.E. Nodir Otajonov, Deputy Prime Minister of Uzbekistan; Mubin Mirzaev, Deputy Minister of Economy of Uzbekistan; Shukhrat Ismoilov, Deputy Minister of Economy of Uzbekistan (2015-2017); Azizbek Urunov, Head of Department for Foreign Trade, Ministry of Economy of Uzbekistan.

The Directorate-General for International Co-operation and Development (DG DEVCO) of the European Commission financed this work and provided importance guidance and support, particularly Pierre Amilhat, Director; Raffaela Iodice, Head of F1 Unit; Frank Hess, Deputy Head of F1 Unit; Bérénice Muraille, Head of Sector, F1 Unit ; Anja Nagel, Head of Sector, F1 Unit; Thomas Boyer, Programme Manager, F1 Unit; Laure Dupin and Anna Berdach, former Programme Managers.

Editorial and visual support was provided by Sally Hinchcliffe, editor; Vanessa Vallée, Communications Manager, Global Relations, OECD; and Anne Gimenez, Communications Officer, Global Relations, OECD. Valuable administrative support was offered by Anna Chahtahtinsky, Mariana Tanova and Orla Halliday, OECD Eurasia Division.

Table of contents

Tables

Figures

Boxes

Acronyms and abbreviations

ADB	Asian Development Bank
AFD	Agence Française de Développement
bn	billion
BEEPS	Business Environment and Enterprise Performance Survey
BLP	Business Linkage Programme
BRI	Belt and Road Initiative
CA	Central Asia
CCI	Chamber of Commerce and Industry
CIS	Commonwealth of Independent States
EBRD	European Bank for Reconstruction and Development
ECP	Eurasia Competitiveness Programme
EEU	Eurasian Economic Union
EPA	Export Promotion Agency
EU	European Union
EUR	Euro (currency)
FAO	Food and Agriculture Organization of the United Nations
FDI	Foreign Direct Investment
GDP	Gross Domestic Product
GIZ	Deutsche Gesellschaft für Internationale Zusammenarbeit (German Society for International Co-operation)
GVC	Global Value Chain
HDI	Human Development Index
ICT	Information and Communication Technologies
IMF	International Monetary Fund
INFE	OECD International Network on Financial Education
IPA	Investment Promotion Agency
IPR	OECD Investment Policy Review
ITC	International Trade Centre
ITF	International Transport Forum
JSC	Joint-Stock Company
KPI	Key Performance Indicator
mn	million
MNC	Multinational Companies
OECD	Organisation for Economic Co-operation and Development
PPP	Purchasing Power Parity
SME	Small and Medium-sized Enterprise
SOE	State-Owned Enterprise
TFI	Trade Facilitation Indicator
USAID	U.S. Agency for International Development
USD	US dollars
VET	Vocational Education and Training
WB	World Bank
WRF	Warehouse Receipt Financing
WTO	World Trade Organization

Executive summary

Central Asia's economies need to diversify

Central Asia has registered **impressive economic growth** since the turn of the millennium. The aggregate gross domestic product (GDP) of Kazakhstan, Kyrgyzstan, Mongolia, Tajikistan, Turkmenistan and Uzbekistan grew at an average annual rate of 7% during 2000-16, despite a sharp slowdown following the drop in global commodity prices in 2014-15. Labour productivity growth averaged almost 5% and poverty rates halved.

Growth has been **driven mainly by exports of minerals and labour**. Their location between Europe and Asia and, in particular, proximity to China allowed Kazakhstan, Mongolia, Turkmenistan and Uzbekistan to benefit from rapidly growing demand for hydrocarbons and metals. Meanwhile, an increasing number of labour migrants to Russia and Kazakhstan generated remittance flows that supported growth and raised living standards in Kyrgyzstan, Tajikistan and, to a lesser extent, Uzbekistan.

The recent slowdown, though, has highlighted **the need for a more sustainable and inclusive growth model**, based on a diversification of economic activity. Successful diversification should bring higher incomes, more jobs and more stable growth.

This requires improvements in governance, connectivity and business environments

In addition to disciplined macroeconomic policies and prudent management of resource revenues, diversification will require reforms in three main areas:

- The Central Asian countries all face important **governance challenges** linked not only to general questions of integrity and government effectiveness but also to the specific challenges that confront largely natural resource-based economies.
- **Better connectivity** is needed to support trade, as diversification will require deeper integration in trade and global value chains. This includes upgrading both transport networks and trade policies to facilitate cross-border flows.
- Stronger, fairer and more reliable **business environments** will favour more entrepreneurship and innovation, as well as encouraging trade and investment.

Access to finance, internationalisation and skills all represent key reform challenges

This report focuses on aspects of the business environment and reflects several years of OECD work with Central Asian countries on access to finance, business internationalisation, and skills. The country-specific case studies that constitute the bulk of this volume suggest that Central Asian governments have an active role to play in addressing co-ordination failures in these areas, by implementing the following measures:

- On **access to finance:** enhance data collection on SMEs, further improve public financial instruments by involving the banking sector more, and implement financial literacy strategies for firms and entrepreneurs.
- On **business internationalisation:** formulate and implement national strategies with sector priorities, including value propositions, improve export promotion and monitor impact, while sustaining a continuous public-private dialogue.
- On **skill gaps:** further stimulate private sector involvement in public-private dialogue on skills and support the implementation of key VET instruments, including national qualification frameworks and workplace training.

Chapter 1. A regional agenda for economic diversification in Central Asia

This chapter analyses the major drivers of economic growth in Central Asia since 2000, notably commodities exports and migrant remittances, and their effects, such as the dependence on a few commodities and on labour migration. It also offers an overview of the challenges ahead to further diversify the Central Asian economies, in particular those related to public governance, connectivity and the business environment. It then highlights the major business environment issues that are the focus of the next chapters.

The need for diversification

The economies of Central Asia (CA) – here defined as the five former Soviet republics of Central Asia (Kazakhstan, Kyrgyzstan, Tajikistan, Turkmenistan and Uzbekistan) plus Mongolia – experienced an unprecedented period of growth from 2000 to 2016, as they bounced back from the transition recession of the 1990s and began to reap the benefits of market reforms. Real gross domestic product (GDP) grew at an average annual rate of 7%, despite a sharp slowdown following the drop in global commodity prices in 2014-15, and GDP per capita in purchasing-power parity (PPP) USD rose by a staggering 14% per year. Labour productivity growth averaged almost 5% and poverty rates halved (Figure 1.1) (World Bank, 2017[1]; IMF, 2017[2]). The CA economies were also able to attract international investors: between 1997 and 2015, net inflows of foreign direct investment increased more than six-fold (World Bank, 2017[1]).

Figure 1.1. Index of real GDP growth in Central Asian countries

1989 = 100

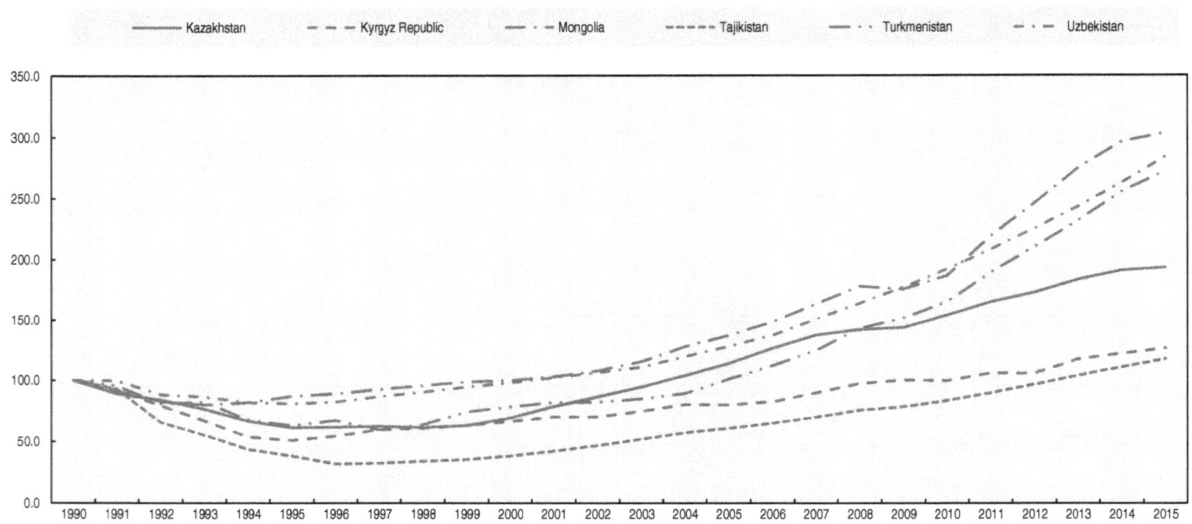

Source: (World Bank, 2017[1])

These growth figures can partially be explained by a "catch-up effect". The theory of convergence suggests that emerging economies' GDP per capita grows faster than developed countries' because diminishing returns, especially of capital, are less important than in capital-rich economies. Catching-up economies can also leverage the know-how in production processes, technology and institutions available to developed economies (Sachs, 1995[3]; Abramovitz, 1986[4]).

Since the turn of the century, most of the Central Asian economies have exhibited a fairly strong convergence dynamic, with hydrocarbon and metal exporters leading the way in closing the distance to OECD levels of income (Figure 1.2). However, with the exception of Kazakhstan (close to Chile's GDP per capita), they remain below the 50% mark in purchasing-power parity (PPP) terms,[1] and their distance from the OECD average is even greater when measured using actual exchange rates. Moreover, the convergence process has largely stalled since 2013. Getting the Central Asian economies back onto a convergence trajectory, in terms of both living standards and productivity, is thus a critical challenge.

Figure 1.2. Convergence progress, 2000-16

GDP per capita as a % of the OECD average (PPP, constant 2011 international USD)

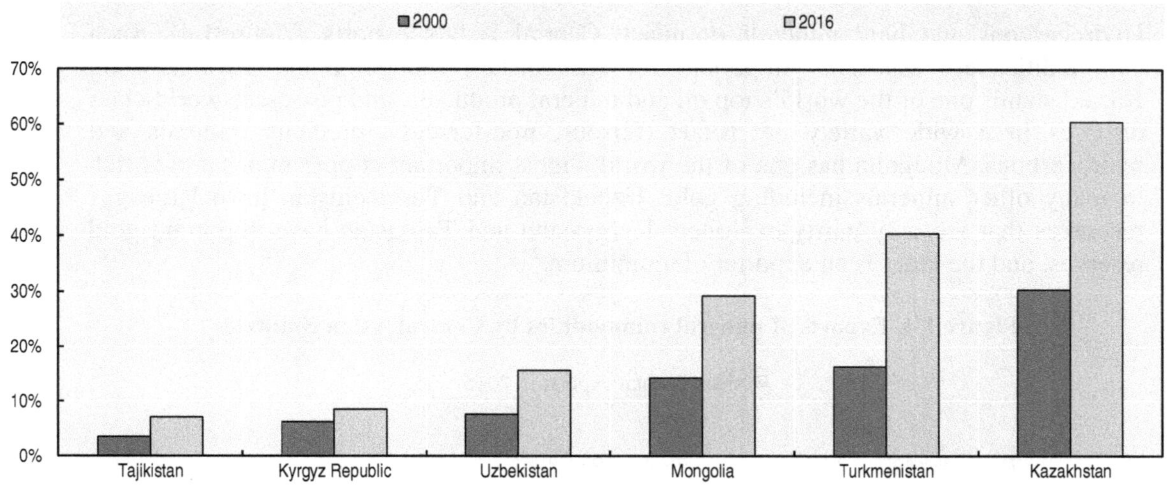

Source: (World Bank, 2017[11])

Figure 1.3. Human Development Index (HDI) as a percentage of OECD average

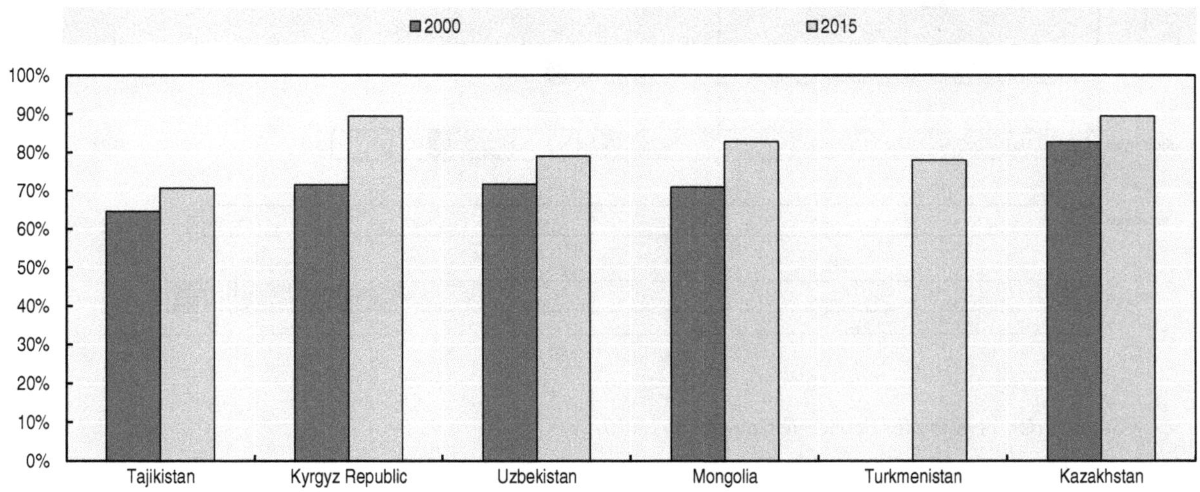

Note: Statistics for Turkmenistan is available only since 2010.
Source: (UN, 2017[5])

Beyond the catch-up effect, other dynamics underlie the strong growth since 2000 in Central Asia: exports of raw materials during a period of exceptionally high commodity prices and significant remittances from labour migrants. Booming Chinese demand was key to this dynamic. China's need for commodities (such as coal, copper, oil and gas) boosted the exports of Central Asian countries and also those of the Russian Federation, which in turn absorbed growing numbers of Central Asian workers, who sent remittances to their home countries. In addition, the recovery from the severe recession of the early 1990s, which followed the collapse of communism and the start of the market transition, owed much to policy reforms that enabled deeper international integration, the growth of private-sector activities and more efficient allocation of resources (IMF, 2014[6]).

Hydrocarbon and mineral commodity exports and migrant remittances have been the main drivers of growth

Hydrocarbons and hard minerals dominate Central Asia's exports (Figure 1.4). Such commodities are especially important for Kazakhstan, Mongolia and Turkmenistan. Kazakhstan is one of the world's top oil and mineral producers, and possesses world-class reserves in a wide variety of metals (ferrous, non-ferrous), precious minerals and hydrocarbons. Mongolia has one of the world's most important copper mines and is rich in many other minerals including gold. Uzbekistan and Turkmenistan have large gas resources that are only partly exploited. Kyrgyzstan and Tajikistan have important gold reserves, and the latter is an exporter of aluminium.[2]

Figure 1.4. Exports of mineral commodities by Central Asian countries

% share of total exports in 2015

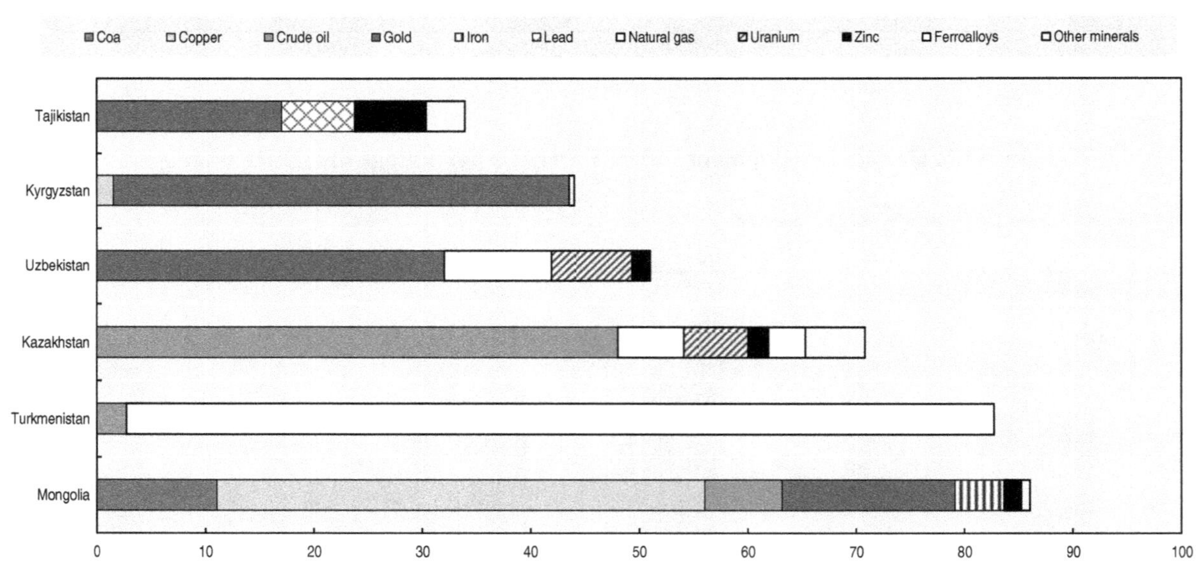

Source: (Observatory for Economic Complexity, 2017[7])

In the first decade of the century, commodity prices consistently rose in what most analysts call the "super-cycle", largely driven by China's rapid economic expansion. Even the global crisis of 2009 did not interrupt this trend for long. From 2000 to 2011 the price of gold (+463%), coal (+396%), copper (+386%), oil (+268%) and natural gas (+207%) (IMF, 2017[2]) all rose sharply. Central Asian countries' exports of such goods rose extremely fast (Figure 1.5).

Figure 1.5. The growth of Central Asia's commodity exports, 2000-11

Increase in USD value of exports from 2000 to 2011[3] (2000 = 100)

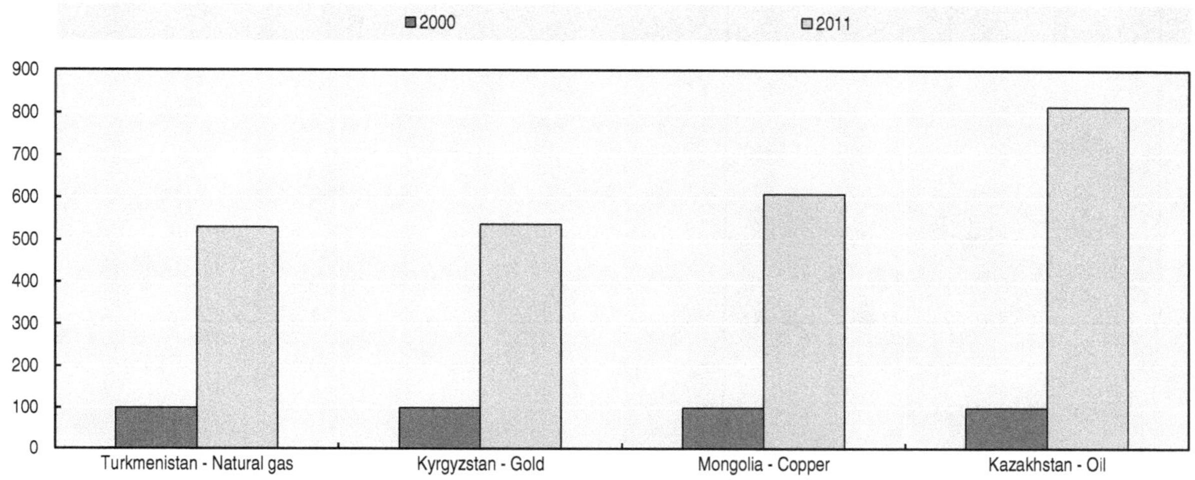

Source: (Observatory for Economic Complexity, 2017[7])

Starting in 2012-13, prices began to fall as China's economy slowed and so did the value of Central Asian exports and real GDP growth rates (see Figure 1.7).

Economic growth was further affected by a fall in remittances. The remittances sent back to families by migrant workers constituted the other major source of growth during the period of high commodity prices. Low salaries and high unemployment prompted millions of workers to move, particularly to the Russian Federation and Kazakhstan: in 2015, the average monthly wage in Russia was roughly 4.5 times the average in Kyrgyzstan and 8.5 times the Tajikistan average; the corresponding figures for Kazakhstan were, respectively, 3.4 and 6.5 times (Ryazantsev, 2016[8]).

Indeed, the scale of remittances is such that for some Central Asian countries, the primary export commodity is really labour. The number of labour migrants from Central Asian countries has been estimated at 2.7-4.2 million, which is 10-16% of the economically active population of the region in 2010 (Ryazantsev, 2016[8]). Remittance flows are particularly important for the less resource-rich economies of the region – Uzbekistan (USD 2.3 billion in 2015), Kyrgyzstan (USD 2.0 billion) and Tajikistan (USD 1.8 billion). In relative terms, remittances were far less important in Uzbekistan (4.6% of GDP), than in Kyrgyzstan (25.7%) and Tajikistan[4] (28.8%) (World Bank, 2017[11]).[5]

The value of remittances in USD increased from the early 2000s until 2013, when it fell sharply as a result of a 50% devaluation of the Russian rouble against the USD and the increasingly strict rules on migration introduced by the Russian Federation, especially for countries outside the Eurasian Economic Union (Figure 1.6).

Figure 1.6. Inflows of remittances to selected Central Asian countries

% of GDP

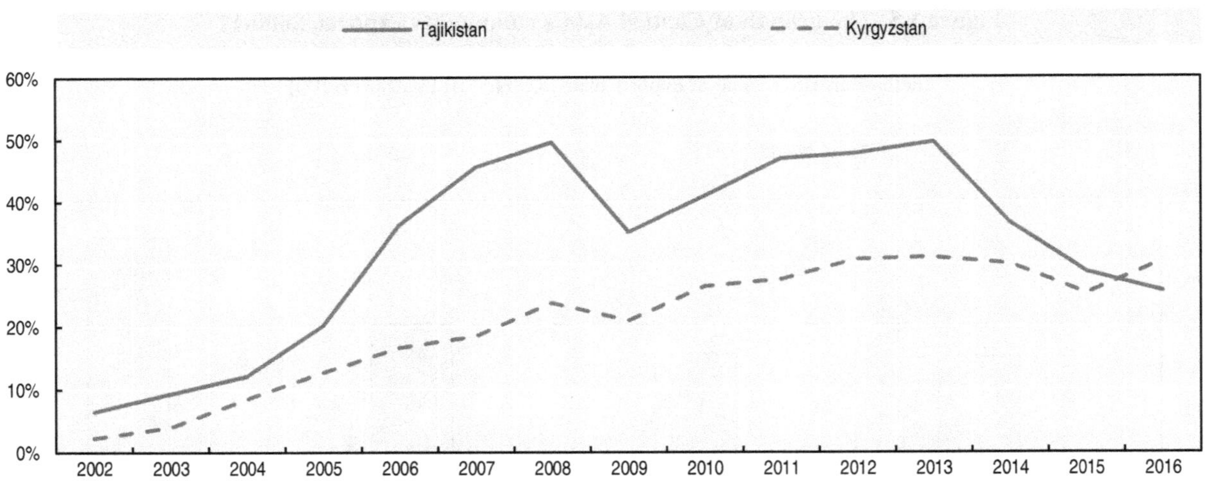

Source: (World Bank, 2017[1]; IMF, 2017[2])

Remittance flows have been economically beneficial but also involve costs

Labour migration has enabled countries with weak export capacities in goods and services to sustain domestic consumption and offset deficits elsewhere in the balance of payments. This is consistent with the Heckscher-Ohlin model of international trade, which holds that a country will export goods that are relatively intensive in the factors that it has in abundance and import goods that are intensive in its scarce factors (Ohlin, 1933[9]). There was, however, one important twist in the transition countries of Central Asia. Domestic conditions, infrastructure and institutions were such that even countries with an abundance of relatively low-cost labour could not move quickly to occupy niches as exporters of labour-intensive goods. Labour thus moved abroad to locations where production conditions were more favourable, both in tradable and non-tradable sectors.

Labour migration has helped to raise household incomes and reduce unemployment in the sending countries. If migrants return with professional skills acquired abroad, they could further benefit their home countries. This depends on the form of migration, however – for example, seasonal agricultural labourers are less likely to return with new skills than those who emigrate for a longer period and in more skill-intensive sectors. There are also opportunities for returning migrants to generate new activities: they often tend to be among their countries' most entrepreneurial citizens. Unfortunately, in many countries, the framework conditions for entrepreneurship do not make it attractive for returnees to invest their remittances and build businesses – indeed, poor framework conditions at home are among the major causes of migration (Marat, 2009[10]; Malyuchenko, 2015[11]).[6] The case study on Tajikistan that follows (Chapter 2) is concerned with policy changes and institutional reforms that can help improve these conditions and maximise the potential contribution of returning migrants to national economies.[7]

There are, however, important economic and social costs associated with such outflows of working-age people. The economies of the sending countries experience the so-called "missing-men" phenomenon, which means a lack of qualified male labour in rural areas, particularly during times of intensive field work. In addition, highly skilled workers also tend to leave. For example, from 1991 to 2005, the number of teachers with higher education in Tajikistan fell from 72 789 to 61 319, and the share of all teachers with higher education thus fell from 77% to 62% (IOM, 2006[12]).

Social costs for migrants and their sending communities may also be significant. First, migrants often live and work in very poor conditions, with little or no access to healthcare or other public services in host countries, where they often work in the informal sector. Second, there are the costs of family separation, which can be substantial (Malyuchenko, 2015[11]). For instance, IOM studies show that about one third of migrants' wives were abandoned by their husbands due to the latter permanently settling in the host country (IOM, 2010[13]; IOM, 2009[14]).

For children, the impact of migration is mixed: remittances increase household income and may thus improve access to health services, education and nutrition, but absent fathers also place emotional and physical burdens on children, who often have to undertake more and heavier work. UNICEF (2012) highlights the negative impact on school performance associated with the reduction of parental control and care, as well as family break-up. These are all challenges sending countries struggle to address, since it is often the low levels of income and institutional development that prompt out-migration in the first place.

At a macro level, dependence on remittances implies a high degree of sensitivity to the performance of the receiving economies, particularly the Russian Federation and Kazakhstan in the case of Central Asia. Consequently, even the resource-poor countries of the region were hit hard by the sharp drop in commodities prices in 2014-15, a shift in the terms of trade that might otherwise have been expected to benefit them as importers of commodities. For example, in Tajikistan in 2013, 89% of remittances were denominated in roubles, amounting to 43% of GDP; weaker demand for Tajik labour in Russia and the depreciation of the rouble against the dollar meant that many businesses and citizens saw their purchasing power fall sharply. Moreover, citizens and businesses found themselves unable to service their debts, as Tajikistan has a strongly dollarised economy, with more than 80% of bank loans and deposits denominated in USD in 2014. The banking and financial crisis that followed in 2015 was in large part a result of this shock and is still hampering growth in the country (IMF, 2016[15]).

Exports are increasingly concentrated, both in terms of commodities and markets

All the countries in the region, except Uzbekistan, have seen an increase in the concentration of their export baskets, as reflected in the Herfindahl-Hirschmann Index[8] over the past 20 years, with fewer products accounting for a larger share of exports (UNCTAD, 2017[16]).[9] Increasing concentration on a limited range of commodities which are often subject to large short-term price fluctuations (mainly hydrocarbons and minerals) entails important risks. For example, Mongolia experienced real GDP growth averaging 11% per year in 2010-14, but after the fall in commodity prices (particularly copper), growth dropped to 2.4% in 2015 and an estimated 1.6% in 2016, with public finances coming under strain as a result. The fall in commodity prices in 2014 slowed growth across the region, although official data for Tajikistan and Uzbekistan do not show much evidence of a slowdown (Figure 1.7). Other major global commodity exporters also experienced an economic slowdown; Chile and South Africa lost more than 2 percentage points of GDP growth between 2013 and 2016 (World Bank, 2017[1]).

Figure 1.7. Growth decrease in Central Asian economies after the commodity price decline, 2013-16

Real GDP growth, annual percentage change

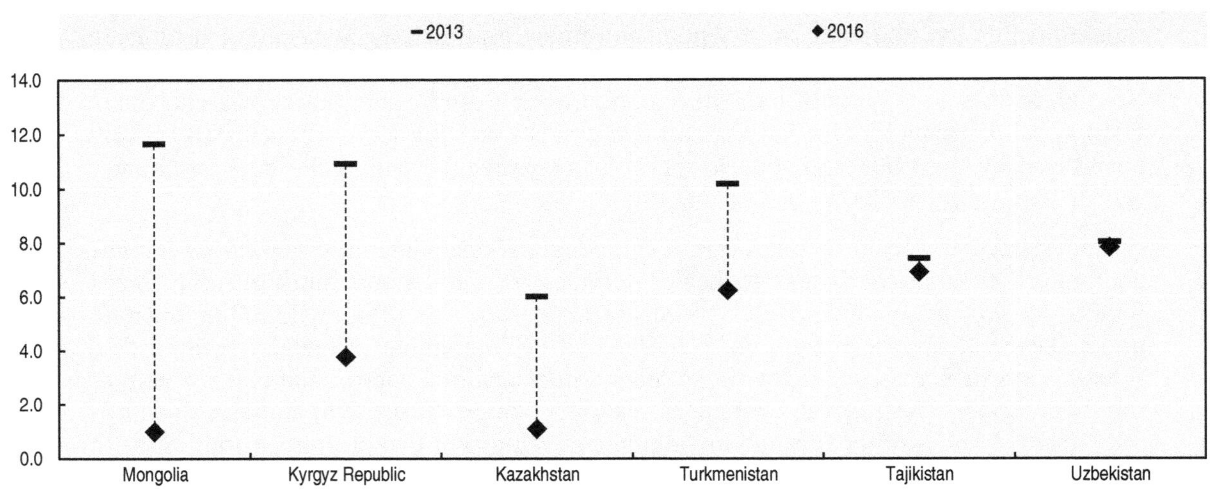

Source: (IMF, 2017[2])

Moreover, the vulnerability of Central Asian countries extends to shocks affecting trade partners, as their exports are concentrated in a limited number of export markets. Landlocked geography and the "distance penalty" mean that a few neighbours almost exclusively make up the export markets for Central Asian economies (Figure 1.8).

Figure 1.8. Export destinations of Central Asian countries

100% = Total export

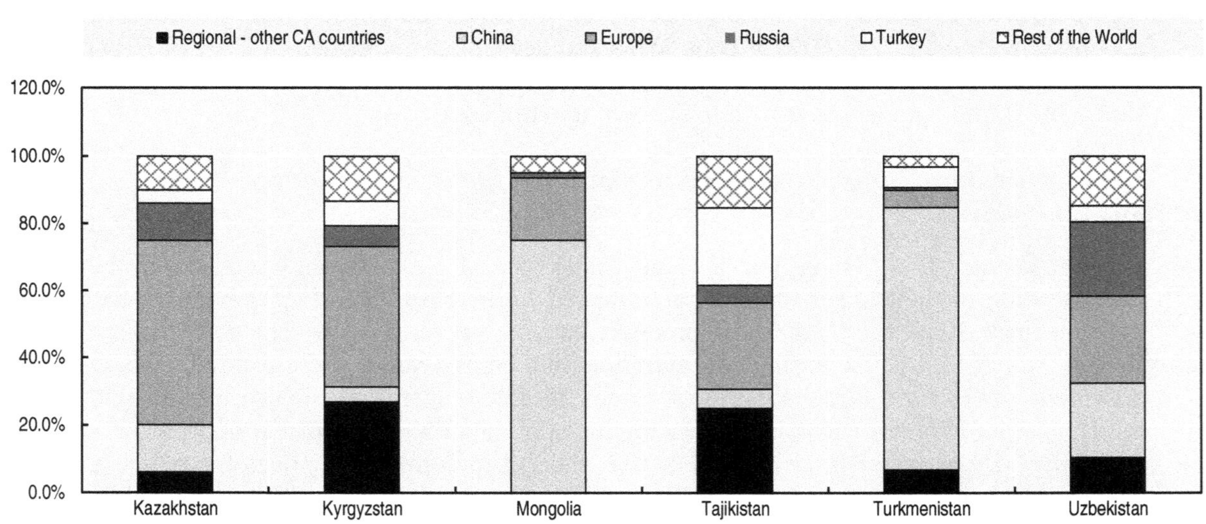

Source: (Observatory for Economic Complexity, 2017[7])

Successful diversification should bring higher incomes and less volatile economic performance

Resource wealth has brought important benefits to Central Asia. The rapid growth of extraction sectors has led to higher incomes and, for most of the last two decades, better growth performance in those Central Asian countries endowed with rich hydrocarbon and hard mineral resources (World Bank, 2017[1]). Proper management of the flow of resources is crucial. A positive example is the National Fund of the Republic of Kazakhstan, with total assets amounting to USD 67 billion as of 2016 (Reuters, 2017[17]; Samruk Kazyna, 2016[18]). Created in 2000 as a stabilisation fund against the fluctuation of commodity prices, the fund manages the financial assets deriving from taxes on oil and gas companies as well as from its own investments. The assets are then accumulated in a government's account at the National Bank of Kazakhstan, with a guaranteed transfer to the national budget that is limited by a fiscal rule (OECD, 2016[19]).[10] Among OECD economies, Chile (the Social and Economic Stabilisation Fund) and Norway (the Government Pension Fund Global) have successfully established such funds to manage natural-resource wealth (OECD, 2008[20]).

Nevertheless, such heavy reliance on exports of hydrocarbons and hard minerals entails significant costs and risks. A large body of empirical research suggests that countries endowed with great natural resource wealth tend to lag behind comparable countries in terms of real GDP growth in the long run. This has given rise to debate about a so-called "resource curse" or "paradox of plenty".[11] At macro level, resource dependence implies a high degree of vulnerability to external shocks, particularly where government revenues rely heavily on export income. More diversified economies also tend to be more resilient to shocks. Their output is less volatile, and lower output volatility is usually associated with higher economic growth in the long run (Ramey, 1995[21]). In the case of Kazakhstan, the OECD has recommended that the government should further diversify its economy to lower its vulnerability towards external shocks (OECD, 2012[22]; OECD, 2016[23]; OECD, 2017[24]). Other resource-rich Central Asian economies face similar challenges.

In addition, the pressures that resource wealth generates on non-resource tradables, particularly when resource booms drive up the exchange rate (the phenomenon known as the "Dutch disease"), can make it hard to generate high-productivity tradable activities outside the resource sector.[12] This is a critical concern, because a large share of employment in Central Asian countries is concentrated in low-productivity sectors, while mining and hydrocarbons are capital intensive and employ relatively few workers. The extraction sector alone will never be able to generate high-productivity employment on a sufficient scale to assure broad-based prosperity – even with very aggressive assumptions about both future commodity prices and the potential to increase resource extraction. A dynamic, non-resource sector is therefore likely to be fundamental to inclusive growth: Central Asian countries need to generate high-productivity activities outside the resource sector.

Diversification is also relevant for the comparatively "resource-poor" countries of the region, since, as noted above, reliance on migrants' remittances is also an unappealing long-term strategy. They can only escape their dependence on foreign labour markets by creating conditions to enable new tradable sectors and activities to emerge and existing ones to grow more quickly.

The importance of diversification is further confirmed if we look at personal income data. Studies leveraging large datasets covering 99 countries (ILO, UNIDO, and OECD) show that sectoral concentration follows a U-shaped pattern. Starting with a very concentrated economy, countries usually diversify to reach higher level of per capita income, only to concentrate again in the sectors with greater competitive advantage at a later stage of development (Imbs, 2003[25]). More recently, on the basis of data covering 178 countries from 1962 to 2010, Papageorgiou et al (2014) found that export diversification is associated with higher per capita incomes, lower output volatility, and higher economic stability (IMF, 2014[26]). This underscores the importance of further diversifying the export structures of Central Asian countries.

Diversification will require better governance, connectivity and framework conditions for business

Sound macroeconomic management – and, in particular, prudent management of resource revenues – will be critical to enabling Central Asian states to diversify their economies and the sources of growth. However, macroeconomic discipline alone will not be enough; policy intervention may also be needed to address co-ordination failures between economic actors, which are leading to underinvestment in infrastructure, modern technologies and human resources (Rodrik, 1996[27]; Rodriguez-Clare, 2005[28]).[13] Reforms in at least three other areas will be essential:

- **Improving the quality of public governance** is a priority. Resource-led development is extremely demanding on national institutions, because of the need to manage the volatile revenues associated with the exploitation of natural resources fairly and productively (IBRD / World Bank, 2014[29]). As a rule, weaknesses in the institutional environment, such as corruption, weak property rights or arbitrary taxation and regulation, have a disproportionate effect on younger firms and sectors, and on small firms. Established incumbents often have the political and financial resources to cope with – or even, in some cases, to profit from – such things, while those engaged in new activities usually lack such resources and, in any case, face higher levels of risk and uncertainty than incumbents. Higher-quality institutions, coupled with proper planning, can turn the "resource curse" into an opportunity (OECD, 2011[30]).
- **Boosting connectivity** to support trade and export diversification. The high cost of access to large foreign markets is a significant impediment to the emergence of new activities in much of Central Asia. This reflects both infrastructure challenges and the often high cost of doing business across borders, which results from tariffs, border procedures and non-tariff barriers. Poor trade and connectivity within the region lead to fragmented markets, making it hard for producers of non-resource tradables to achieve critical mass and to realise economies of scale, while poor connections to the rest of the world undermine access to the largest markets and inhibit integration into global value chains.
- **Enhancing the business environment** is an effective way to support the diversification of economic activity (Lederman, 2012[31]). In particular, the development of small and medium-sized enterprises (SMEs) in sectors such as manufacturing, trade and services can also help economies to diversify away from natural resource sectors in which large companies are over-represented (OECD, 2016[32]). In a stable and predictable environment, businesses can operate with longer time horizons, and face reduced risks in trying innovative activities. In the absence of such conditions, rational agents will focus on short-term gains, and there is likely to be little investment in any activity that does not generate very rapid returns (OECD, 2006[33]).

Improving the quality of public governance

Government effectiveness across much of Central Asia is relatively low

A substantial body of research suggests that resource dependence can have important implications for governance, which can, in turn, constrain prospects for diversification. Competition for natural resource rents across different levels of government can make the whole political system malfunction, as there is usually less public scrutiny and political accountability (Gelb, 2010[34]). Moreover, in a situation of limited institutional control, the struggle among elite groups to obtain the most from resource windfalls can cause an increase in fiscal redistribution strong enough to offset any increase in the raw rate of return from resource windfalls, ultimately hampering growth (Tornell, 1999[35]).

When a state's production and export profile is highly concentrated, the characteristics of its leading sector can significantly influence its institutions, and this is especially evident in countries that specialise in extractive sectors (Chaudry, 1989[36]; Shafer, 1994[37]). Hydrocarbons and mining are typically dominated by a small number of players, with high barriers to entry and exit, and a high degree of asset specificity. Faced with the need to govern these sectors, the state develops special, highly centralised institutions and practices to capture resource rents and deal with the leading sector. The centralised, sector-specific character of the state to some degree mirrors that of the economy. Many oil-producing countries, for example, have created specialised tax agencies to tap (and spend) the oil rents and specialised agencies to monitor, regulate, and promote the activities of big oil companies.[14] At the same time, they often fail to strengthen the institutions needed to promote other sector, or to create a business environment conducive to experimentation and entrepreneurship.

This point is extremely important in the larger resource curse debate, as some research suggests that state ownership rather than resource wealth lies at the root of resource exporters' apparently chronic under-performance (Auty, 2004[38]; Ross, 1999[39]; Jones Luong, 2004[40]). State ownership of resource industries may soften states' budget constraints and encourage fiscal indiscipline. In any case, state-owned minerals producers are likely to be less efficient and less transparent, and also to be subject to more political interference.[15]

In addition, the expropriability of resource rents creates a climate of uncertainty that discourages foreign investment. For instance in Kazakhstan, the new Mining Code includes one notable drawback. The state's pre-emptive right to mineral resources ("strategic deposits") was understood in the past to be of significant concern to potential and existing foreign investors in Kazakhstan, particularly in the field of solid minerals. The list of eligible minerals and their respective amounts is fairly exhaustive in terms of Kazakhstan's resources. Even under the new mining code, some observers fear that any significant deposit would be potentially eligible for inclusion in the "strategic" category.

Institutional design and governance are also a product of domestic choices: they are not wholly determined by factors intrinsic to the sector (Jones Luong, 2004[40]). Nevertheless, the predominance of state ownership in major hydrocarbon and minerals sectors across the world over the last 40-50 years – despite wide variation in the political circumstances of mineral-exporting states – suggests that the characteristics of the sector itself are important in structuring the choices politicians make in response to domestic political opportunities and constraints. These choices, in turn, affect the prospects for developing governance models that are less centralised and more responsive to the needs of a wide range of interests and sectors. In the context of Central Asia, it is important to note that the impact of *remittance* flows on institutions is likely to be very different, since labour remittances, in contrast to oil rents, typically bypass both state institutions and formal banking systems. Remittances can engender an independent and affluent private sector but also provide opportunities for the government to tap remitted funds indirectly through import duties and other restrictive measures. In either case, the risk is that "extractive institutions and their ancillary legal, fiscal, and information-gathering bureaucracies" may atrophy (Chaudry, 1989[36]).

Whatever one makes of the resource curse arguments, Central Asian states do broadly conform to the general patterns found in the literature on resource- and remittance-dependent economies. Businesses and international indexes consistently report that Central Asian countries have weak institutions. For instance, they score well below the OECD average in the World Economic Forum Global Competitiveness Indicators of institutional quality, including resource-rich countries such as Canada, Chile and Norway (World Economic Forum, 2017[41]). Central Asian countries also lag behind in quality of governance, ranking in the bottom 35% in the World Bank Governance Indicators. Assessment of Central Asia's governance points in particular towards:

- low government effectiveness, which reflects the perceived quality of public services, civil service, policy formulation and implementation
- low regulatory quality, which reflects the government's ability to formulate and implement policies for private sector development (Figure 1.9).

Figure 1.9. Worldwide Governance Indicators for Central Asian and selected countries

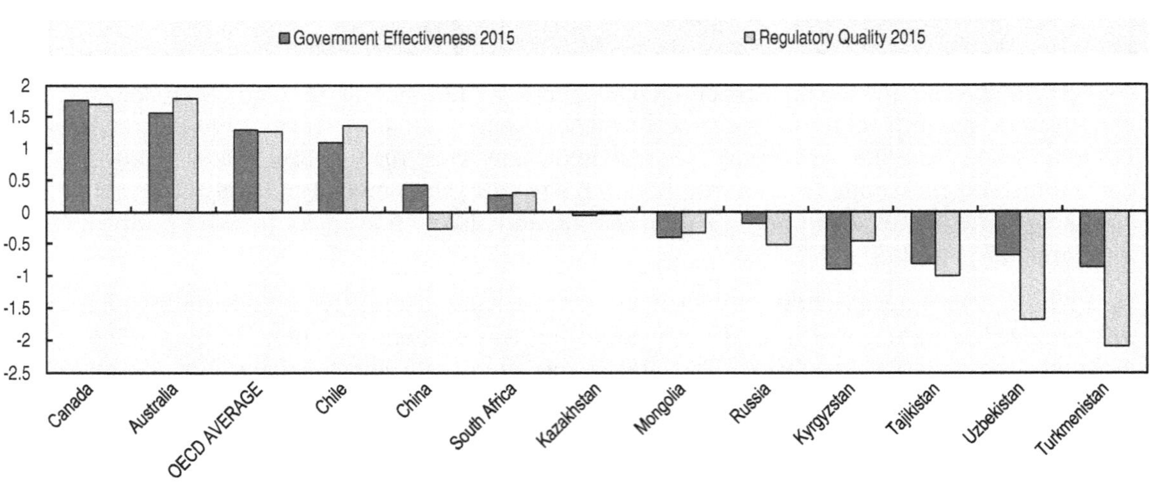

Note: The Worldwide Governance Indicators, published by the World Bank on a yearly basis, estimate the quality of governance in over 200 countries. They cover six dimensions of governance, ranking their performance from -2.5 (weak) to 2.5 (strong). The 6 aggregate indicators are based on several hundred underlying variables obtained from 31 different data sources
Source: (World Bank, 2017[42])

Such evidence of institutional weakness implies not just a need for reforms to strengthen public-sector integrity or government effectiveness, which are major challenges in themselves, but also a need to create new capacities and institutions that are better suited to the needs of an emerging non-resource sector. The Asian Development Bank (ADB) refers to a "modern industrial and service economy" as the goal of diversification (ADB,

2013[43]). Such institutions, in fields as diverse as export-promotion and human-capital development, are the focus of discussion in the chapters that follow.

Countries in the region are strengthening their institutional capacities at different rates. Governments have had difficulty in implementing approved plans (Box 1.1). Ministries often have to operate with relatively limited resources and insufficient institutional capacity. They often lack reliable, accurate micro-level data which makes it difficult to structure precise Key Performance Indicators (KPIs) for implementation. The result of this is that governments and other public agencies produce ambitious strategic plans, which usually fall short at implementation. The Regional Civil Service Hub in Astana, a co-operation platform aimed at proposing partnerships, capacity building and peer-to-peer learning among governments in the region, is one good initiative in this area (RHCS, 2017[44]). Participation by Uzbekistan and Turkmenistan – and more active participation by Kyrgyzstan, Tajikistan and Mongolia – in this hub might help tackle this issue.

Box 1.1. OECD review of the Central Administration of Kazakhstan

The review of the Central Administration of Kazakhstan, carried out by the OECD in 2014, focused on the capacity of central government and line ministries in Kazakhstan to implement national objectives and priorities. To this end, the review offered recommendations on how to re-assess the role and capacity of the ministries; review the function and roles of central agencies; promote transparency in policy making, monitoring and evaluation; improve horizontal co-ordination at central level; and improve human resource management and accountability for management results.

One of the main policy recommendations was to give ministries and agencies greater autonomy to reduce centralisation and the cost of bureaucracy. The OECD recommended enhancing the role and capacities of ministries to generate strategic policy documents, perform policy analysis, and deliver government priorities. As part of the Strategy Kazakhstan-2050, Kazakhstan aims to improve and streamline the system of state planning and forecasting, and further professionalise its civil service.

Kazakhstan already had a law on Local Government (2001) including the division of power and responsibilities between the central and local government but problems in implementing the law stopped the transition. Decentralisation is also at the core of the Strategy Kazakhstan-2050, and in particular how to divide decision-making powers between central government and regions. To overcome most of the issues, the OECD suggested a long-term development of human resources to prepare staff in all the junctions of this model. This would also enhance service delivery at a local level, with local authorities being closer to citizens.

Source: (OECD, 2014[45]; Government of Kazakhstan, 2017[46])

Corruption is perhaps the most important governance challenge today

Public sector corruption and business integrity are major issues for Central Asian countries, all of which except Mongolia are found in the bottom quarter of the Transparency International Corruption Index. Although the degree of corruption varies across the region, all countries are ranked below 40 (on a scale of 0-100) (Figure 1.10). This is far below the OECD average and in particular below several OECD countries that are successfully managing vast natural resources, including Australia, Canada and Chile (Transparency International, 2016[47]).

The OECD has worked extensively with governments in the region to tackle corruption. In particular, in 2003 the OECD Anti-Corruption Network (ACN) for Eastern Europe and Central Asia launched the Istanbul Anti-Corruption Action Plan, a regional peer review programme focusing on Central Asia and Eastern Europe. The plan offers country reviews and monitors follow-up on recommendations concerning anti-corruption legislation. It targets nine countries, including Kazakhstan, Kyrgyzstan, Mongolia, Tajikistan and Uzbekistan. During 2003-05, all of the Central Asian countries underwent baseline reviews based on anti-corruption standards established by the United Nations, the OECD and the Council of Europe. Since this baseline review, they have undergone three further rounds of monitoring of the implementation of anti-corruption reforms and their impact on levels of corruption.

Figure 1.10. Corruption Perception Index in Central Asian and reference countries

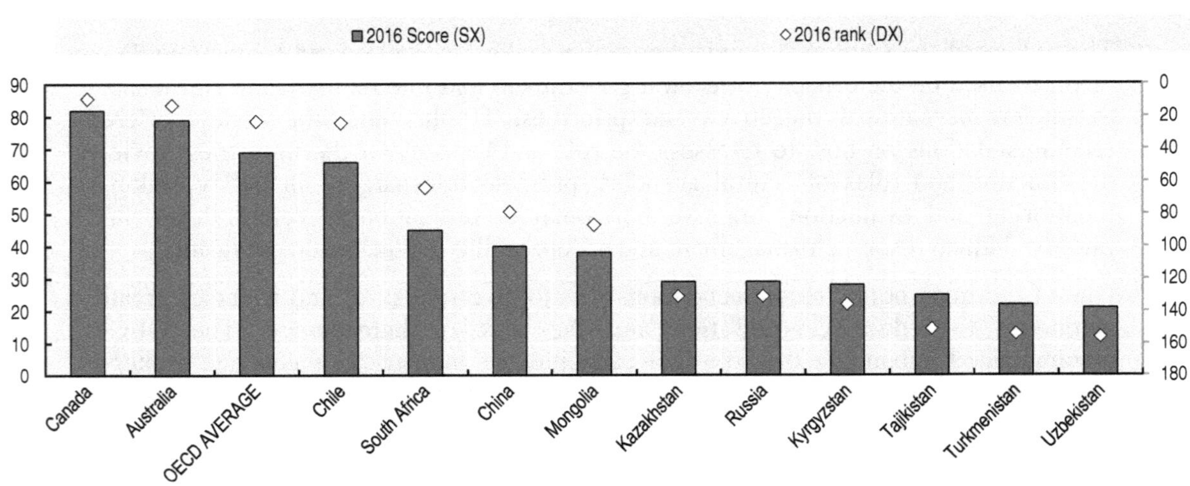

Source: (Transparency International, 2016[47])

The 2013-15 monitoring round demonstrated that the region has made some progress in preventing and punishing corrupt practices. Yet considerable challenges remain with respect to anti-corruption policies and institutions, the criminalisation of corruption and law-enforcement, and measures to prevent corruption in public administration and the business sector. The lack of specific timelines and measurable indicators to assess the effectiveness and impact of the reforms and ineffective law enforcement are still holding the countries back (OECD, 2016[32]).

Competition in many markets is weak

To allow businesses to thrive, competition law and policy and should create a level playing field, especially between state-owned enterprises (SOEs), large private companies (foreign and domestically owned), and SMEs. The pressure of competitors is one of the strongest incentives for a company to try to allocate resources efficiently and to innovate. This is particularly important in a region where incumbents and SOEs often benefit from uncompetitive advantages (Box 1.2).

The EBRD has developed an indicator that looks at the quality of competition policy and its enforcement, with scores ranging from 1 (no competition legalisation or institution) to 4+ (best standards and effective enforcement of competition policy are applied).[16] Central Asian countries started to introduce competition legislation after independence, with different patterns (Figure 1.11): Mongolia currently leads the way, with a score of 2.7, followed by Kazakhstan and Kyrgyzstan at 2, Tajikistan and Uzbekistan at 1.7 and Turkmenistan still at 1 (EBRD, 2017[48]).

Box 1.2. OECD Competition Law and Policy Peer Review of Kazakhstan

In 2016, Kazakhstan was the first country in the region to undergo its OECD competition law and policy peer review, which was attended by almost 90 delegations from around the world. In that context, the OECD provided key recommendations to the government of Kazakhstan on enforcement prioritisation, tools to detect collusive practices, analysis of mergers, procedural rules to increase overall transparency of proceedings and how to align to Eurasia Economic Union (EEU) standards.

The Government of Kazakhstan was advised to reduce the number of state monopolies, since many of the commercial activities considered to be state monopolies and conducted by state enterprises under tight regulation could be offered competitively by private companies. It was recommended, wherever possible, to subject these monopolies to a critical assessment and open them to private actors and competition.

The OECD also suggested reforms regarding control over dominant enterprises. In particular, the Kazakh government should shift from the current "State Register for Dominant Undertakings" (based exclusively on market share analysis and not constantly updated) to a case-by-case analysis of an undertaking's market position only if there is a reason to suspect abusive behavior. Analyses have to include not only the market share criteria but barriers to entry, the nature of the products, competitors and competition on the market, technological developments, the market phase and history, and foreseeable developments in the market.

Recommendations on tackling the abuse of dominant positions concentrated on shifting focus from price control to abusive practices that foreclose markets and erect barriers to entry. The OECD recommended focusing action on the reasons for non-competitive market structures, which would have much more lasting effects than interventions directed at prices.

As seen in Figure 1.10, the other Central Asian countries share the need to increase competition. After a first wave of legislation in the 1990s the indicators show that only Mongolia has progressed in its competition law since 2000.

Source: (OECD, 2016[49]; EBRD, 2017[48])

Figure 1.11. Competition law indicators since independence

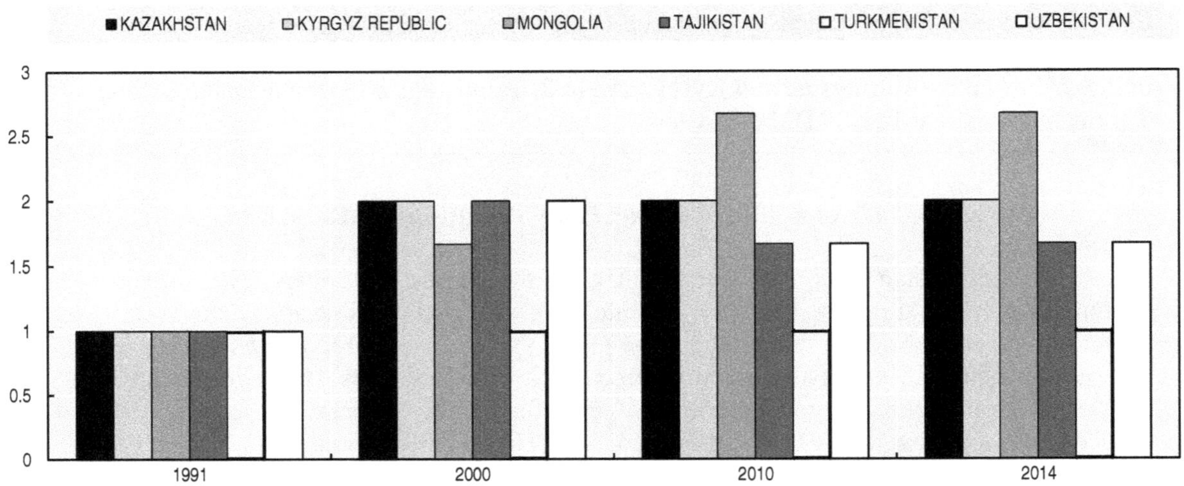

Source: (EBRD, 2017[48])

Boosting connectivity

With the development of global value chains (GVCs), countries in search of diversification today cannot hope to develop fully integrated industries from scratch (e.g. in the automotive or computer sector) that can compete with efficient GVCs. They need to find particular tasks within GVCs in which they enjoy a competitive advantage and work to create the conditions for the development of those activities (Baldwin and Taglioni, 2011[50]) (Baldwin, 2016[51]). Import substitution industrialisation policies, which tried to replace imports with domestic products by diversifying the domestic production structure and imposing high trade barriers, have proved to be an inefficient strategy (Sachs, 1995[52]). This is true even of some large emerging economies and even more so of smaller countries, like those in Central Asia, where limited market size means that any real move towards diversification needs to be outward oriented. Improving transport and information and communications technology (ICT) infrastructure, while reducing the soft barriers to trade (e.g. inefficient customs) will reduce trade costs, make countries more attractive as regional and global value-chain participants, and ultimately support the diversification of Central Asian economies (Pomfret, 2014[53]).

Connectivity is one of the great challenges facing the countries of Central Asia. Despite the region's historical role as a centre of global trade, it is largely peripheral to global trade flows today. The region's integration is limited by low density of settlement and economic activity, infrastructure bottlenecks, and long distances to major markets, as well as numerous regulatory and policy barriers to cross-border flows of trade and investment. Flows of trade, investment and people – both within the region and with the rest of the world – are far smaller than one might expect. Moreover, the connectivity framework that does exist is largely a product of the region's current reliance on exports of primary products, particularly agricultural commodities, hydrocarbons, metals and rare earth minerals. That is not surprising, but this may need to change if the Central Asian countries wish to diversify their economic structures so as to rely less on the primary sector.

Transport infrastructure in the region is far from adequate

Infrastructure investment needs in Central Asia[17] are estimated at USD 492 billion over the period 2016-30, implying an increase in spending from the current 4% to 6.8% of the region's GDP (ADB, 2017[54]). Central Asian countries have relatively poor roads, which undermine the connectivity potential of the region. Of the roads identified by the United Nations Economic and Social Commission for Asia and the Pacific (UNESCAP) for the realisation of the Asian Highway, 23% in Uzbekistan lack asphalt or cement concrete, and this figure rises to 48% in Tajikistan, 54% in Kazakhstan, 60% in Mongolia, 60% in Kyrgyzstan and 97% in Turkmenistan (UNESCAP, 2017[55]). This is also reflected in a high level of infrastructure risk (the probability of losing income because of deficiencies in transport, power and communication facilities). On a scale from 0 (low risk) to 100 (high risk), the average value of infrastructure risk in Central Asia has been estimated by the Economist Intelligence Unit at 67,[18] compared with 19 for OECD member countries (EIU, 2016[56]).

Governments in Central Asia, with the support of neighbouring countries and multilateral financing organisations, have invested in the improvement of transport infrastructure such as railways and roads in recent years. Central Asia is a key area for China's "Belt and Road Initiative" (BRI; Box 1.3). In 2008, the Central Asia Regional Economic Cooperation (CAREC) completed the upgrade of the road linking Bishkek and Almaty, thus making it easier and safer to transport goods between the two cities. The governments of Kazakhstan, Turkmenistan and Iran, with the support of organisations such as the ADB and the Islamic Development Bank, have opened an economic corridor linking Uzen in Kazakhstan with Bereket and Etrek in Turkmenistan and eventually stretching up to Gorgan in Iran, thanks to the railway opened in 2014.

Applying the Global Freight Model of the OECD International Transport Forum (ITF) to Central Asian countries could offer policy-makers unique insights into the costs, benefits and trade-offs of various options when it comes to transport infrastructure, enabling them to make more informed choices.

More can be done to increase digital connectivity

Central Asia has experienced a sharp increase in the penetration of ICT in recent years. The average number of mobile cellular subscriptions per 100 people was 124 in 2015, in line with levels in the United States (118), the European Union (123) and Japan (125) (World Bank, 2017[1]). These figures should be viewed with caution, however, as the very high number of mobile subscriptions is also caused by poor landline services and multiple contracts per person, as competing suppliers have different least-cost services. However, Central Asia is enhancing ICT connectivity and performance thanks to the construction of new infrastructure, such as the cable installed in 2009 between Tajikistan and Kyrgyzstan, and the planned Trans-Eurasian Information Super Highway (TASIM) connecting Frankfurt to Hong Kong and passing through Central Asia.

Box 1.3. China's Belt and Road Initiative (BRI)

This ambitious project, announced in 2013 by China's President Xi Jinping, aims to increase China's weight in the global economy by facilitating the shipment of Chinese goods to destination markets, promoting China's energy security and spreading Chinese investments in foreign countries.

Several billion dollars have already been invested in Central Asia within the OBOR initiative. In 2015, the Chongqing-Duisburg railway (inaugurated in 2011) offered a regular thrice-weekly service, enabling cargo to travel between China and Europe through Kazakhstan in only 16 days, instead of the 36 days required by maritime routes. China and Kazakhstan are also investing in a second rail link through Kazakhstan to Almaty, hence opening the prospect of another route to Europe south of the Caspian Sea. The China-Pakistan Economic Corridor is also important as it will make Kashgar into a hub for Central Asia once the Kashgar-Osh-Uzbekistan railway has been built.

In 2013, the construction of the Dushanbe-Chanak highway was completed, with 80% of the financing coming from the Chinese Development Bank (Cooley, 2016[57]). This last project not only boosts Chinese exports but also increases regional connectivity by linking major Tajik cities such as Dushanbe and Khujand with neighbouring Uzbekistan.

Source: (CGTN, 2017[58]; Cooley, 2016[57]; World Bank, 2016[59])

However, Central Asian countries still have few trans-border fibre optic links. This limits their connection to global communication networks, reduces the availability of internet bandwidth for local users and increases the costs they face. The number of fixed broadband subscriptions per 100 people in Central Asia is comparatively low. While the European Union and the United States had 31.8 and 31.5 fixed broadband subscriptions respectively per 100 people in 2015, there were just 13.1 in Kazakhstan, 7.1 in Mongolia, 3.7 in Kyrgyzstan, 3.6 in Uzbekistan, and around 0.1 in Tajikistan and Turkmenistan (World Bank, 2017[1]).

Trade policies can strengthen both connectivity and competition

Membership of the World Trade Organisation (WTO) implies a harmonisation of customs regulation, standards, certification and tariffs that help countries' trade policies to become more open and predictable. Most of the countries in the region have become members of the WTO in the past 20 years: Mongolia in 1997, Kyrgyzstan in 1998, Tajikistan in 2013 and Kazakhstan in 2015. Uzbekistan has an observer status with an accession working party that last met in 2005. Turkmenistan has also shown some interest in the possibility of joining, setting up a government commission in 2013 to analyse the possibility of accession. In addition, the accession of China in 2001 and of the Russian Federation in 2012 made membership more valuable for Central Asian countries.

Box 1.4. Sustainable electricity provision through energy integration in Central Asia

Access to electricity is the 7th Sustainable Development Goal proposed by the UN, to which all Central Asian governments have committed, and a core pre-condition to unlock economic development and diversification of the economy. Central Asia's energy infrastructure was well integrated under the Soviet Union, thanks to the Unified Energy System (UES). After the breakup of the USSR, the UES weakened and became fragmented.

However, in recent times there has been a growing consensus in Central Asia about the need to recreate such a unified power grid. After high-level meetings in May 2017, Uzbekistan decided to allow Turkmen electricity exports to flow again across its territory towards Kyrgyzstan and southern Kazakhstan (and, maybe, in winter months, also to Tajikistan). This is a breakthrough, since it partially re-establishes a Central Asian unified energy system. Moreover, the recently-inaugurated project CASA-1000, which is to export electricity produced by hydropower plants in Kyrgyzstan and Tajikistan to Pakistan and Afghanistan, is expected to be finalised soon thanks to the financial support of several international financial institutions. A high-level inter-governmental council has been established to make the 1 222 km CASA-1000 transmission project happen.

Source: (CASA-1000, 2017[60])

Regional integration has also increased forward through the creation of the Eurasian Economic Union (EEU), which includes two Central Asian states among its members, Kazakhstan and Kyrgyzstan. Tajikistan and Mongolia are currently discussing the possibility of joining. The benefits of EEU accession are still being assessed for current members and potential new entrants (Box 1.5).

Given the limited size of Central Asian domestic markets, regional trade integration may facilitate enterprise growth and promote the development of manufacturing sectors.

Box 1.5. The Eurasian Economic Union (EEU)

The establishment of the Eurasian Economic Union (EEU) in 2014 (following the formation of a customs union (CU) comprising Belarus, the Russian Federation and Kazakhstan in 2010) partly addresses the need to smooth customs procedures and facilitate the passage of cargo across borders. The EEU's goal is to create a common space for the free movement of goods, services, capital and labour, while at the same time promoting co-ordination among member states in sectors such as agriculture, energy and fiscal policy. The EEU currently has five member states: Armenia, Belarus, Kazakhstan, Kyrgyzstan and Russia

The EEU's efforts to promote competitiveness through measures such as the unification of customs procedures, the reduction of customs duties and the removal of non-tariff barriers are intended to promote trade among member states. Before the introduction of the customs union, the average border crossing time between Kazakhstan and Russia was about 7 hours, but it has since fallen to only 2 hours.

Nevertheless, trade facilitation in the framework of the EEU is an ongoing process that still faces several challenges. Some of the measures introduced to foster trade among CU/EEU member states seemed to have a negative effect on trade dynamics between these states and non-member countries. For instance, average border crossing time for cargos from non-CU countries to Kazakhstan rose from 8 hours before the introduction of the CU to 21 hours afterwards. In addition, the common external tariff means some partners have had to adopt higher tariff levels. However, the impact of this will abate somewhat as WTO-mandated annual tariff reductions are implemented. There have also been conflicts among EEU members concerning the imposition of *ad hoc* restrictions and non-tariff barriers that disadvantage them.

Furthermore, the EEU should foster the creation of new export possibilities for local enterprises within its common space, since today's export structure remains unidirectional. In 2015, exports to Russia represented 89.6% of Kazakhstan's exports towards EEU member countries, and this figure rises to 94.6% for Armenia and 96.1% for Belarus. Mutual trade between EEU member states as a percentage of their total foreign trade has increased from 12.3% in 2014 to 13.5% in 2015.

Source: (CAREC, 2012[61]; Vinokurov, 2017[62]).

Experience suggests that increased market access and liberalisation should progress gradually, giving Central Asian governments some scope to help local companies to adjust during the first stages of integration. The protection should be limited in scope and with a specific timeframe for the subsidies to begin and end, to limit market distortion once private enterprises become big enough to compete in the enlarged common market. In designing such transitional assistance, policy-makers should aim to reduce the costs of structural change rather than – as is too often the case – to try to forestall it. Evidence shows that defensive policies are usually driven by short-term interest and are more likely to be successful if they have precise conditionality and a clear exit strategy (Warwick, 2013[63]).

Central Asian countries still face difficulties when it comes to trading across borders. They record low scores on many dimensions of the OECD Trade Facilitation Indicators (TFIs). The TFIs offer a clear picture of the specific issues faced by Central Asian countries along 11 dimensions, offering a synthetic quantitative representation of inherently qualitative data (OECD, 2017[64]).

This assessment suggests that Central Asian countries need to prioritise:

- simplification of trade documents; harmonisation in accordance with international standards; acceptance of copies ("Formalities – Documents");
- streamlining of border controls; single submission points for all required documentation - single windows; post-clearance audits; authorised economic operators ("Formalities – Procedures");
- governance and operations of customs: customs structures and functions; accountability; ethics policy ("Governance and Impartiality").

Figure 1.12. The OECD Trade Facilitation Indicators

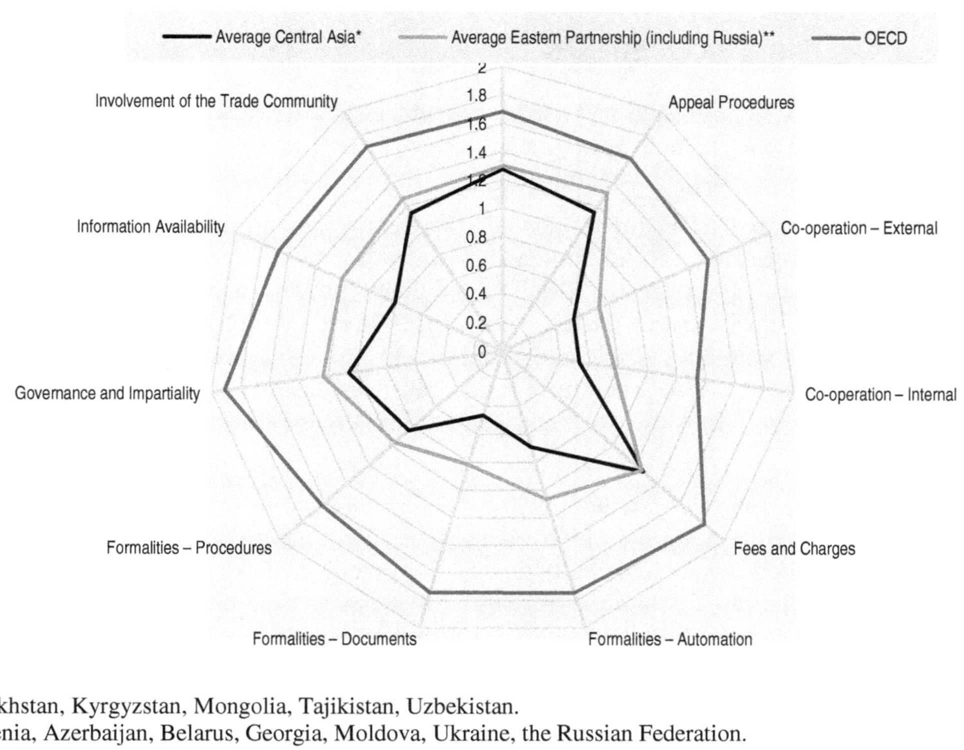

1. Kazakhstan, Kyrgyzstan, Mongolia, Tajikistan, Uzbekistan.
2. Armenia, Azerbaijan, Belarus, Georgia, Moldova, Ukraine, the Russian Federation.
Source: (OECD, 2017[64])

Enhancing the business environment

A general measure of the quality of the business environment in Central Asia is provided by the World Bank's Doing Business reports. Despite overall progress across the region in recent years, the most recent data reveal striking contrasts, with Kazakhstan ranking 35th (just below Japan), Mongolia 64th (close to Chile, 57th) and Kyrgyzstan 75th (just below South Africa); the latter two both fell back around 10 positions in 2017, while Uzbekistan is stable at 87th and Tajikistan rose 4 positions to 128th. There are also divergences across indicators. For example, procedures to start a business in the region are relatively easy and close to the best in the world, especially with the development of online procedures and one-stop shops in Central Asia, while performance on paying taxes varies widely, with Kazakhstan and Mongolia scoring far better in this respect (World Bank, 2016[59]).

Another measure of the quality of the business environment in Central Asian economies is offered by the position of SMEs. SMEs tend to suffer more from business climate issues than larger firms. They can less afford to bear the costs arising from poor enforcements of contracts, burdensome regulations, non-competitive procurement practices, and frequent inspections, which often serve as opportunities for corruption (OECD, 2014[65]; 2015[66]; 2015[67]). This may also limit economic diversification and the attraction of foreign capital. For example, Kazakhstan is moving forward on addressing some of these issues (Box 1.6).

Box 1.6. OECD Investment Policy Review of Kazakhstan

In 2012 the OECD published its first Investment Policy Review of Kazakhstan, based on the OECD Policy Framework for Investment and focusing on the critical policy objective of diversifying the economy.

In the review, the OECD recommended increasing support to SMEs; in particular regarding access to finance and human capital development, as well as investment and export promotion. Moreover, the OECD Guidelines for Multinational Enterprises were leveraged to address major issues regarding effective corporate governance and business ethics, including disclosure requirements of environmental and other non-financial performances. An important point raised in the review was that in all these policy areas the way in which the decisions are implemented is crucial in shaping their outcome.

In 2017 Kazakhstan was invited by the OECD to become adherent to the OECD Declaration on International Investment and Multinational Enterprises and its investment policy was reviewed again. It emerged how Kazakhstan's strong performance in terms of economic growth has been supported by its continuous efforts to liberalise and simplify investment regulation which helped spur capital inflows. Again, the main recommendation was to continue on the path to diversification, away from the over-reliance on natural resources (oil and gas sector generates as much as 30% of GDP currently).

Source: (OECD, 2012[22]; OECD, 2017[24])

In Central Asia, the contribution of SMEs to the economy is comparatively low, albeit with a good deal of variation between countries. They represent more than 90% of total businesses but their contribution to GDP is only between 25% and 41%, except in Uzbekistan, which is closer to OECD average of around 55%. They employ 78% of the workforce in Uzbekistan but only 38% in Kazakhstan. SMEs are mostly concentrated in low-value added sectors, especially agriculture and trade. Because of this concentration, they make a limited contribution to exports, while natural resources exported by large companies represent the bulk of exports in the region. In addition, as will be seen in Chapter 3, they often face particular barriers when it comes to accessing foreign markets.

Strategic approaches to industrial policy can be used to support SME development. These can be categorised as either *comparative advantage-following* or *comparative advantage-developing*, and according to whether the country or industry is in *catch-up* mode or at the *frontier*. Subsequently, tailored instruments of industrial policy could be selected to perform "softer" interventions, bringing industry and government together in setting strategic priorities, improve business networking opportunities and improve productivity. A crucial condition of the success of such an approach would be the planning for clear monitoring and evaluation from the very first conception of the industrial policies (Warwick, 2013[63]).

SMEs represent important untapped potential for economic diversification. They are a key engine of economic growth, generating output, trade, employment and productivity gains (OECD, 2000[68]). In OECD economies, they represent 99% of companies and from 50% to 60% of value added, and they provide more than 70% of jobs (OECD, 2016[69]). In resource-rich countries such as Australia, Canada, Chile and Norway, they also represent more than 99.75% of companies, around 60% of value added and close to 80% of jobs (OECD, 2016[69]). In the private sector they are important contributors to trade, as they generate more than half of the valued added in international trade in OECD countries, either as direct exporters or as suppliers to multinational companies (MNCs).

Recent OECD work suggests that as SMEs start up and grow, skills, access to financial resources and internationalisation are among the most critical challenges they face (OECD, 2017[70]). Governments have a key role to play in helping SMEs overcome such barriers. OECD governments are active in supporting SME development through dedicated institutions, such as SME agencies, a wide range of programmes targeted to SMEs and public-private dialogue mechanisms (OECD, 2017[71]).

The OECD has worked extensively in Central Asia to advise governments on policies to support SMEs and address co-ordination failures, focusing on access to finance, human internationalisation, and skills and human capital. The next chapters provide eight country-specific case studies that build on three years of OECD work with the governments of the region.

Access to finance: SMEs in most Central Asian countries report difficulties in accessing finance as a major obstacle for doing business. Bank credit is the main source of external funding for SMEs in Central Asia and the focus of most of the difficulties faced by SMEs. Other sources of financing are still underdeveloped, including microcredit, credit co-operatives, venture capital and asset-based financing instruments. Both supply and demand issues hamper access to finance for SMEs. On the demand side, SMEs are exposed to high interest rates, stringent and systematic collateral requirements, and cumbersome procedures to obtain a loan. On the supply side, banks regularly mention the poor financial literacy of SMEs as an important obstacle (OECD, 2013[72]; 2016[73]). The case studies in Chapter 2 will look at:

- **Mongolia**: enhancing SMEs' **access to finance**
- **Tajikistan**: facilitating the productive use of **remittances** and supporting return **migrant entrepreneurship**
- **Kyrgyzstan**: improving **supply-chain financing in agriculture**.

Business internationalisation in Central Asia is hindered by connectivity issues inherent to the region. Inadequate hard and soft infrastructure hamper access to foreign markets and SMEs bear relatively higher transport costs as they lack economies of scale, cannot develop their own infrastructure network, and are more affected by complex trade and customs procedures (OECD, 2009[74]). Exporting SMEs also report insufficient knowledge of foreign markets, a lack of advisory services, especially on certification and standards, and insufficient financial support to export. In an increasingly connected world, SMEs could also further participate in GVCs by building linkages with MNCs. The case studies in Chapter 3 will cover:

- **Uzbekistan**: improving **SMEs export promotion**
- **Kyrgyzstan**: revamping the **investment promotion system**
- **Tajikistan**: enhancing **export policies in agriculture**.

Skills: SMEs in Central Asia frequently cite an inadequately educated workforce as an obstacle to development. They have difficulty identifying, recruiting and training workers, in part because of limited connections between the private sector and education institutions. The available workforce does not meet their skill needs, both in terms of general business skills and specific occupational competencies. The relevance and quality of education and training opportunities to develop skills appear to be limited, leading SMEs to focus mostly on-the-job-training (EBRD, 2017[75]; OECD, 2016[76]). The case studies in Chapter 4 focus on:

- **Kazakhstan**: public-private co-operation in defining **occupational standards**
- **Kyrgyzstan**: implementing reforms of **workplace training**.

Notes

[1] Purchasing power parities (PPPs) are the rates of currency conversion that equalise the purchasing power of different currencies by eliminating the differences in price levels between countries" (OECD, 2017). Real exchange rates exhibit both short- and long-run deviations from PPP values, largely illustrated in the Balassa–Samuelson theorem.

[2] However, Tajikistan has to import alumina and other materials, so the net earnings from export of this commodity are significantly lower than those from the other raw commodities (and it is not included in Figure 1.4).). Besides, Tajikistan's aluminium exports can be considered de facto water-based exports as hydroelectricity is the main input from imported aluminia to Tajikistan's aluminium exports.

[3] Turkmenistan's natural gas export rose from USD 850 mn to USD 4.5 bn, Kyrgyzstan's export of gold from USD 186 mn to USD 1 bn, Kazakhstan's exports of crude oil from USD 5.5 bn to USD 44.8 bn and Mongolia's copper export (considering 2001, as 2000 was virtually 0) from USD 162 mn to USD 987 mn.

[4] The relative weight of remittances went sharply down in Tajikistan in 2015, owing to the recession in Russia and, in particular, the contraction in its construction sector: during 2010-14, remittance flows averaged 46% in Tajikistan.

5 Tajikistan and Kyrgyzstan are the 3rd and 4th highest receivers of remittances in the world as a share of GDP.

6 That said, it is important to note that even if they do not become entrepreneurs, migrants may return with new technologies, goods and ways of doing business (Kireyev, 2006[331])

7 It should be noted that migration has likewise brought significant economic benefits to *receiving* countries, though these are not the focus of the present study. A great deal of economic activity in receiving countries now depends on foreign labour. This is particularly true of Russia, where it helps offset very low fertility, an ageing population and the consequent reduction in local labour forces.

8 The Herfindahl-Hirschmann Index (Product HHI), calculated by UNCTAD, ranges from 0 (more diversified) to 1 (more concentrated).

9 It is worth noting that there are some data issues in this context. For example (as in Figure 1.8), most of the gold sold by Kyrgyzstan went to intermediaries in Switzerland, without a clear indication of the final destination. The same was the case for the cotton sold in international exchanges by producing countries such as Tajikistan.

10 An important issue, beyond the scope of this paper, is how to adjust those guaranteed transfers in the face of macro-economic disturbances as a result of low commodity prices. The Kazakh authorities have wrestled with this recently and have, indeed, revised the regime governing the fund in an effort to put the country onto a more sustainable fiscal path (IMF, 2017[356]).

11 See the classic statement of the resource curse hypothesis by Sachs and Warner (Sachs, 2001[332]); many recent studies have also focused on the resource curse (Frankel, 2010[333]; van der Ploeg, 2011[334]; Venables, 2016[335]); on the "paradox of plenty", see Karl (Karl, 1997[336]). Numerous hypotheses have been advanced to explain this phenomenon, with most falling into one of two categories: those that focus on the impact of resource wealth on the competitiveness of other tradables and those concerned with the effect of resource wealth on the quality of institutions, political processes and governance. Other analyses focus on the consequences of commodity-price volatility, particularly for fiscal revenues, and on the interaction of commodity-price volatility with financial market imperfections, which can lead to inefficient specialisation. For an overview of explanations of the resource curse, with particular emphasis on the issue of weak financial markets, see Hausman and Rigobon (Hausmann, 2003[337]).

12 The Kazakhstan Sovereign Wealth Fund described on page 19 was instrumental in forestalling any serious "Dutch disease" for the country's economy after the fall in commodity prices.

13 Co-ordination failures stem from discrepancies between production and investment decisions in the upstream and downstream part of an industry. Suppliers and customers of intermediary goods may not produce and invest in higher tech goods, leading to a lower-tech equilibrium. Government interventions can co-ordinate, subsidize and encourage upstream and downstream companies to invest in value added technology, skills and capabilities, thus reaching a higher-tech equilibrium.

14 If a government can easily control resource rents, then it does not need public approval (e.g. through a parliament) for public finance decisions. This happened in Uzbekistan and Turkmenistan in the 1990s: the governments could control the cotton gins, and hence pay farmers less than the global price and keep the difference as state revenue. It was harder for Kazakhstan, Kyrgyzstan and Mongolia because they had to negotiate agreements with foreign companies with good know-how.

15 This proposition has not undergone much empirical analysis, for the simple reason that most of the literature focuses on minerals sectors in the period from the 1960s through the 2000s – a period during which the vast majority of mineral-rich countries opted for state ownership and control of

mineral reserves. In other words, there is too little variation in the variable of primary interest to allow a deeper analysis.

16 The scoring system ranges goes as follows: 1 - No competition legislation and institution; 2 - Competition policy legislation and institutions set up; some reduction of entry restrictions or enforcement action on dominant firms; 3 - Some enforcement actions to reduce abuse of market power and to promote a competitive environment, including break-ups of dominant conglomerates; substantial reduction of entry restrictions; 4 - Significant enforcement actions to reduce abuse of market power and to promote a competitive environment; 4+ - Standards and performance typical of advanced industrial economies: effective enforcement of competition policy; unrestricted entry to most markets

17 The ADB's definition of Central Asia includes Armenia, Azerbaijan and Georgia and excludes Mongolia.

18 Kazakhstan (41), Kyrgyzstan (69), Turkmenistan (72), Uzbekistan (75), Mongolia (78) and Tajikistan (84).

References

Abramovitz, M. (1986), "Catching up, forging ahead, and failing behind", *The Journal of Economic History*, pp. 385-406. [4]

ADB (2013), *Asia's economic transformation: Where to, How, and How Fast?*, Asian Develpment Bank. [43]

ADB (2017), *Meeting Asia's infrastructure needs*, ADB Publishing. [54]

Auty, R. (2004), *Patterns of Rent-Extraction and Deployment in Developing Countries: Implications for Governance, Economic Policy and Performance.* [38]

Baldwin, R. and D. Taglioni (2011), "Gravity chains: estimating bilateral trade flows when parts and components trade is important", *NBER Working Paper No. 16672.* [50]

Baldwin, R. (2016), *The Great Convergence: Information Technology and the New Globalization*, Harvard University Press. [51]

CAREC (2012), *Corridor performance measurement and monitoring annual report 2012*, Asian Development Bank. [61]

CASA-1000 (2017), *CASA-1000.org*, http://www.casa-1000.org/MainPages/CASAAbout.php#objective. [60]

CGTN (2017), *CGTN news*, https://news.cgtn.com/news/3d63544d3363544d/share_p.html. [58]

Chaudry, K. (1989), *The Price of Wealth: Business and State in Labour Remittance and Oil Economies*, International Organisation. [36]

Cooley, A. (2016), *The Emerging Political Economy of OBOR*, Center for Strategic & International Studies. [57]

EBRD (2017), *Forecasts, macro data, transition indicators*, http://www.ebrd.com/what-we-do/economic-research-and-data/data/forecasts-macro-data-transition-indicators.html. [48]

EBRD (2017), *EBRD Transition Report 2016-2017*, EBRD. [75]

EIU (2016), *One Belt, One Road: an economic roadmap*, EIU. [56]

Gelb, A. (2010), *Economic Diversification in Resource Rich Countries*, IMF. [34]

Government of Kazakhstan (2017), *Strategy Kazakhstan 2050*, https://strategy2050.kz/en/multilanguage/. [46]

IBRD / World Bank (2014), *Diversified development - making the most of natural resources in Eurasia*, The World Bank. [29]

Imbs, J. (2003), "Stages of diversification", *American Economic Review*, pp. 63-86. [25]

IMF (2014), *25 Years of Transition*, IMF. [6]

IMF (2014), *Sustaining long-run Growth and Macro-Economic Stability in Low-Income Countries*, IMF Policy Paper. [26]

IMF (2016), *Republic of Tajikistan - Financial System stability assessment.* [15]

IMF (2017), *IMF World Economic Outlook - April 2017*, https://www.imf.org/external/pubs/ft/weo/2017/01/weodata/index.aspx. [2]

IOM (2006), *External labour migration in Tajikistan: root causes, consequences and regulation*, International Organisation for Migration. [12]

IOM (2009), *Abandoned wives of Tajik labour migrants*, International Organisation for Migration. [14]

IOM (2010), *Tajik labout migration during the global economic crisis: causes and consequences*, International Organisation for Migration. [13]

Jones Luong, P. (2004), *Rethinking the Resource Curse: Ownership Structure and Institutional Capacity.* [40]

Lederman, D. (2012), *Does what you export matter?*, IBRD / World Bank. [31]

Malyuchenko, I. (2015), *Labour migration from Central Asia to Russia: Economic and social impact of the societies of Kyrgyzstan, Tajikistan, and Uzbekistan*, Central Asia Security Policy Briefs. [11]

Marat, E. (2009), *Labor Migration in Central Asia: Implications of the Global Economic Crisis.* [10]

Observatory for Economic Complexity (2017), http://atlas.media.mit.edu/en. [7]

OECD (2000), *OECD Small and Medium Enterprise Outlook*, OECD Publishing. [68]

OECD (2006), *OECD Investment Policy Reviews: Russian Federation 2006*, OECD Publishing. [33]

OECD (2008), *To benefit from plenty: lessons from Chile and Norway*, OECD Development Centre. [20]

OECD (2009), *Top Barriers and Drivers to SME Internationalisation*, OECD Publishing. [74]

OECD (2011), *The Economic Significance of Natural Resources: key points for reformers in Eastern Europe, Caucasus and CEntral Asia*, OECD Publishing. [30]

OECD (2012), *Kazakhstan - Investment Policy Review*, OECD publishing. [22]

OECD (2013), *Fostering SMes' participation in Global Markets*, OECD Publishing. [72]

OECD (2014), *Review of the Central Administration of Kazakhstan*, OECD Publishing. [45]

OECD (2014), *Regulatory Policy in Kazakhstan: Towards Improved Implementation*, OECD [65]

Publishing.

OECD (2015), *SME Policy Index - Eastern Europe and South Caucasus*, OECD Publishing. [66]

OECD (2015), *Enhancing Access to Finance for SME Development in Tajikistan*, OECD Publishing. [67]

OECD (2016), *Sixth meeting of the policy dialogue on natural resource-based development.* [19]

OECD (2016), *Multi-dimensional Review of Kazakhstan: Volume 1. Initial Assessment*, OECD publishing. [23]

OECD (2016), *Anti-corruption reforms in Eastern Europea and Central Asia - Progress and Challenges 2013-2015*, OECD Publishing. [32]

OECD (2016), *Competition Law and Policy in Kazakhstan*, OECD Publishing. [49]

OECD (2016), *Entrepreneurship at a glance 2016*, OECD Publishing. [69]

OECD (2016), *Enhancing Access to Finance for MSMEs in Mongolia*, http://www.oecd.org/globalrelations/eurasia-week-roundtable.htm#prs_2016. [73]

OECD (2016), *Monitoring competitiveness reform in Kyrgyzstan.* [76]

OECD (2017), *OECD Investment Policy Review: Kazakhstan 2017*, OECD publishing. [24]

OECD (2017), *OECD Trade Facilitation Indicators*, http://www.oecd.org/trade/facilitation/indicators.htm. [64]

OECD (2017), *Small, Medium, Strong. Trends in SME Performance and Business Conditions*, Organisation for Economic Co-operation and Development, http://www.oecd-ilibrary.org/content/book/9789264275683-en. [70]

OECD (2017), *Financing SMEs and Entrepreneurs 2016: an OECD scoreboard*, OECD Publishing. [71]

Ohlin, B. (1933), *Interregional and international trade*, Harvard University Press. [9]

Pomfret, R. (2014), *Global Value-Chain and connectivity in developing Asia - with application to the central and west asian region*, ADB Publishing. [53]

Ramey, G. (1995), "Cross-country evidence on the link between volatility and growth", *American Economic Review*, pp. 1138-1151. [21]

Reuters (2017), *Kazakh wealth fund says over 120 firms sold in privatization drive*, http://www.reuters.com/article/us-kazakhstan-swf-privatisation-idUSKBN1772OK. [17]

RHCS (2017), http://www.regionalhub.org/. [44]

Rodriguez-Clare (2005), *Coordination Failures, Clusters and Microeconomic interventions*, Inter-American Development Bank. [28]

University, C. (ed.) (1996), *Coordination failures and government policy: A model with applications to East Asia and Eastern Europe*, Journal of International Economics. [27]

Ross, M. (1999), "The Political Economy of the Resource Curse", *World Politics*, pp. 297-322. [39]

Ryazantsev, S. (2016), *Russia Global Affairs*, http://eng.globalaffairs.ru/valday/Labour-Migration-from-Central-Asia-to-Russia-in-the-Context-of-the-Economic-Crisis-18334. [8]

Sachs, J. (1995), *Economic convergence and economic policy.* [3]

Sachs, J. (1995), "Natural Resource abundance and economic growth", *National Bureau of Economic Working Paper 5398*. [52]

Samruk Kazyna (2016), *Annual Report*. [18]

Shafer, D. (1994), *Winners and Losers: How Sectors Shape the Development Prospects of States*, Ithaca: Cornell University Press. [37]

Tornell, A. (1999), "The Voracity Effect", *American Economic Review*, pp. 22-46. [35]

Transparency International (2016), *Corruption Perception Index*, http://www.transparency.org/news/feature/corruption_perceptions_index_2016. [47]

UN (2017), *Human Development Data*, http://hdr.undp.org/en/data. [5]

UNCTAD (2017), http://unctadstat.unctad.org/EN/. [16]

UNESCAP (2017), *UNESCAP.ORG*, http://www.unescap.org/our-work/transport/asian-highway/about. [55]

Vinokurov, E. (2017), "Eurasian Economic Union: Current state and preliminary results", *Russian Journal of Economics*, pp. 54 - 70. [62]

Warwick, K. (2013), "Beyond Industrial Policy: Emerging Issues and New Trends", *OECD Science, Technology and Industry Policy Papers*, p. No. 2. [63]

World Bank (2016), *Doing Business 2017 - Equal opportunity for all*, World Bank. [59]

World Bank (2017), *World Development Indicators*, http://data.worldbank.org/data-catalog/world-development-indicators. [1]

World Bank (2017), *Enterprise Surveys*, The World Bank, http://www.enterprisesurveys.org/. [42]

World Economic Forum (2017), *The Global Competitiveness Report 2016-2017*. [41]

Chapter 2. Business environment in Central Asia: Access to finance

This chapter explores the demand- and supply-side issues relating to access to finance for firms in Central Asia, ranging from stringent collateral requirements to high interest rates and limited financial literacy. The OECD has helped several countries in the region to enhance access to finance for private businesses, including Mongolia, Kyrgyzstan and Tajikistan. The findings from this work suggest that Central Asian governments could enhance data collection on small and medium-sized enterprises (SMEs), further improve public financial instruments via greater involvement of the banking sector, and implement financial literacy strategies for SMEs.

Setting the stage

Firms in Central Asia face barriers in accessing finance, particularly SMEs

Firms and entrepreneurs in Central Asia often identify difficulties in access to finance as a major barrier to starting, sustaining and growing their businesses (OECD, 2015[1]). As in OECD countries, SMEs in Central Asia face strong headwinds in accessing finance. Around one-quarter of SMEs in Central Asia[1] identify access to finance as a major constraint to doing business. The numbers vary strongly by economy, with more than one-third of Mongolia's SMEs struggling with access to finance, while just 4% of Uzbekistan's SMEs cite this as an issue (Figure 2.1.) (World Bank, 2017[2])[2]. In particular, small and medium-sized enterprises (SMEs), generally face higher interest rates and tighter borrowing terms, and they are more likely to be credit-rationed than large firms and have less access to formal sources of finance (Beck, Honohan and Demnirguç-Kunt, 2007[3]).

On the supply side, financial institutions see lending to SMEs as riskier. This is often due to the opacity of SME operations and their high transaction costs, under-collateralisation, limited credit history and, in many cases, lack of knowledge of financial products and lack of the expertise needed to produce sophisticated financial statements (OECD, 2006[4]; 2017[5]).

On the demand side, SMEs are also more sensitive to complex and cumbersome administrative and lending processes (OECD, 2015[1]). Agricultural SMEs, which represent the bulk of SMEs in the region, often face risks related to high collateral requirements that can barely be met by farmers whose main asset are land and buildings, which are usually located in remote rural areas and hence without significant market value. The need for collateral to secure loans also constrains innovative start-ups and SMEs whose business models rely on intangible products (OECD, 2004[6]).

While SMEs often rely on personal finance, bank finance is the most widely used external financing tool in Central Asia. However, only a small number of SMEs in Central Asia are actively using banks to finance their working capital and investment. With the exception of Mongolia, less than 25% of companies are using banks to finance their working capital, compared to around 30% in middle income countries and 33% in OECD countries (World Bank, 2017[2]). In the region overall, credit to the private sector stood at 28% of gross domestic product (GDP) in 2015 compared to 147% of GDP in OECD countries and 95% of GDP in middle-income countries (World Bank, 2017[2]) Other options for financing, such as early stage financing through business angels, venture capitalists or credit unions, are very limited.

Microfinance institutions (MFIs) are active in all countries of Central Asia with more than 100 MFIs in each country of the region, but their importance varies across countries (Box 2.1). They represent a limited share of assets in most of the region (under 5% of total assets), but account for up to 17% of outstanding loans in Tajikistan. Their role in supporting the local economy should not be underestimated, especially for regions where bank branches are scarce and for underserved populations, like women entrepreneurs. The sector shows high growth prospects but also faces several challenges, including raising more funding denominated in local currencies, diversifying product lines (various loan products, deposits, money transfers, remittances), and further consolidating and strengthening the financial management of existing institutions.

Figure 2.1. Share of Central Asian SMEs identifying access to finance as a major constraint

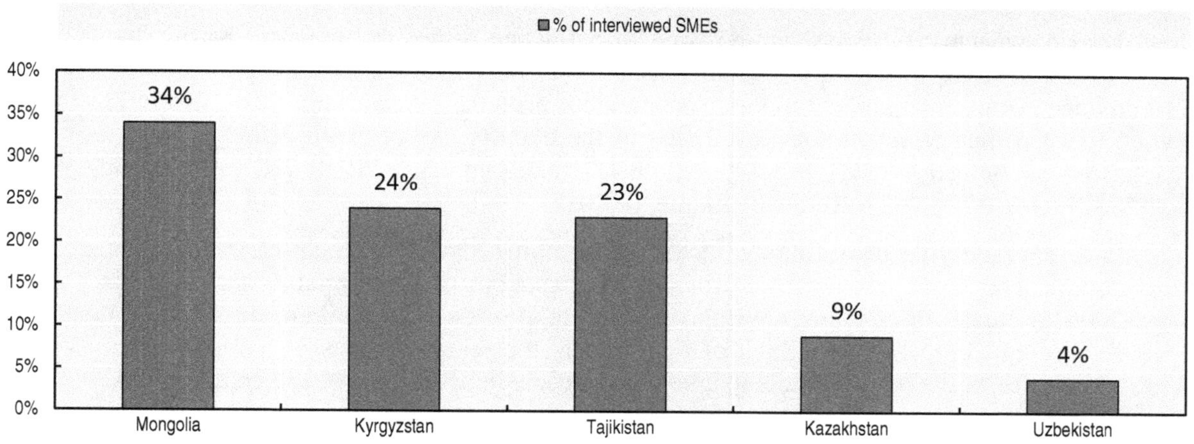

Note: Data for Turkmenistan were not available
Source: (World Bank, 2017[2])

The perception among banks that lending to SMEs is high risk is a major hurdle. To cover this risk, banks in Central Asia systematically impose high collateral requirements. Limited availability of information and a lack of financial infrastructure such as credit bureaux and collateral registries contribute to high collateral requirements for SMEs in the region (OECD, 2015[1]). Between 85% and 100% of loans require collateral and the value of the collateral required ranges from 170% to 227% of the loan amount (Figure 2.2) (World Bank, 2017[2]). Private and public credit registries in Central Asia cover between 27% and 52% of adults (World Bank, 2017[2]).

OECD/G20 high-level principles on SME financing provide a framework to support access to finance for SMEs

In 2015, at the request of the G20, the OECD developed high-level policy principles on SME financing, outlined in Box 2.2. The principles aim to support government efforts to enhance access to a diverse range of financing instruments for SMEs, including micro-enterprises, and entrepreneurs. The principles are cross-cutting and build on existing international financial principles and guidelines. They consist of 11 actions that should help SMEs gain access to finance.

Most OECD members have established additional financing institutions and programmes to help SMEs access finance (OECD, 2016[7]). Figure 2.3 provides an overview of the instruments and levers available to policy makers.

Box 2.1. Overview of microfinance institutions in Central Asia

In Kazakhstan, the Association of Microfinance Organizations of Kazakhstan (AMFOK) aims to ensure sustainable access to financial services for the population to reduce poverty and support economic growth. According to AMFOK, 136 microfinance institutions are active in the country. As of April 2017, their total assets amounted to KZT 135 478 million (Kazakhstani tenge; EUR 370 million) and had increased by 7% since the beginning of 2017.

In Kyrgyzstan, the microfinance sector was established with the help of international donors. The Association of Microfinance Organisations of Kyrgyzstan was founded in 2005 to create an enabling environment and support capacity building in the sector. According to the National Bank of Kyrgyzstan, the sector consists of 5 microfinance companies, 232 microcredit companies, 74 microcredit agencies and 172 credit unions.

Mongolia's microfinance sector is mainly supported by the Microfinance Development Fund. In 2002, the Mongolian Parliament enacted laws defining the roles and responsibilities of non-bank financial institutions and legalising savings and loan co-operatives. In 2001, a consortium of these institutions became XacBank, 47% of whose customers were rural clients. From 2002 to 2010, XacBank's assets grew by 26 times, loans increased by 43 times and savings by 25 times and it held assets worth over MNT 2 257 billion (Mongolian tugruk; EUR 773 million) as of 2016.

In Tajikistan, microfinance institutions are mainly grouped under the Association of Microfinance Organizations of Tajikistan. MFIs represent a key player in financing the Tajik economy, holding 17% of outstanding loans. Tajikistan's MFIs, which have increased to a total of 124 institutions in 2012, bear a special commitment to social goals and women's empowerment. Women account for 39% of their clients and 32% of loan disbursements.

In 2011, Turkmenistan passed legislation on "microfinance institutions and microfinance" intended to help attract financial resources. However, the institutional framework related to the microfinance sector is not fully developed, and information remains limited on the sector.

In Uzbekistan, the government is directly involved with microfinance operations through several micro-lending programmes managed through specific funds as well as through a number of commercial banks. In 2006, the government reorganised the state-run Tadbirkor Bank as the first specialised microcredit bank. Overall the country has 28 microcredit organisations, while non-bank credit organisations had assets amounting to more than UZS 123.7 billion (Uzbekistani som; EUR 27 million), 46% more than in 2015 (Central Bank of Uzbekistan, 2016[8]).

Sources: (AMFI, 2017[9]; AMFOK, 2017[10]; Central Bank of Uzbekistan, 2016[8]; National Bank of Kazakhstan, 2017[11]; UNDP, 2016[12]; Investment and Export Promotion Agency Kyrygzstan, 2017[13])

Figure 2.2. Collateral requirements for SMEs in Central Asia

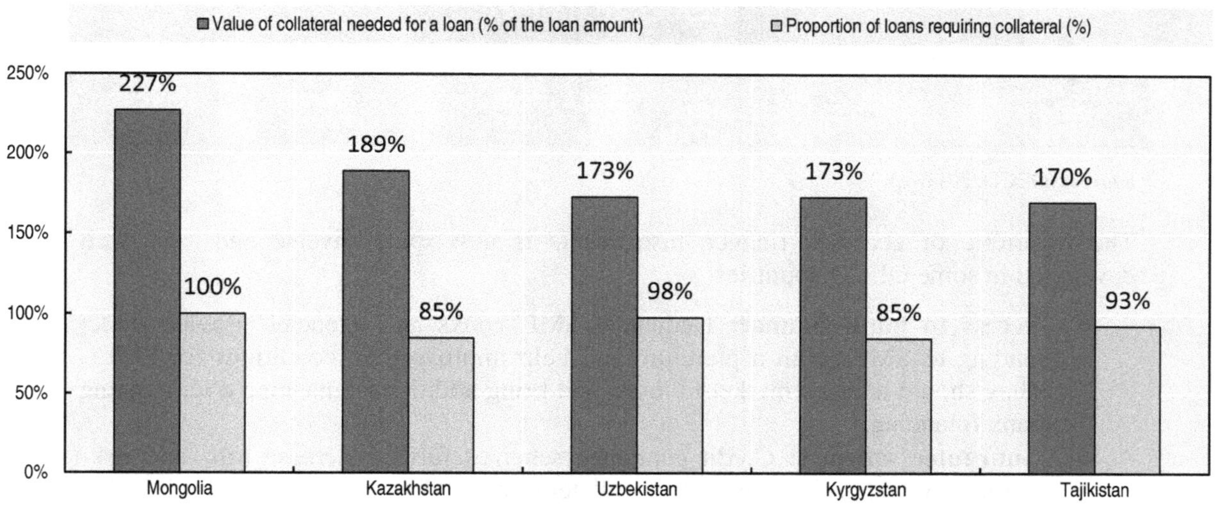

Note: Data for Turkmenistan were not available
Source: (EBRD, 2017[14]; World Bank, 2017[2])

Box 2.2. The G20/OECD high-level principles on SME financing

1. Identify SME financing needs and gaps and improve the evidence base
2. Strengthen SME access to traditional bank financing
3. Enable SMEs to access diverse non-traditional financing instruments and channels
4. Promote financial inclusion for SMEs and ease access to formal financial services, including for informal firms
5. Design regulation that supports a range of financing instruments for SMEs, while ensuring financial stability and investor protection
6. Improve transparency in SME finance markets
7. Enhance SME financial skills and strategic vision
8. Adopt principles of risk sharing for publicly supported SME finance instruments
9. Encourage timely payments in commercial transactions and public procurement
10. Design public programmes for SME finance which ensure additionality, cost effectiveness and user-friendliness
11. Monitor and evaluate public programmes to enhance SME finance

Source: (OECD, 2015[1])

Figure 2.3. Access to finance policy framework

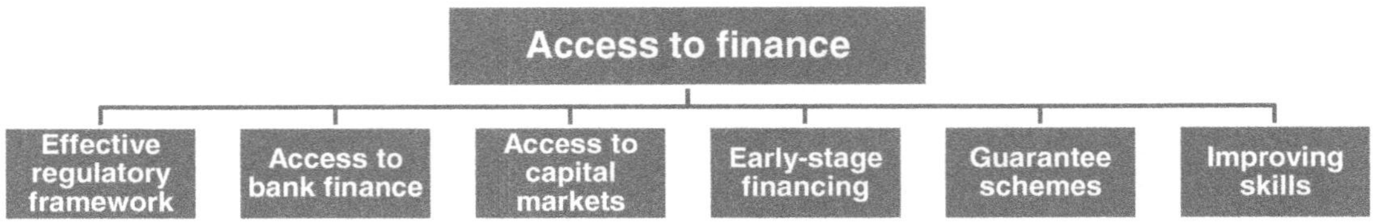

Source: (OECD, 2011[15])

The repertoire of access-to-finance instruments is now quite diverse and very well developed in some OECD countries:

- **Access to bank finance:** Dedicated SME banks and agencies provide direct lending to SMEs with a premium and help improve loan conditions for SMEs. They should address market failures, and bring additional financing over existing bank financing.
- **Guarantee schemes:** Credit guarantee schemes further increase trust and risk-sharing by addressing the lack of collateral that SMEs can offer and by insuring banks against potential credit losses and insolvencies by SMEs.
- **Improving skills:** Financial education programmes for SMEs help them become aware of financing opportunities and financial risks and opportunities. This enables them to make informed business plans and manage their financial records, planning and risks effectively.
- **Effective regulatory framework**: The legal and regulatory framework for bankruptcy helps to protect creditors' rights and to support debt recovery in case of insolvency. Credit and collateral registries also help to reduce information asymmetries by providing potential lenders with reliable information on the existing credit exposure of entrepreneurs and companies.
- **Early-stage financing:** several instruments that help start-ups, small farms and entrepreneurs. **Microfinance** institutions and **co-operatives** can help facilitate access to finance in underserved populations, particularly in the agricultural sector. **Supply chain financing** can help facilitate access to finance for companies that lack collateral, particularly in the agricultural sector where warehouse receipt systems can help overcome this barrier. **Business angels and venture capital** are important sources of capital for start-ups, as they provide initial capital and advice.
- **Access to capital markets**: capital markets can help SMEs raise funds to finance their development. SMEs can issues equity or debts securities on the main capital market or on dedicated stock exchanges. The small size of stock markets in Central Asia is however a strong barrier to this policy option in the region at this stage.

OECD work on SME financing in Central Asia suggests a need for better data, improved governance of SME support institutions and greater financial literacy

Peer reviews on access to finance in Kyrgyzstan and Mongolia were carried out at the OECD Eurasia Competitiveness Roundtable in 2013 and 2016 respectively, as well as a monitoring on Tajikistan in 2017. The example of Mongolia provides insight into how to enhance a full set of financial institutions supporting for access to finance for SMEs. Tajikistan has supported the development of early-stage financing, in particular micro-finance institutions, to help SMEs and entrepreneurs. Kyrgyzstan has designed warehouse receipt systems to facilitate supply chain finance and hence access to finance in the agricultural sector. Key recommendations that could benefit other countries in the region include:

- **Better data collection on SME access to finance:** reliable, precise and coherent data will help inform policy making on access to finance. Mongolia, Kyrgyzstan and Tajikistan could consider adhering to the OECD financial scoreboard to enhance the quality of data on SMEs, and better monitor SME business financing conditions. They could also benchmark their existing situations and programmes on access to finance for SMEs against other countries.
- **Increasing public-private co-operation in managing institutions and instruments that affect access to finance:** public financial institutions need to further involve banks and non-banking financial institutions as well as SMEs and business associations. Mongolia could improve the product offer and scope of its SME Development Fund, as well as the risk management of its Credit Guarantee Fund by further involving banks. In Tajikistan, associations of micro-finance organisations play a pivotal role in reforming the sector, and could be involved with other business associations in the governance of public funds. In Kyrgyzstan, the Chamber of Commerce and Industry and banking associations have been active in designing warehouse receipt financing (WRF), and further support will be needed from them as the WRF is implemented beyond the pilot phase.
- **Expanding financial literacy among SMEs:** aligning national strategies and initiatives with the good international practices of members of the OECD International Network on Financial Education (INFE) could foster local SMEs' understanding of financial instruments and documents, ultimately helping them to get better access to finance. For example, Mongolia needs to implement its financial literacy strategy and add a specific section and actions on SMEs. Tajikistan could help entrepreneurs, especially returning migrants, train on business cases and financial options. Kyrgyzstan could develop capacity building sessions to mobilise and train agricultural SMEs on the new financial instruments.

Table 2.1. Access to finance instruments in Central Asia

	Kazakhstan	Kyrgyzstan	Mongolia	Tajikistan	Uzbekistan
SME funding agency	Enterprise Development Fund (DAMU), the SME funding agency of Kazakhstan, provided loans to 24 000 borrowers	Not in place	SME Development Fund of Mongolia providing loans to SMEs, but operations could be improved	The Entrepreneurship Support Fund (ESF) provides subsidised loans to SMEs, but better governance is needed	Dedicated export support funds for SMEs through the Export Promotion Fund (EPF)
Public credit registry	In place	Not in place	In place	Not in place	Not in place
Private credit bureau	In place	In place	In place	In place	In place
Credit guarantee schemes	Credit guarantee scheme for SMEs under DAMU	A new local credit guarantee fund has been established. The Asian Development Bank (ADB) provided grants to create a credit guarantee scheme	The Mongolian Credit Guarantee Fund has been established, and is expanding with the support of the ADB	Credit guarantee fund in place under the name of Credit Guarantee Fund Tajikistan (CGFT)	A credit guarantee fund (the Small Entrepreneurship Guarantee Fund) is in place
Financial literacy programmes	The Ministry of Finance created the financial social network www.1ccc.kz to support entrepreneurs and increase their financial literacy. KazMicroFinance (KMF) implemented projects to enhance people's and SMEs' financial literacy.	The National Bank of Kyrgyzstan (NBKR) implemented the 2016-2020 Programme for the Increase in Financial Literacy of the Population and created the online platform www.finsabat.kg.	A draft National Financial Literacy Strategy has been prepared, and a dedicated working group set up. The Bank of Mongolia has joined the OECD / INFE	Financial literacy strategy being drafted by the National Bank of Tajikistan with the support of the World Bank. Many projects implemented by Tajik institutions along with international development partners.	Several activities organised under the framework of the project Increase in the Financial Literacy of the population in Uzbekistan, co-ordinated by the Central Bank of Uzbekistan.
Insolvency framework	Strong insolvency framework: ranks 37th in the Doing Business (DB) ranking for this dimension. Recovery rate of 41.4 cents in the dollar, 1.5 years needed to resolve insolvency.	Weak insolvency framework: ranks 130th in DB for this dimension. Recovery rate of 34.3 cents in the dollar, 1.5 years needed to resolve insolvency.	Robust insolvency framework: ranks 91st in DB for this dimension. Recovery rate of 17.1 cents on the dollar, 4 years needed to resolve insolvency.	Weak insolvency framework: ranks 144th in DB for this dimension. Recovery rate of 35.9 cents in the dollar, 1.7 years needed to resolve insolvency.	Robust insolvency framework: ranks 77th in DB for this dimension. Recovery rate of 39.5 cents in the dollar, 2 years needed to resolve insolvency.
Supply-chain finance	Various supply chain financing initiatives, including warehouse receipt finanoing for grain producers.	Successful pilot warehouse receipt mechanism, currently being expanded; legislation being drafted		Discussions to reform the secured lending legal regime under way	A collateral registry was established in 2015
Early stage financing	Active micro-credit institutions. Existing network of credit co-operatives (RCC) managed by state holding Kazagro AKK	Important role played by micro-finance and micro-credit organisations and credit unions	Limited microfinance institutions and network of co-operatives. Business angels and venture capital mostly active in the mining sector	Active associations of MFIs, current consolidation of MFIs	

Source: (OECD and ADB, 2014[16]; ADB, 2013[17]; ADB, 2015[18]; Business World, 2017[19]; Central Bank of Uzbekistan, 2017[20]; CGFT, 2017[21]; KMF, 2017[22]; Pressreader, 2017[23]; National Bank of Tajikistan, 2017[24]; Sultanov, 2017[25]) (World Bank, 2016[26])

Mongolia: Enhancing access to finance for micro, small and medium-sized firms

Access to finance is a crucial issue for micro, small and medium-sized enterprises (MSMEs) in Mongolia. In 2016, the OECD prepared five main recommendations that include: diversify the loan products on offer, improve the risk assessment tools of the Mongolian Credit Guarantee Fund, streamline the administrative procedures involved in applying for a loan and build the financial literacy of MSMEs. This sub-chapter also looks at how these recommendations could be applied to the cases of the cashmere and textile sector.

Context: Resource dependence and vulnerability

In 1990, Mongolia's peaceful revolution put an end to 70 years of one-party communist rule, opening the doors to the democratic multi-party system that has since been in place. The ensuing economic transition proved extremely difficult. In 1987 around 97% of Mongolia's trade was with Soviet-bloc countries (Earnshaw, 1987[27]), so when the Soviet Union collapsed, a severe contraction followed: real GDP fell by more than one-quarter over four years. The country turned to the international financial institutions for help and for a time Mongolia became the fifth-highest recipient of international aid per capita in the world, while undertaking deep and wide-ranging market reforms in order to secure multilateral support.

After the recession bottomed out in 1993, Mongolia's economy started growing again, driven mainly by the mining sector. Growth averaged 3.2% per year from 1994 to 2000, rising to 7.2% per year from 2001 to 2008 on the back of rising global commodities prices. Following a brief contraction in 2009 (-2%), Mongolia's economy became one of the fastest-growing in the world with real GDP growth averaging +11% per year from 2010 to 2014, driven largely by rapid growth of its mining sector – before slowing sharply to 2.3% in 2015. Declining Chinese demand for mining products and falling commodity prices, however, slowed real GDP growth to 2.3% in 2015, and to 1.0% in 2016 (IMF, 2016[28]; World Bank, 2017[29]).

Today the mining sector accounts for 17% of GDP. Most of the coal, copper and ore dug from the country's vast mineral reserves are exported to China, which is the destination for 88% of all Mongolia's exports. This dependency on a single sector and export destination is a crucial economic challenge for the country. Diversifying the economy is an urgent priority for achieving sustainable growth.

Most of the large companies operating in the country are concentrated in the mining sector, while micro, small and medium-sized enterprises (MSMEs) are the main players in all other economic sectors, especially agriculture, wholesale trade and manufacturing. Overall they generate 25% of GDP and 52% of employment (National Statistical Office of Mongolia, 2016[30]). Policies to build their educational and financial capacity could therefore be one key to diversifying the economy.[3]

A 2015 Bank of Mongolia (BoM) survey of MSMEs revealed that their main constraints were related to their "social, political and macroeconomic environment" (Bank of Mongolia, 2015[31]): 1) the limited purchasing power of the majority of the population;[4] 2) political instability, which has been the norm since 1990, with a new government every two years on average; 3) widespread mistrust of state institutions, which are often perceived as corrupt by the population and by MSMEs;[5] and 4) high vulnerability to external economic conditions. Along with these macro-level issues, access to finance was reported by MSMEs as the main micro-level constraint to doing business (Bank of

Mongolia, 2015[31]; 2015[32]; 2015[33]). A recent joint survey by the European Bank for Reconstruction and Development (EBRD) and the World Bank also found that access to finance was the barrier most frequently cited by MSMEs (31% of respondents), followed by tax rates (12%) and inadequate education of the workforce (9%); (EBRD and World Bank, 2015[34])). In 2015, domestic credit to the private sector as a percentage of GDP was 55%, compared with averages of 96% for Europe and Central Asia, and 147% for the OECD. Loans to MSMEs accounted for less than one-fifth of the total (17%), compared to 39% in Turkey and a median value of 44% in OECD countries (OECD, 2016[7]; Bank of Mongolia, 2015[33]; World Bank, 2016[35]; 2016[36]).

Credit conditions and access to finance in Mongolia are naturally influenced by the monetary policy set by the BoM. The monetary base expanded rapidly in 2013-14, when the BoM directly injected liquidity into both the financial and corporate sectors. The share of BoM credit among total liabilities for commercial banks rose to 21% in 2013, from 2% in 2012. However, this share had fallen to less than 10% by the end of 2015, partially because of the phasing out of the Price Stabilisation Programme (PSP)[6] and the tapering off of the BoM's quantitative easing programmes. At the same time, the role of local currency deposits as an alternative source of funding for banks has weakened, showing negative growth in the second half of 2015. This has further strained banking sector liquidity. The rapid growth of non-performing loans – from 4.3% of outstanding loans at the end of 2012 to 8.6% in the second quarter of 2016 – is an additional indicator of a substantial deterioration in credit conditions that has been particularly detrimental to MSMEs.

The Mongolian financial sector consisted of 14 commercial banks, 17 insurance companies, 271 credit unions, 434 non-bank financial institutions (NBFIs) and 58 securities and brokerage firms as of the first quarter of 2016. The banking system provides 97% of total lending and 93% of MSME lending. Alternative sources of financing in Mongolia have a very limited role.[7] While the number of NBFIs has grown considerably since the late 1990s, they remain very small, accounting for just 2% of financial sector lending; savings and credit co-operatives account for another 1%.

The banking sector is not particularly concentrated. The top five banks (all privately owned except State Bank, the smallest of the five) held 90% of the sector's total assets of USD 9.2 billion, and 90% of the loans (out of the total USD 5 billion) as of the first quarter of 2016 (Figure 2.4), (EPCRC, 2016[37]). The Herfindahl-Hirschman index (HHI)[8], calculated as the sum of the squares of the market shares, is equal to 1 985 (in a scale from 0 to 10 000), which indicates only moderate concentration.[9] Indeed, it might be argued that concentration is lower than one would expect for such a small economy, given the economies of scope and scale in banking. In any case, bank concentration is not considered to be a reliable proxy for (lack of) competition. The theory of contestable markets in fact suggests that the main players can be non-collusive and compete with each other in an environment with prospective new entrants (Box 2.3). This could lead to desirable outcomes from a consumer welfare perspective (OECD, 2011[38]).

Figure 2.4. The relative diversity of Mongolia's banking sector

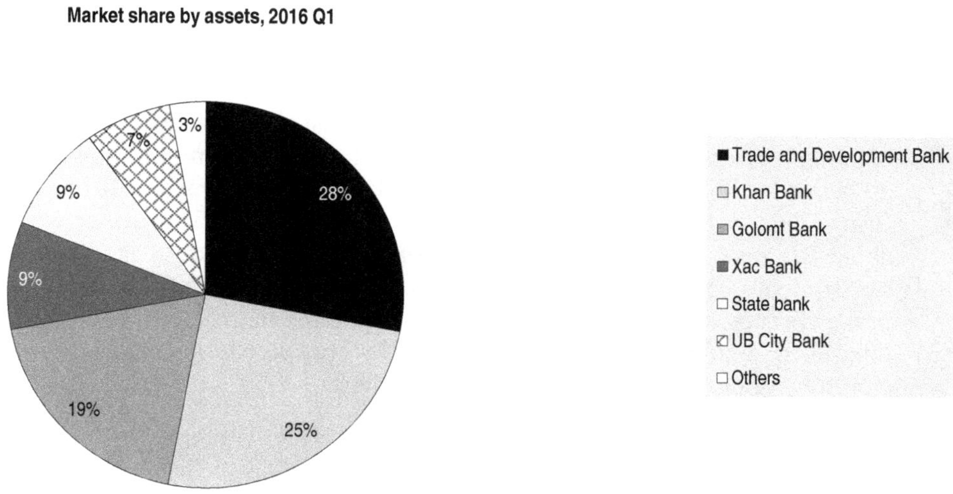

Note: 100% of banking assets = 21 557 bn Mongolian Tugruk (= 9.2 bn US Dollars, exchange rate of 24-10-2016 of USD/MNT = 2 331.5); Q1: first quarter
Source: (EPCRC, 2016[37])

Overall objective: Diversify and grow the economy by enhancing MSMEs' access to finance

To create a better business environment for MSMEs, Mongolia should focus primarily on enhancing access to finance by leveraging the role of the banking system. A system offering better loan conditions and guarantees would help to build trust among the players involved: MSMEs, financial institutions, individuals, and public institutions, such as the Mongolian Credit Guarantee Fund and the SME Development Fund. Easier credit would allow MSMEs to invest and expand both in internal and external markets, with positive effects on growth and employment.

Challenges: Access to finance

The latest Business Environment and Enterprise Performance Survey (BEEPS V) found that 56% of Mongolian MSMEs do not apply for loans because they are discouraged by the credit conditions (EBRD and World Bank, 2015[34]). MSMEs face a wide range of difficulties when accessing finance, including high interest rates (23% of respondents), collateral requirements (13%), size and maturity of loans (8%), and complex application procedures (7%) (Figure 2.5). Moreover, interviews with financial institutions operating in the market show that their ability to trust MSMEs and extend credit is hindered by MSMEs' lack of financial knowledge (EBRD and World Bank, 2015[34]).

Box 2.3. Competition in retail banking

In the absence of market imperfections, competition should drive the market towards efficiency by allocating resources in the most profitable market segments, thus encouraging agents to enter them. Banking competition should play a role in improving the loan offer for MSMEs, such as lower interest rates for loans or a lower degree of collateralisation. However, some research suggests that market power can in fact be associated with easier access to credit and better terms for small new and unknown firms. This is because large banks have the resources to create private information about borrowers that is unavailable to other players, which makes them able to lend over time on better terms and conditions (reducing the high default premium/rationing in the absence of that information). In a competitive market with frequent switches, this long-term, mutually beneficial relationship between large banks and small clients would be rarer, with increased costs for the latter.

Moreover, prudential regulation often conflicts with the aim of promoting competition. The banking business is inherently based on the trust of the consumers/clients in the financial system as a whole being stable. This means that allowing retail banks to fail, as would be necessary in a truly competitive environment, may make contagion more likely than in other sectors. An individual bank's failure to internalise risks imposes an externality on all other banks, as a run on one bank can spread fear about all the others, including healthy ones.

That is why the OECD Competition Committee has concluded that a focus on barriers to entry would moderately strengthen competition in the market without putting stability at risk. In particular, a main determinant of entry barriers is consumer behaviour. Inelastic consumer demand is often directly caused by lack of understanding of complex products, of credit conditions and of financial concepts that reduce consumer confidence and raise switching costs. The OECD suggests that the most effective ways of supporting competition would be to take steps to increase clients' financial literacy and simplify the administrative procedure for switching (see recommendations to improve financial literacy in this note).

Source: (OECD, 2011$_{[38]}$; OECD, 2008$_{[39]}$; Petersen and Rajan, 1995$_{[40]}$)

Overall, these constraints can be categorised either into supply side or demand-side problems. The main supply-side issues include unattractive and costly loans, the high and ubiquitous requirement for immovable assets to be used as collateral, and the overly complicated administrative procedures. Low financial literacy is the main demand-side problem. This assessment was also confirmed by the Economic Policy and Competitiveness Research Centre (EPCRC), a Mongolian think-tank that carried out a horizontal policy assessment for the OECD in 2015-16.[10] Moreover, the lack of coherent and accessible data on MSMEs and on their financing is an additional general issue for policy makers. These issues are discussed and Box 2.7 uses the example of the cashmere and textile sector to illustrate their impact on a sector with diversification potential.

Figure 2.5. Mongolian MSMEs obstacles to access of finance

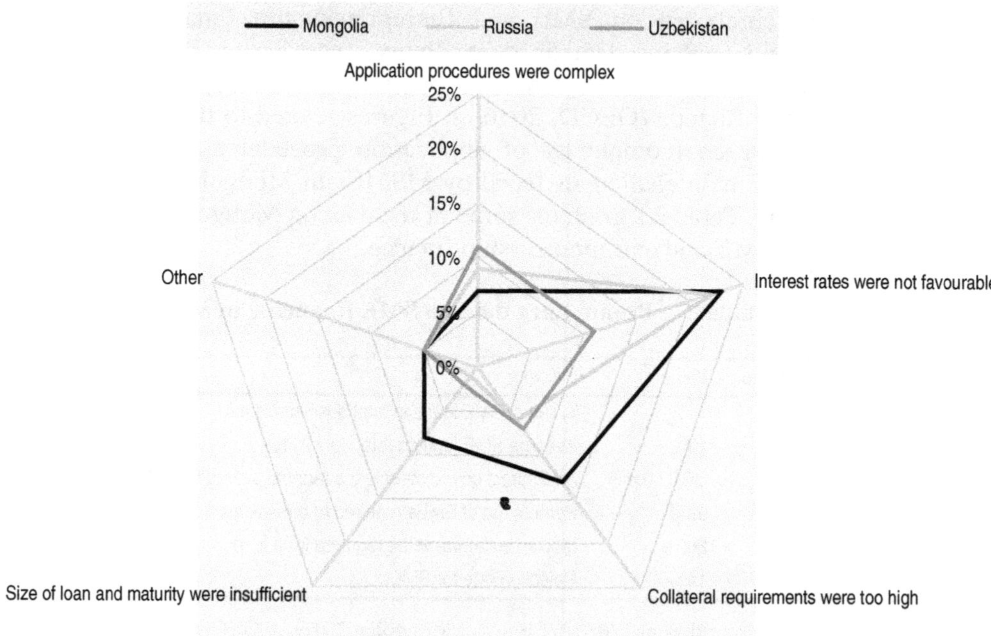

Source: (EBRD and World Bank, 2015[34])

Data on MSMEs are fragmented and lack coherence

Data on Mongolian MSMEs are gathered by a number of public institutions with limited or no co-ordination amongst them. Responsibility for data collection and analysis is currently shared by the Bank of Mongolia (e.g. data on financing, but also on behaviour and perceived difficulties of MSMEs), the National Statistical Institute (e.g. number, size, sector, geographical location) and the line ministries and their agencies, such as the Mongolian Credit Guarantee Fund (e.g. loan guarantees, SME guaranteed loans) and the SME Development Fund (e.g. financial needs, participation in government programmes). Additional data on MSMEs are gathered by the Chamber of Commerce through surveys among its members and by international organisations, such as the BEEPS survey conducted by the EBRD and the World Bank. These independent surveys offer a specific service, disseminating data to the public and to researchers; they should be encouraged.

This lack of co-ordination makes it difficult to present a clear, transparent picture of MSMEs' situation. Moreover, institutions gather data based on different definitions of MSMEs, thus creating inconsistencies among data on the various aspects of their activities and structure. The SME law of 2007 defines MSMEs on the basis of staff headcount, sector of activity and turnover, while the National Statistical Institute focuses exclusively on staff headcount. By comparison, the EU definition uses staff headcount and turnover but it does not differentiate by sector. To the extent possible, the data pulled together from different sources for this report have been selected to reflect the OECD Scoreboard on SME and Entrepreneurship Finance, which provides a comprehensive framework for assessing the financing needs of SMEs and entrepreneurs and the degree to which these are being met (Box 2.4).

Box 2.4. Key indicators for MSMEs' access to finance in Mongolia

The OECD Scoreboard on SME and Entrepreneurship Finance currently covers 37 countries, and contains data on debt, equity, asset-based finance and framework conditions. These data are complemented by an overview of policy measures to ease SMEs' access to finance (OECD, 2016[7]). Figures related to the loan offer, collateral and loan application (complexity of application procedures and financial literacy) contribute to the main challenges faced by MSMEs in Mongolia and are addressed in the next sections. Table 2.2 contains some of the data on Mongolia based on the OECD Scoreboard on SME and entrepreneurship finance.

Table 2.2. Preliminary data on SME financing in Mongolia

SME financing variable	Value	Indicator
Loan offer	14%	Share of SME loans in total business loans
	19%	Average SME lending rate (July 2016)
	USD 50 mn	SME direct government loans (annual average, 2011-2015)
Collateral	99%	Percentage of SMEs required to provide a collateral on their last bank loan
	200%	Median collateral value required for a loan
Loan application	14%	Rejection rate for SMEs

Source: (EBRD and World Bank, 2015[34]; Bank of Mongolia, 2016[41]; OECD, 2016[42])

The loan offer is not suited to the needs of MSMEs

Most MSMEs report that the loans on offer from banks and NBFIs do not meet their needs in terms of interest rates and duration. Interest rates are considered too high (average 19.6% in 2016), their maturities are too short (less than a year on average) and while the loans are large enough to provide working capital, they are usually insufficient to finance investment. The BEEPS V survey confirms that the share of MSMEs discouraged from seeking loans is the highest in the region (Figure 2.6).

Undoubtedly, macroeconomic conditions influence the high rates and the profitability of lenders. With a base rate set by the Bank of Mongolia of 12% (increased again to 15% in August 2016), the interest rate spread for bank loans in Mongolia was 6.6% in 2015. This was in line with that of Russia (6.5%), but below the average for low and middle-income countries (6.9%). Moreover, since the tapering off of quantitative easing by the BoM, banks have been financing themselves with short-term, volatile and costly deposits (close to 12% on average in 2015). Their liquidity management is thus challenging, and explains their limited options for offering MSMEs the long-term loans required to invest and expand.

Figure 2.6. Credit conditions discouraging Mongolian MSMEs

MSMEs who did not apply for a loan in the last year before the survey, reasons

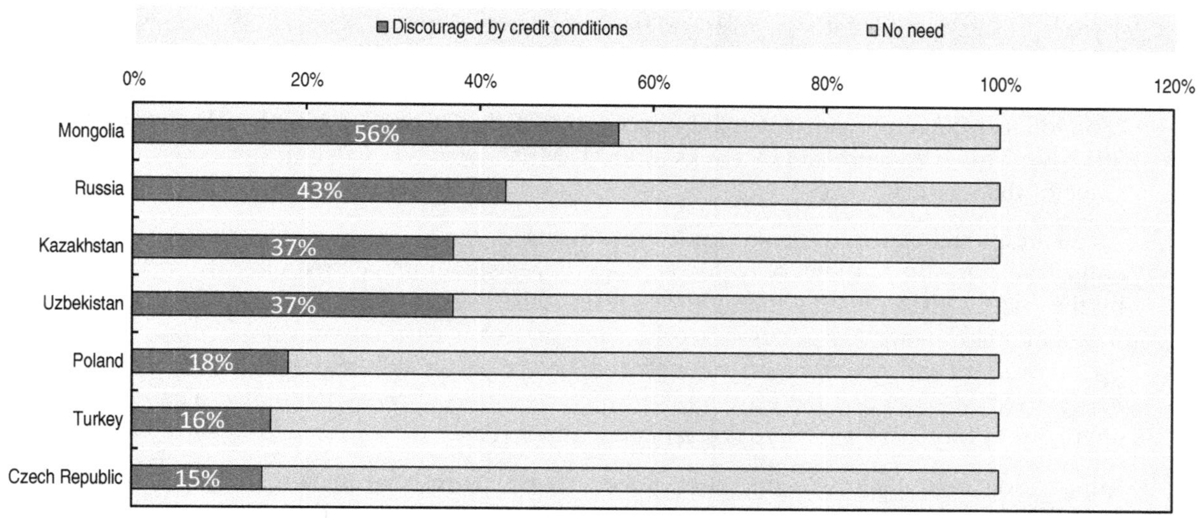

Source: (EBRD and World Bank, 2015[34])

Mongolia has established the SME Development Fund (SMEDF) to support financing for MSMEs. Its role includes providing long-term concessional loans for MSME operations, helping MSMEs to access production equipment through financial leasing, promoting the activities of subsidised MSMEs, organising workshops and training, and offering double guarantees for credit. However, following every election the new government changes the status, location and responsibilities of the SMEDF which leads to instability in its function and structure. Prior to 2012 it was an agency within the Ministry of Agriculture and Light Industry, while from 2014 it was a department within the Ministry of Industry. Today it operates from the Ministry of Food, Agriculture and Light Industry.

Between 2013 and 2016 the SMEDF provided MNT 276.1 billion in loans (USD 142 million) to 1 864 MSMEs. The government has recently approved another MNT 200 billion allocation to the SMEDF. However, compared to similar funds in other countries, the SMEDF has a limited portfolio of products and is less developed. Most OECD countries have set up similar public funds to finance MSMEs and to compensate for market failures. These tend to provide a better loan offer to SMEs, including credit interest rate support.

Collateral requirements are ubiquitous and restrictive

In 99% of cases in Mongolia, banks require collateral to guarantee a loan. This is the highest percentage in Central Asia and far higher than the median of OECD countries (where only 40% of SME bank loans require collateral). Furthermore, Mongolia has the highest median collateral value required in the region, at 200% of the value of the loan. In OECD member countries the median value is 148% (OECD, 2016[7]; EBRD and World Bank, 2015[34]).

These tough requirements reflect the deep distrust by financial institutions when lending to MSMEs. Means of enforcing creditor rights are not particularly strong in Mongolia.

The World Bank's Doing Business 2015 rankings give Mongolia a score of 7 out of 8 for the strength of its credit reporting systems, but only 5 out of 12 for the effectiveness of collateral and bankruptcy laws in facilitating lending (World Bank, 2016[35]). The same study finds that the recovery rate for creditors in Mongolia is 17.4 cents on the dollar over 4 years,[11] compared with an average in Europe and Central Asia of 38.3 cents over 2.3 years, and 72.3 cents over 1.7 years in OECD countries (World Bank, 2016[35]).[12] Moreover, the World Bank's survey on financial literacy reveals the inability of Mongolian MSMEs to present reliable accounts of their financial history (World Bank, 2012[43]). This is exacerbated by banks' and MSMEs' reported difficulties in assessing the value of their assets.

As an additional constraint, only immovable assets (e.g. real estate, plant) are accepted as collateral, since they are the only goods properly registered in the credit registry managed by the Bank of Mongolia. Although Mongolia lacks a registry of movable assets, a joint International Finance Corporation/World Bank project is currently developing one in co-operation with the government, through the Law on Movable and Intangible Property Pledges (MIPP law) and the Law on the Implementation of the MIPP Law. These were approved in July 2015 and have not yet come into force.

Information asymmetry is the core reason that commercial banks ration credit to MSMEs.[13] In this context, credit guarantee schemes (CGSs) can help banks accurately identify lending risk and improve their ability to make appropriate lending decisions (Levitsky, 1997[44]). Public intervention is justified, because weak co-ordination among private sector providers may prevent them entering the market for credit guarantees (De la Torre, Gozzi and Schmukler, 2008[45]). There is some evidence that CGSs are a cheaper way to expand access to finance than direct lending. CGSs are also market friendly, as the lending institution usually has sole responsibility for deciding whether to issue the guarantee (Beck, Klapper and Mendoza, 2008[46]). Moreover, CGSs can be a mechanism for risk transfer and diversification – by covering part of the default risk, the lender's risk is lowered. CGSs are particularly relevant in emerging markets and developing economies as they can encourage banks and NBFIs to get into the MSMEs market, thus improving the institutions' lending technologies and risk-management systems (World Bank, 2015[47]). Provision of credit guarantees is also the most widely used policy instrument in the 34 countries included in the OECD Scoreboard on SME and Entrepreneurship Finance which reviews policy measures to support SME finance (OECD, 2016[7]).

The Mongolian Credit Guarantee Fund (MCGF) was established in 2013. It is the main institution in charge of providing guarantees to MSMEs in Mongolia. From 2013 to 2015 it issued guarantees to the tune of MNT 31.2 billion (USD 16 million), unlocking a total of MNT 76.2 billion in loans (ADB, 2015[18]). However, limited resources and unreliable operations have hindered its capacity to support the credit market, and operations have halted since mid-2015 due to the limited guarantee funds available and the decrease in applications sent by banks (Box 2.5). Banks lost confidence since some guarantees were not repaid by the MCGF; during interviews with the OECD they underlined that no guarantee was paid by the MCGF in 2016.

MCGF representatives also stated that fees amount to 3% of the loan and coverage is up to 60% of the total amount borrowed; this is in line with the OECD average. However, at 12%, defaults appear to be higher than similar schemes in other countries, such as Turkey's Credit Guarantee Fund (around 5%), and Estonia's KredEx (around 2%). This is even more striking given MCGF's high rejection rate for applications (26% compared to

KredEx's 20%[14]). In 2016, the OECD carried out a short analysis of the MCGF's risk scoring tool. While the tool appeared robust, staff's lack of practice and capacity to use the tool to reduce the rejection and default rate appear to be a substantial problem. The fund's team is currently working on improving internal operations with the support of international organisations.

Box 2.5. Mongolian Credit Guarantee Fund's protocol for working with banks

The MCGF has a bilateral agreement that governs its relations with the banks. It also has an operational protocol with banks based on the following procedure. The MCGF establishes a co-operation agreement (called a framework agreement) with banks prior to operation. Once a bank submits an SME-borrower's loan guarantee application to the MCGF for approval, the MCGF will revise the loan application as necessary, assess the risk and decide whether to provide the guarantee. Based on the decision of the MCGF Committee, which includes representatives from banks, the MCGF establishes a tripartite agreement with the bank and the borrower. After the guaranteed loan is issued, the MCGF conducts monthly monitoring and evaluation of loan utilisation, business operations and the repayment process. The bank subsequently submits monthly reports to the MCGF on loan repayment.

Source: OECD interviews, 2016.

OECD interviews with banks suggest that there is limited trust in the guarantees offered by the MCGF. There are reported cases of the MCGF refusing to pay out the guarantee and preferring to go to trial instead. Without examining the specifics of these cases, it is apparent that trust in the MCGF can be heavily undermined in such circumstances, reducing the institution's effectiveness in sustaining the credit market. This is also confirmed by the results of the OECD survey on MSMEs, which indicates that bank officers are often not interested in the possibility of a guarantee by the MCGF as a substitute for collateral.

The administrative process to obtain a loan is cumbersome

Cumbersome procedures were the fourth most important reason given by Mongolian businesses for not applying for a loan (Figure 2.6): 7% of Mongolian businesses declare that they were discouraged from applying for a loan because of the procedures involved (EBRD and World Bank, 2015[34]). This is similar to Kazakhstan (8%) and Russia (9%), but higher than some OECD countries, including Poland (4%) and the Czech Republic (2%). MSMEs and business associations interviewed by the OECD confirmed that MSMEs need to submit five different administrative documents, often involving multiple interactions with several public agencies and certification bodies (including the tax administration, local administration, and environment agencies). According to an OECD survey of MSMEs, the complexity of this process stems from insufficient co-ordination among and within government agencies, and with the SMEDF and banks; unnecessary documents being requested; the same documents being asked for several times; the requirement for burdensome and costly notarial seals; the limited knowledge of agency staff; and lack of information provided by the administration.

MSMEs also face a complex process when applying for a subsidised loan from the SMEDF. The whole process takes between six and nine months according to MSMEs, and the uncertainty surrounding the various steps can be discouraging and make their application irrelevant. With very limited support, MSMEs must prepare a total of 30 documents for the 2 institutions (the private bank and SMEDF). Of these, seven are actually administrative documents that the MSME must submit to different public agencies (Table 2.3). Most official documents are available as online forms, except the social insurance statement which requires additional documents to be presented in person.

Table 2.3. Documents required for MSMEs' subsidised loan application in Mongolia

	Mongolian bank	SMEDF
Entrepreneurs	A copy of citizen identification card	Civil documents
	Statement of residential Khoroo[1]	Statement of residential Khoroo[1]
	Collateral information (copy of certificate)/inquiry whether it is already collateral	State registration certificate of rights to the collateral property
	Application of executive official	
	Photo size 3x4	
Project	Business plan (extensive)	Business plan (extensive)
	Agreements related to the main operations (supply, purchase")	Proposed sale plans and contracts
	Calculation of loan profit and repayment source	Loan repayment graphics
	Photos related to the main operations	List of photos of equipment
	Ordering agreement	
	Official letter for the loan request	
	Shareholders' meeting resolution	
	Calculation of loan disbursement	
	Forms and contracts related to loan request	
Company	State Registration Certificate of Enterprise	State Registration Certificate of Enterprise
	Statement of Tax Administration	Statement of Tax Administration
	Company charter	Company charter
	Brief introduction of the company	Information about current business
	Number of employee	Structure, number of employees
	Financial statements of previous years (by quarter)	Financial statement of previous year
	License for manufacturing and services	
	List of work done in the past, and estimated profit	
	Audit of financial statement	
	Annual report for 2012, 2013	
		Social insurance statement, record
		Location of enterprise
		Employees' major and professional qualification
		Annual turnover, sales, percentage of export
		Name, type and photos of products to produce
Total administrative documents required,	6	6
of which overlapping	5	5
Total other documents,	19	12
of which overlapping	8	8
Total	25	18
Total overlapping	13	13
Total of 7 administrative docs + 23 additional docs = 30 total documents to be presented by SMEs		

1. Administrative subdivision of Ulaanbaatar.

Source: (OECD, 2016[48])

This administrative process is costly for companies in both time and resources. This is particularly acute for MSMEs which do not have dedicated staff and time to deal with these procedures. Interviews conducted by the OECD suggest that in some cases the complexity of the process discourages MSMEs from even attempting to access the financial system.

Various bank officials complained about the poor quality of the projects submitted to them during interviews with the OECD, but also reported a reluctance to refuse projects that had been approved by the SMEDF. They also said that the quality and robustness of loan applications supported by the SMEDF were questionable, and they underlined the lack of transparency of the process leading to this list (Box 2.6).

Box 2.6. The SMEDF's operational protocol

In the current setup, loan applications are assessed by the SMEDF, approved by the Ministry of Industry and submitted to banks as a list of selected loan applications. Following a decree issued by the ministry, the SMEDF and ministry's SME policy officers in district offices prepare the tenders and disseminate information to the public. MSMEs prepare applications and send them to district offices. District offices select those that meet the requirements and submit them to the Project Selection Committee (and Sub-committee) of the SMEDF. These committees, mainly composed of representatives of the SMEDF and the local administration (but not of banks), review and submit the list of selected projects to the Minister of Industry for approval. After receiving the approval, this list is transferred to the commercial bank or NBFIs.

Source: (Ministry of Industry, 2016[49]).

Since 2007, Mongolia has established 41 one-stop-shops (OSSs) for citizens, with support from the Swiss Development Cooperation (SDC). These aim to increase the accessibility and transparency of public services related to social services, land, employment and notary procedures and programmes in all regions and most districts of Mongolia (ILO, 2016[50]). In the first half of 2014 they served 845 000 customers, and the rate of satisfaction was high (SDC, 2015[51]). However, they do not include business-relevant information and business associations; MSMEs interviewed by the OECD had little or no knowledge of these one-stop-shops. Various partners of the OSSs have identified areas for improvement, including streamlining bureaucratic procedures further, improving co-ordination with local authorities, and giving the OSS a wider remit than simple information provision (ILO, 2016[50]).

Box 2.7. Access to finance in the Mongolian textile sector

Cashmere is a key resource for the Mongolian economy. The country produces about 2 500 tons of raw cashmere each year, making Mongolia the world's second largest producer of raw cashmere (15% of global production) after China (75%). The sector is the top non-mining related sector in Mongolian exports, representing 6% of national exports. Annual export revenues from cashmere and textiles are close to USD 300 million but they could be higher – a significant share of production is smuggled into China. Mongolia is currently concentrating on the production and export of raw cashmere – it would benefit from further developing local manufacturing of textiles and garments, and from targeting exports of higher value-added cashmere products. Only an estimated 30% of raw cashmere is converted into finished products in Mongolia (National Statistical Office of Mongolia, 2015[52]).

Cashmere and textiles could play an important role in the diversification of the Mongolian economy. However, access to credit is holding them back. The Mongolian government has distributed USD 68.8 million to the sector in the form of Chinggis Bonds – state-issued bonds distributed through Golomt Bank. However, this approach, while benefiting SMEs, risks crowding out private investors and distorting market competition. The difficulties faced by businesses in the cashmere and textile sector when accessing finance reflect the four issues faced by MSMEs across the economy (the fifth issue – data quality – is only indirectly relevant for MSMEs):

1. **The loan offer is not suitable.** Loans have relatively short maturities and capital is expensive. For example, herder loans are provided for a maximum of two years. Interest rates on domestic currency loans fluctuate around 20%, twice the rate of foreign currency loans. Textile and garment manufacturing companies also face high interest rates, and the small sizes of loans prevent them from upgrading their equipment.
2. Herders and manufacturing companies in the cashmere sector also **lack collateral**. Herders face high risks due to climate vulnerability, nomadism and the absence of real property. Their lack of immovable collateral leads banks to undervalue assets and eventually stop lending to herders. Manufacturing companies also complain of undervaluation of their fixed assets, especially factories used as collateral. Banks interviewed by the OECD underlined the difficulty of valuing assets on the fluctuating real estate market. MCGF intermediation is therefore crucial to sustain lending to both targets. The cashmere sector represents 5% of MCGF users and 8% of guarantees, but is over-represented for high-risk loans (17%) compared to its share in national production (close to 10%). The MCGF also records a relatively high rate of non-performing loans (28%) in the cashmere sector.
3. **The procedure for obtaining a loan** can also be a barrier both for herders and textile manufacturing firms. More than 30 documents are required, and the process can take between two and nine months. More specifically, herders suffer from a lack of clear information and the difficulty of providing proof of permanent residence. Manufacturing companies interviewed by the OECD reported a lack of training and information on the part of both banks and public agencies.

4. The cashmere sector suffers from low financial literacy. There is a correlation between low financial literacy scores and high presence of herders in several regions (World Bank, 2013[53]). Financial literacy difficulties vary along the value chain. While herders lack basic financial education, especially to make savings and investment decisions, manufacturers and exporters need training in advanced financial auditing and reporting, as well as developing a global financial strategy for their expansion.

Sources: OECD analysis, questionnaires and interviews; (World Bank, 2013[53]; National Statistical Office of Mongolia, 2015[52]; UNESCO, 2013[54]) (Bank of Mongolia, 2015[31])

Understanding of complex financial concepts is limited

A financial literacy survey carried out by the World Bank in 2012 revealed that Mongolian adults had limited understanding of basic financial concepts, although the vast majority of the population was aware of financial products and had mastered basic arithmetic (World Bank, 2013[53]). For example only 39% understood inflation correctly, in contrast to an average of 44% in the other countries included in the survey and 60% in advanced economies (World Bank, 2013[53]). Another survey found that agricultural SMEs (mostly herders) were less familiar with financial concepts than firms operating in Ulaanbaatar and in regions with mining activities and companies. The Financial Regulatory Committee (FRC), the Bank of Mongolia and the Ministry of Finance have prepared a National Strategy for Financial Literacy that was approved in 2016; however, it does not include provisions explicitly designed for MSMEs. In addition, the strategy does not map the various initiatives around the country to expand financial literacy (such as the Banking Academy on the supply side and the National Incubation Centres Association on the demand side). Having an overview of these initiatives would allow them to be leveraged to unlock possible synergies and could avoid overlap (Bank of Mongolia, Financial Regulatory Commission and Ministry of Finance, 2016[55]).

Recommendations to enhance MSMEs' access to finance

In 2015, the OECD adopted the G20/OECD High-Level Principles on SME Financing, following a request from the G20 Finance Ministers and Central Bank Governors (G20/OECD, 2015[56]). These principles form the basis for much of the analysis in this sub-chapter, and the Mongolian government could consider them when developing its long-term strategy for SME development, as they give an all-encompassing view of the most relevant policy areas. These include improving the evidence base; strengthening SME access to bank financing; promoting financial inclusion; improving transparency in SME finance markets; including risk-sharing principles in publicly supported SME finance instruments; and the best way to monitor government programmes.

In particular, in order to improve the ability of MSMEs to obtain loans for their working capital and investment projects, it is recommended that the Government of Mongolia design and implement a consistent plan aimed at streamlining the loan offer and making them more affordable. At the same time, the government also has a fundamental role to play in providing entrepreneurs and MSMEs with a stronger grounding in financial planning to ensure that loans can be repaid thanks to companies' healthy financial management. Credit conditions and accessibility (especially in rural areas) should be tackled with a comprehensive national strategy that should be included in the next national SME strategy.

Specific recommendations are as follows:

- gather and disseminate more coherent and reliable data on MSMEs through a co-ordinated approach by the Bank of Mongolia, National Statistical Institute and line ministries, while also leveraging the OECD Scoreboard on SME and entrepreneurship finance;
- develop the conditions for a better and less costly loan offer to MSMEs by diversifying the products offered by the SME Development Fund (SMEDF);
- overcome the collateral issue by improving the Mongolian Credit Guarantee Fund's risk appraisal techniques and building the trust of banks;
- make it easier for MSMEs to request loans by streamlining the banks' and SMEDF's administrative processes through a one-stop-shop backed up by support and training, and enhancing the co-operation between the SMEDF and partner banks and
- increase financial literacy through public-private co-ordination, including activities for MSMEs in the National Strategy for Financial Education, and creating tailored tools to meet MSME needs, also leveraging the expertise of the OECD International Network for Financial Literacy.

The remainder of this sub-chapter provides more details on each of these recommendations. It also applies these recommendations to the case of the cashmere and textile sector.

Recommendation 1: Develop and disseminate coherent data on MSMEs

Reliable and coherent data are a necessary precondition for effective policy design. It is recommended that Mongolia increase co-ordination across the various institutions in charge of MSME data collection. To this end, the OECD Scoreboard on SME and Entrepreneurship Finance could provide a comprehensive and internationally comparable framework.

Action A: Develop a co-ordinated approach among public institutions and consider joining the OECD Scoreboard on SME and entrepreneurship finance

The varying definitions of MSMEs used by the various state institutions, in some cases differing from the 2007 SME law, should be harmonised. A whole-of-government approach will help to overcome the lack of co-ordination among the public bodies collecting and working on MSMEs data. The OECD Scoreboard could provide a basis not only for ensuring harmonisation of practice across government bodies, but also for enabling Mongolia to develop data better suited to international comparisons. A list of core indicators is presented in Table 2.4.

Table 2.4. Core indicators of the OECD Scoreboard on SME and entrepreneurship finance

Core indicators of the OECD Scoreboard	Data availability (Y/N)	Mongolia: Source of Data
1 – Share of SME loans in total business loans	Y	Bank of Mongolia
2 – Share of SME short-term loans in total SME loans	N	Not published (Bank of Mongolia)
3 – SME loan guarantees	Y	Not published (Mongolian Credit Guarantee Fund)
4 – SME guaranteed loans	Y	Not published (Mongolian Credit Guarantee Fund)
5 – SME direct government loans	Y	SME Development Fund
6 – SME rejection rate	Y	BEEPS – EBRD/World Bank
7 – SME loans used	Y	BEEPS – EBRD/World Bank
8 – SME NPLs/SME loans	N	Not published (Bank of Mongolia)
9 – SME interest rate	Y	BEEPS – EBRD/World Bank
10 – Interest rate spread between large and small enterprises	N	Not published (Bank of Mongolia)
11 – Percent of SMEs required to provide collateral	Y	BEEPS – EBRD/World Bank
12 – Venture and growth capital	N	Various privet equity funds
13 – Asset-based finance	N	-
14 – Payment delays	N	-
15 - Bankruptcies	N	-

Source: (OECD, 2016[7])

Recommendation 2: Diversify the products offered by the SME Development Fund

The SMEDF is best placed to support a better and more extended loan offer to MSMEs through direct lending and co-financing with banks. The operations of the fund are being re-organised, and the Department for Coordination of SME Policy Implementation is now under the Ministry of Food, Agriculture and Light Industry. This is expected to ensure greater stability of resources and governance, which would allow continuity in the operations and more reliability for all its partners, especially banks and MSMEs. A good example for Mongolia to follow is that of KOSGEB, the Turkish SME development organisation (Box 2.8). KOSGEB supports loans to SMEs through credit interest subsidies and has a diversified loan offer which responds to the needs of MSMEs.

Action B: Diversify SMEDF's products

Currently the SMEDF's offer through the partner banks is limited to a few types of loans and leases. SMEDF's management should expand this offer to better address the needs of MSMEs throughout their life cycles (e.g. seed capital, export, cash flow, long-term investment). According to international experience, the loan portfolio should therefore include: new start-up loans, express loans (cash flow), fixed capital loans, international development loans, green loans, innovation loans and export loans, among others. Double guarantees should be designed in mutual partnership with the private sector, also including the MCGF when necessary. A single MSME should be able to request more than one type of loan, depending on the goal of its project or investment plan. Each type of loan should vary in its maturity, size, rates and collateral requirements (ideally none) to tailor it to need. In addition, specific loan programmes could be created to target priority MSME types, such as start-ups. As start-ups are particularly sensitive to external financing conditions, they may benefit strongly from programmes such as seed financing and long-term innovation loans, as well as possibly equity financing.

Box 2.8. Financial services for SMEs in Turkey

According to the OECD Scoreboard on SME and Entrepreneurship Finance, SME loans in Turkey increased by 23% in 2014 compared to 2013, to reach a total of 38% of total business loans. Non-performing loans (NPLs) have remained limited since 2010 and were recorded at 3% of total loans (OECD, 2016[7]). Public support for access to finance for SMEs in Turkey is mainly provided by KOSGEB, the Turkish SME development organisation affiliated to the Ministry of Science, Industry and Technology. It supports the development of more than 850 000 registered SMEs in the country. KOSGEB offers a wide range of financial products to improve access to finance for SMEs, including credit interest support, guarantees, training and equity.

Regarding credit interest support, KOSGEB works in close co-operation with banks. KOSGEB pays the loan interest for SMEs which receive loans from banks under a contractual agreement with KOSGEB. Loans supported by KOSGEB cover various SME needs, such as working capital, exports, investment, new employment and energy efficiency. Since 2003, more than 214 000 SMEs have benefited from the programme, representing USD 370 million in loan interest support and USD 4 billion of credit volume created.

To enhance SMEs' access to its services, KOSGEB has an extensive network of branches, 88 service centres and 33 technology development centres. It is present in all Turkey's provinces. This large network is also leveraged to offer many different forms of non-financial support to MSMEs: from enabling Turkish companies to take part in international trade fairs, to training and mentoring – especially through the adoption of the "Entrepreneurship Support Programme". KOSGEB has also signed 83 research and development innovation protocols.

KOSGEB also offers a very interesting example of financial literacy promotion. It has established e-learning infrastructure called "SME Campus", a dedicated platform for SME e-training. Moreover, an agreement between KOSGEB and the Council of Higher Education underpins university-business co-operation involving a dedicated platform (USIMP).

Sources: OECD interviews with the KOSGEB; (OECD, 2016[7])

BPIfrance, the French public bank for SMEs, gives access to a vast portfolio of loans from which SMEs can select through the website or directly in agencies. Moreover, BPIfrance has recently incorporated a private equity division that focuses on French companies with good growth potential. DAMU, the SME fund in Kazakhstan, has organised its loan offer by sector, regional presence, and target (e.g. programme to support the manufacturing industry, programme to support regional priority projects, microcredit for women's entrepreneurship).

Recommendation 3: Ease collateral demands by making the Mongolian Credit Guarantee Fund more effective

In order to reduce the need for overly demanding collateral requirements, the Mongolian Credit Guarantee Fund (MCGF) needs to improve its risk assessment techniques and product offer. It also needs to increase co-ordination with and build the trust of private sector players. This may require modifying the provisions in the current law on the Credit Guarantee Fund. International experiences may offer viable models for increasing reliability for all stakeholders (government, banks and MSMEs). Most successful CGSs in OECD countries involve frequent visits to banks' offices and exchanges with management and loan officers. For example, broad international experience in CGS management, especially appropriate funding and best practices for monitoring the fund, could be drawn on, especially the World Bank's high-level Principles for Public Credit Guarantee Schemes for SMEs (World Bank, 2015[47]). The MCGF should expand its operations to support development, and could consider including banks on its board and involving them in the guarantee appraisal. Finally, the MCGF should improve its claims management.

Action C: Strengthen trust between MCGF and banks by including bank representatives on MCGF's board, by implementing financial agreements and by sharing risk assessments

The MCGF could update its operational protocol and start co-operation with banks on risk procedures prior to drafting the framework agreement, in order to reflect agreed upon practices in the agreement. In addition, it is recommended that the MCGF engage in frequent interactions with banks to discuss and adjust risk assessment policies and to share practices and views on applications. This would ensure a mutual understanding of the guarantee assessment and provision, and better management of default. Including banks on the board of the MCGF would increase trust and allow the financial sector to have shared ownership of the instruments, with positive effects on MCGF's expansion and effectiveness. International experiences like those of DAMU and BPIfrance have illustrated the potential of this arrangement. This would be complementary to the financial capacity needed to implement the financial agreements with private players.

BPIfrance has a network of regional offices which include banks on their governing boards so they can participate in decisions on loan and risk assessment policies. Moreover, BPIfrance loan officers are required to show a good understanding of the sector and the business operations of the SME, in addition to having loan assessment skills. Staff always visit the SMEs' facilities when assessing the loan, sometimes jointly with banks. Moreover, BPIfrance meets with partner banks almost weekly to agree on the loan assessment and ensure that its processes and policies are aligned with those of each partner bank.

Action D: Enhance risk appraisal using risk assessment tools from banks and institutions with international experience

The MCGF could improve its risk assessment tools by leveraging international experiences. Most of the operational indicators of the fund are in line with international experience: the share of total MSME loans covered by guarantees is, at 1.4%, similar to DAMU and higher than Estonia's KredEx (0.5%) and Turkey's CGF (0.2%). Pricing mechanisms should be linked to risk exposure, usually charging a guarantee commission fee covering administrative and management costs.[15] The MCGF's fees can go up to 3% of the value of the guarantee, comparable to Turkey's CGF, while KredEx's go up to 1% and DAMU's to 0.1%. Coverage of the guarantees is up to 60%: this is somewhat lower than, but still in line with, international players (DAMU, KredEx and CGF of Turkey are at 70%, 75% and 85% respectively). A comparison of 70 schemes worldwide revealed an average coverage ratio of 80%, although coverage is lower for more risk-averse schemes (without public funds) or schemes exposed to higher risks (Beck, 2010[57]).

The MCGF could benefit from further capacity building and support in implementing risk assessment tools and procedures. It should also consult with banks before and during the risk assessment to align methods, and to agree on the risk-scoring results and the decision on providing (and later paying) the guarantee. This will be key for building the trust of the banks. In principle, all parties involved (SMEs, banks, credit guarantee schemes) should retain a sufficient share of the risk and responsibility to avoid moral hazard (OECD, 2013[58]). Concerning the late payment of the guarantee, the World Bank's Principles for Public Credit Guarantee Schemes for SMEs, especially Principle 13, give general guidelines for structuring an efficient claim management process, providing incentives for loan loss recovery and aligning with the legal and regulatory framework (World Bank, 2015[47]).

BPIfrance uses a dedicated computerised instrument for risk assessment, which assigns a score to counterparty risk, project risk and transaction risk. The rating obtained is only a support to decision making, which also takes into account immaterial elements, such as qualities and weaknesses of the project, the entrepreneur profile, and market perspectives. BPIfrance also leverages its extensive experience by combining statistical data on defaults of past projects, observed over long periods, to infer the most appropriate multiplier for each fund.

Recommendation 4: Streamline administrative procedures for loan applications

The government could undertake several actions to simplify the administrative process of obtaining key documents for loan applications to banks and the SME Development Fund and make it more business friendly, not least by reducing the number of required documents and making them more easily accessible.

Action E: Increase co-ordination between SMEDF and partner banks

The SMEDF should allow banks to join the decision-making process at the earliest possible stage by organising regular knowledge-sharing meetings. It may consider including them on both the loan selection committee and the board (possibly as rotating members, to ensure the independence of the institution). While loan applications are currently first assessed by the SMEDF and then by banks, the SMEDF has indicated that it might change its process for spending new funds so that loan applications would be assessed by banks before being reviewed by the SMEDF, a practice that offers considerable advantages. The review would involve regular discussions and knowledge sharing between the banks and the SMEDF. The SMEDF should hold discussions with the banks to agree on the documents and forms to be requested by each partner bank. The procedure could be aligned with that of partner banks, so that the MSME does not need to produce additional documents for the bank and for the SMEDF. This practice would not only strengthen trust relations with banks, it would also simplify the process and reduce the number of administrative documents required to apply for subsidised loans. It could mean that at least 13 documents would only have to be submitted once (instead of twice as is currently the case – see Table 2.3). It would also better align the procedure to reduce the remaining 17 documents that need to be submitted (see next action point).

BPIfrance's more established practice allows SMEs to negotiate either with the bank or with BPIfrance – the application is sent to the other co-financer once approved by the first institution. As the documents required by the banks and BPIfrance are similar, they are requested only once by the first institution in contact with the MSME to avoid duplication of procedures. This model requires deep trust between banks and BPIfrance. In the case of DAMU, the bank receives and analyses the request, and transmits it to DAMU if the case is strong enough. DAMU checks the quality of applications and either accepts or rejects the co-financing. DAMU's board membership includes its partner banks (Box 2.9).

Box 2.9. DAMU's support for SME development in Kazakhstan

The role of SMEs in Kazakhstan's economy has become more and more important in recent years. The number of SMEs more than doubled between 2005 and 2014. In the same period, SMEs' share of employment increased from 26% to about 32%. Similarly, whereas in 2005, SMEs generated 11% of Kazakhstan's GDP, by 2014 this figure had risen to about 25%. Kazakhstan's Entrepreneurship Development Fund (DAMU) was established in 1997 by the Government of the Republic of Kazakhstan. To start with, DAMU mainly managed state budget funds for the programme of measures to support domestic commodity producers. It was only in 2002 that the fund started to provide small businesses with financial resources.

DAMU has two key goals. The first is to ensure and strengthen financial support for SMEs. The increase in the volume of financial support for SMEs is achieved through co-operation with second-tier banks, the recourse to a subsidised fee rate for credits, the provision of loan guarantees, the development of the microfinance sector, and the attraction of extra funding from domestic and external markets (e.g. ADB Fund, National Fund of Kazakhstan etc.). Secondly, DAMU aims to promote SME competencies. It pursues this goal by offering training opportunities to entrepreneurs, extending the outreach of consulting services (more than 200 centres have already been set up all around Kazakhstan), and introducing new forms of distance consulting methods, such as call centres and business portal services.

DAMU provided financial support to 23 995 borrowers for a total amount of KTZ 1 391 billion (USD 4.2 billion). Furthermore, 1 484 projects for a total loan amount of KTZ 293 billion (USD 885 million) were financed from the National Fund in the manufacturing and services sector.

Sources: (DAMU, 2014[59]; DAMU, 2014[60]; DAMU, 2016[61])

Action F: Reduce the number of documents required by banks

In order to stimulate demand for loans, the government could consider reducing the number of official documents required by banks from MSMEs. In France, the number of documents required by banks is generally slightly lower, with up to 18 documents related to the project, the entrepreneur and the company. In particular, French banks only require three administrative documents to be submitted, compared to five in Mongolia (Table 2.5).

Table 2.5. Documents required to obtain a loan in Mongolia

	Mongolian Bank	French bank
Official documents required	A copy of citizen identification card	Identification
	Statement of tax administration	Recent fiscal statements / tax bill
	State Registration Certificate of Enterprise	Recent Kbis (state registration of enterprise)
	Statement of residential Khoroo[1]	
	Licence for manufacturing and service	
Total	**5**	**3**

Note: [1]Administrative subdivision of Ulaanbaatar

Source: OECD interviews with Mongolian banks (March 2016); OECD interviews with French banks (April 2016).

Action G: Consider implementing one-stop-shops for MSMEs

The principle of a one-stop-shop is to bundle in a single physical/online space all the procedures required for business administrative processes. The gain in efficiency is two-fold: a one-stop-shop should not only simplify the procedure for the entrepreneur, it should also help co-ordinate the various ministries involved in the process. Creating one-stop-shops for businesses would save the MSMEs a considerable amount of time. By providing a single interface for questions and clarification, this would strongly simplify the administrative part of the process, avoid contradictions and make the timings more predictable. It would also optimise costs for the public administration. Georgia provides a good example of a successful one-stop-shop for businesses (Box 2.10).

Mongolia could extend its current citizens' OSSs to include services to businesses. New OSSs may also be needed. To set these up, the government could consider the following steps:

- Secure high-level political support and buy-in through discussion and government endorsement. The launch of this project will also require a wide media campaign by the government to inform businesses, and will also require the support of business associations including the Chamber of Commerce and Industry.
- Give a clear mandate to the Ministry of Food, Agriculture, and Light Industry to co-ordinate the work with other administrations, and to identify which administrative processes should be handled by the one-stop shops. This could be done by selecting the processes and documents which are the most used by MSMEs, and by leveraging the procedures currently supported by the existing OSS.
- Consult widely to identify the needs, key missing procedures and access limitations for businesses in the current OSSs. Identify those procedures that can be dealt with by the OSS on behalf of businesses, revising and simplifying protocols and guidelines with the relevant administrations, and agreeing on the transfer of authority from the administration to the one-stop-shop for approving and rejecting applications.
- Agree on clear, transparent and shared business pricing and location of the shops, potentially in different locations from the existing OSSs (OECD, 2013[62]).
- Staff the OSSs by detaching staff from line ministries and providing additional staff (OECD, 2010[63]).
- Establish information technology tools and a database to address and store requests (ILO, 2016[50]).

- Launch two pilot OSSs – one in Ulaanbaatar and the other in a district outside the capital – to test the robustness of the model in two different contexts.

In the future, the government could also consider launching an electronic one-stop-shop to allow businesses to conduct all procedures online, as was done in Kazakhstan. Kazakhstan has also developed an efficient e-government system that delivers all licenses electronically through a single website. Most administrative procedures can now be conducted be online, which saves time and resources for businesses (OECD, 2014[64]).

Box 2.10. One-stop-shops for businesses in Georgia

In 2012, the Georgian government introduced a "single window principle" by creating the Public Service Hall; a large centre where all certificates needed to launch a business are provided. After creating the first one-stop-shop in Batumi, Georgia replicated this initiative across the country – to 13 other cities and regions. The large diversity of services provided, 400 in total, as well as the effectiveness of this organisation, explain its success.

Starting a business in Georgia now only requires two procedures and takes on average two days. In 2012, the Public Service Hall was awarded the United Nations Public Service Award in the category Improving the Delivery of Public Services. The World Bank Doing Business report 2016 ranked Georgia 6th in 2016 for its ease of starting a business.

Sources: (Government of Georgia, 2016[65]; OECD et al., 2015[66]; World Bank, 2016[35])

Recommendation 5: Improve financial education by ensuring the national strategy is tailored to MSMEs

Good financial literacy is an important element in improving access to finance. It is defined as the ability of individuals to make informed judgements about financial products and behaviour and to take part in financial decisions (OECD, 2013[58]). A high level of financial literacy not only contributes to financial well-being and to financial market stability, it also helps improve access to finance through a better understanding of financial products. Low financial literacy remains a major obstacle for MSMEs in Mongolia, because they are generally considered un-bankable due to their weak management skills and poor financial reporting (World Bank, 2012[43]).

In 2016 Mongolia started to implement a national strategy for improving citizens' financial literacy, further building their capability to make sound financial decisions, increasing long-term saving, and enhancing trust in the banking system and promoting long-term, sustainable economic development in the country (Bank of Mongolia, Financial Regulatory Commission and Ministry of Finance, 2016[55]). The structure of the strategy follows quite closely the High-level Principles on National Strategies for Financial Education developed by the OECD International Network on Financial Education (Box 2.11). The strategy has been approved and is now being implemented. Mongolia has set up permanent public-private co-ordination working groups, which are critical to avoid unnecessary overlap and to ensure effective and sound implementation.

The country now needs to ensure that the structure of the national strategy involves all relevant stakeholders and addresses all relevant target groups: currently it focuses only on personal and household finances. Although younger people and rural dwellers are addressed as target groups, the national strategy does not refer to entrepreneurs or MSMEs. This would also encourage competition in the banking sector, as more informed customers (citizens and MSMEs) would be able to assess more precisely which offers might be the most convenient for them and if and when it is worth switching banks/financial provider. It may also push commercial banks to develop "switching packs" that allow a smooth transition between different bank accounts.[16]

Box 2.11. OECD/INFE High-Level Principles on National Strategies for Financial Education

Within a fast-evolving financial landscape, where access to financial services is made easier as more risks are being transferred to citizens, financial literacy has become a key life skill for individuals. Financial education can help enhance financial literacy and contribute to individuals' participation in financial, economic and social life. As a complement to financial inclusion and financial consumer protection policies, financial education is also important to restore confidence and trust in financial markets, and can support financial stability. An increasing number of countries have started developing nationally-coordinated financial education policies as a way to bring together the relevant stakeholders, avoid duplication and save resources.

Mongolian public institutions involved in financial education should consider joining the OECD International Network for Financial Education (INFE). In 2012, the OECD/INFE (comprising representatives from over 110 countries, including all G20 members, and relevant international organisations) developed high-level principles addressing governments and public authorities and providing non-binding international guidance and policy options for the efficient development of national strategies for financial education. The principles provide guidance on the preparation, governance, roadmap development and implementation of national strategies. These principles were endorsed by the G20 leaders at the 2012 Los Cabos Summit.

As a follow-up to the High-level Principles, in 2015 the OECD/INFE developed a Policy Handbook on National Strategies for Financial Education to support governments and key stakeholders in addressing challenges linked to the implementation of national strategies for financial education. It provides an overview of the status of national strategies worldwide, an analysis of relevant practices and case studies and identifies key lessons learnt.

Sources: (OECD/INFE, 2012$_{[67]}$; OECD/INFE, 2015$_{[68]}$)

Action H: Build synergies by mapping and co-ordinating all existing initiatives on financial literacy for MSMEs

The government should create a precise map of all the main initiatives carried out by public and private players in the country. These players should be involved in implementing the national strategy in order to empower them, increase their effectiveness within established structures, and find the most appropriate approach for each target group.

Several organisations are offering financial literacy training but with little (or no) co-operation with other institutions such as the SMEDF, the MCGF or the working groups on financial literacy set up by the Bank of Mongolia and the Financial Regulatory Commission:

- Many banks have launched numerous initiatives to support financial literacy – these need to be better co-ordinated. This would ensure public participation and supervision.[17]
- The Banking and Finance Academy was established in 2010 with the participation of the country's eight largest banks and supported by the Mongolian Banking Federation. In 2012 it absorbed the Bank Training Institute of the Bank of Mongolia. It aims to increase education by providing training services and certification for banking and finance professionals, including specific training for dealing with MSMEs. The academy could also expand its operations by "training trainers": training current or former banking officials, as well as employees from relevant ministries and government agencies so they can in turn train MSMEs.
- The Mongolian National Business Incubator Federation, established in 2008, includes 12 business incubators funded by the Ministry of Labour and Social Welfare. Its aim is to generate employment opportunities and alleviate poverty through financial education and support to Mongolian MSMEs. In addition, another four Small to Medium Enterprise Development Centres are funded by the Department of Agriculture.

Action I: Include financial education for MSMEs in the national strategy and consider joining the OECD International Network for Financial Literacy

Mongolia should include a dedicated pillar and implementation tools for building MSMEs' financial literacy in the national strategy. A strategy tailored to MSME needs, with appropriate tools and actions, would be more effective than hoping that building citizens' financial literacy will trickle down to entrepreneurs and MSMEs as well. Public and private training programmes for MSMEs would give them the skills required to present their financial statements and formulate reliable financial plans so that they become more "bankable". Online information and tools – either on a comprehensive national strategy website or a dedicated MSME website – could complement other measures. Various OECD countries (like Australia and Portugal) and non-members (like Indonesia) have started to target MSMEs in their national strategies (Box 2.12).

Sector focus: Enhancing access to finance in Mongolia's cashmere and textile sector

Better data on SME financing, when available to policy makers, could improve the effectiveness of policies in the cashmere sector. As of today only fragmented statistics are available especially regarding nomadic herders and their financing opportunities and capabilities.

Box 2.12. Australia's financial literacy strategy and tools

Australia aims to provide the right environment for SMEs, including financial and education conditions, as pointed out by the OECD Scoreboard on SME and Entrepreneurship Finance. Loans to SMEs represent 32% of total business loans in 2014, and interest rates declined to 6.2% in 2014, down from 8.3% in 2010. In addition to providing loan guarantees and support to SMEs, the Australian government pays close attention to consumer protection and financial education through public institutions like the Australian Competition and Consumer Commission (ACCC) and the Australian Securities & Investment Commission (ASIC) (OECD, 2016[7]).

Australia's National Financial Literacy Strategy has a section that specifically focuses on MSMEs, as part of a comprehensive approach that encompasses all Australians. The strategy uses tools designed to reach self-employed people, entrepreneurs and SMEs. An extensive website for financial literacy improvement provides information, tools and training, including:

- MoneySmart website: MoneySmart is the reference website for increasing financial knowledge and includes financial information, videos, online training and calculators.
- Being Money Smart Certificate IV: a competency that companies can obtain online that covers establishing a small business, being a contractor, business planning, and managing business finance and compliance.
- Guidance for self-employed people: MoneySmart also gives guidance on how to manage cash flow, and savings for taxes and retirement
- Online teaching resources for educators addressing students in vocational training.
- The Australian Business Portal: provides information on planning, starting and growing your own business.
- Financial reporting quiz for directors: a free 10-question multiple choice quiz to test knowledge of financial reporting. It provides explanations of answers after the test.

Sources: (ASIC, 2016[69]; ASIC, 2016[70])

Enhancing SMEDF's portfolio for the cashmere sector would ease access to finance by herders and cashmere-producing SMEs and reduce the sector's public investment dependency without setting the private sector aside. The SMEDF's portfolio could be better tailored to the sector, such as through a greater focus on cash flow history and projections, express loans, and loan maturity to match the cycle of herding activities.

The MCGF could continue to support the textile sector with customised guarantee products that would also leverage movable assets and past and future cash-flow statements. It should also refine risk assessment criteria in the sector to reduce the rate of payment defaults.

Simplifying administrative procedures of both banks and public funds would also increase the sector's access to finance. This should include clearer information and removing the need for herders to provide proof of permanent residence. The government could expand information about government programmes and training in rural regions, and centralise information and procedures in the form of one-stop shops located in both cities and rural areas.

Financial education tools for MSMEs in the sector could be tailored to herders and manufacturers respectively. For instance, online training and information on loan and saving decisions and opportunities might better suit herders, while manufacturers might also benefit from workshops on advanced financial reporting and business management. Following Australia's example (Box 2.12), the creation of an extensive financial literacy website available through smart phones and covering MSME business planning and financial management could help improve financial literacy among herders and manufacturers alike. Considering the relatively high penetration of mobile phone technology in Mongolia, including in rural areas, its use could support the dissemination of financial information, training and calculators. Facilitating the productive use of remittances and supporting return migrant entrepreneurship.

The way forward

Table 2.6 outlines an indicative roadmap for implementing the policy recommendations. This roadmap takes into account the need to strengthen co-operation among public credit institutions, to increase evidence-based policy on SME financing, to further build capacity at the public credit institutions, and to increase exposure and knowledge sharing with international experience especially by joining the OECD Scoreboard on SME and entrepreneurship finance and the OECD International Network on Financial Education.

Table 2.6. Suggested implementation roadmap for Mongolia

Recommendations	Indicative implementation timing		
	Short term < 1 year	Medium term 1-3 years	Long term > 3 years
Gather and disseminate coherent data on MSMEs			
A – Develop a co-ordinated approach among public institutions and consider joining the OECD Scoreboard on SME and entrepreneurship finance	■	■	
Diversify the products offered by the SME Development Fund			
B – Diversify SMEDF's products	■		
Overcome collateral issue by making the Mongolian Credit Guarantee Fund more effective			
C – Strengthen trust relations between MCGF and banks by including bank representatives on MCGF's board, by implementing financial agreements and by sharing risk assessments	→	→	→
D – Enhance risk appraisal using risk assessment tools from banks and institutions with international experience	■	■	
Streamline administrative procedures for loan applications			
E – Increase co-ordination between SMEDF and partner banks	→	→	→
F – Reduce the number of documents required by banks	■		
G – Consider implementing one-stop-shops for MSMEs	■	■	
Improve financial education by ensuring the national strategy is tailored to MSMEs			
H – Build synergies by mapping and co-ordinating all existing initiatives on financial literacy for MSMEs	■		
I – Include financial education for MSMEs in the national strategy and consider joining the OECD International Network for Financial Literacy	→	→	→

Tajikistan: Facilitating the productive use of remittances to finance entrepreneurship

Remittances play an important role in the economy of Tajikistan. The government should develop policies to facilitate their productive use in the domestic economy and boost access to finance for entrepreneurs and SMEs. The OECD developed recommendations in this area in 2014 and monitored their implementation in 2017. This sub-chapter is the result of that monitoring. It records the progress made and suggests further solutions to better use remittances to finance small firms and entrepreneurs in the country, such as improving the banking of remittances and enhancing financial literacy and business skills.

Context: Remittances as a driver of growth

Remittances play a key role in Tajik economy and amounted to 31% of gross domestic product (GDP) in 2016. This is lower than the 44% registered in 2013, mostly due to the depreciation of the Russian rouble (RUB) as most remittances are denominated in roubles (ADB, 2017[71]; World Bank, 2017[72]).

Unemployment remains high, at 11%, and limited job opportunities continue to encourage workers to migrate. The bulk of Tajik migrants still work in Russia, where 79% of the Tajik diaspora resides, followed by Ukraine (5.0%), Germany (4.9%) and Kazakhstan (2.7%) (United Nations, 2015[73]). As a result, 76% of the USD 2 259 million remittances sent to Tajikistan in 2015 came from Russia, significantly more than the flows from Kazakhstan (6.3% of the total), Ukraine (4.0%) and Germany (3.7%) (World Bank, 2017[72]). The slowing of the Russian economy has reduced the number of labour migrants from 800 000 (16% of the working population) in 2013 to 467 000 (9%) in 2016, with a corresponding negative effect on remittances.

Studies conducted on a wide set of emerging economies show that a consistent flow of remittances promotes financial development, which in turn stimulates growth and poverty reduction. In particular, financial development is connected to the effect of remittances on the aggregate level of deposits and credit intermediated by the local banking sector (Aggarwal, Demirguç-Kunt and Martinez Pería, 2010[74]). The use of the formal financial sector to transfer remittances plays an important role by increasing transparency and accountability.

However, the use of the formal financial sector might be unpopular in the absence of incentives for migrants, as money transfer organisations (MTOs) cost less to use and there is no deposit insurance scheme (Grigorian and Kryshko, 2017[75]). Incentives are particularly important in Tajikistan, as the 2015 banking crisis inflicted a severe blow to public trust in the stability of the financial system. In fact a significant, if decreasing, share of migrants' remittances are still transferred through MTOs (Figure 2.7).

The banking crisis that hit Tajikistan during the monitoring period (Box 2.13) worsened conditions for migrants' families receiving remittances. It pushed many to withdraw their bank deposits and reduced their willingness and ability to save, as well as reduced Tajikistan's already low levels of financial inclusion. The National Bank of Tajikistan (NBT) recently surveyed the population about their savings and 68% of respondents said that they were not able (56%) or not willing (12%) to accumulate savings, 20% that they kept them under their pillow and only 12% said that they were keeping their money in credit institutions or banks (National Bank of Tajikistan, 2017[76]).

Box 2.13. The banking crisis in Tajikistan

Traditional banks in Tajikistan are facing severe capital issues, as the ratio of capital to risk-weighted assets fell to just 5.4% in 2015, against the required 12%. In December 2016, the government recapitalised four banks, to a total of USD 400 million (7.1% of GDP). Turmoil in the financial sector has tightened credit conditions for small and medium-sized enterprises (SMEs). Borrowers have already been hit hard by the depreciation of the Tajikistani Somoni (TJS), which lost almost half its value between the end of 2014 and May 2017, as almost 60% of outstanding loans are denominated in USD. The share of non-performing loans (NPLs) in bank portfolios jumped to 55% in 2015, from 30% in 2014. Credit to the private sector shrank from 23% of GDP in 2015 (in line with Kyrgyzstan's share but well below Kazakhstan's 38%) to around 10% at the end of 2016.

Sources: (World Bank, 2017[77]; ADB, 2017[71]; National Bank of Tajikistan, 2017[76])

Nevertheless, there is evidence that receivers of remittances are subject to a wealth effect which makes them more likely to invest their savings in micro-enterprises, usually in self-employment, overcoming liquidity constraints (Woodruff, 2007[78]; Mesnard and Ravallion, 2006[79]). The studies do not suggest that the majority of remittances are used for productive investment, but over time their cumulative impact is still significant. Most remittances were and are used for consumption, but the OECD recommendations focused on how these financial resources could be used productively, in particular as a form of internal financing of SMEs (OECD, 2015[80]).

Overview of 2014 recommendations

In 2014, the OECD recommended taking advantage of migrants' remittances and returning migrants' skills to improve access to finance and support entrepreneurship. The 2014 OECD recommendations focused on ways to enhance access to finance for SMEs, by designing and implementing policies to support both the supply side (loan offers) and demand side (financial literacy) (OECD, 2015[80]).

Recommendation 1: On the supply side, facilitate the banking of remittances

Most remittances in 2014 were channelled through MTOs such as Western Union, Money Gram and Golden Crown. Money was withdrawn directly in cash, without passing through Tajikistan's financial system. The OECD recommended three specific steps (OECD, 2015[80]):

- To create a technological platform to connect these MTOs to the financial system and link the country's payment system[18] to migrant destination countries' payment systems, especially Russia's. This would also have the effect of encouraging financial inclusion and the take up of official bank accounts. At present only a very small minority of the population (12%) has a bank account (World Bank, 2017[81]).
- To consolidate the microfinance institution (MFI) sector to allow MFIs with stronger capitalisation to offer better products to SMEs, transform themselves into micro deposit institutions (MDIs) or even request banking licences.

- To improve the operational management of the Entrepreneurship Support Fund to offer better financing alternatives to SMEs in the country.

Recommendation 2: On the demand side, support business creation and create a one-stop-shop for migrants

The 2014 review suggested two steps to the government (OECD, 2015[80]):

- To organise and promote financial literacy in the country, both for the general population and for SMEs. Citizens and returning migrants with better financial skills would be keener to open bank accounts, hold savings and access credit. The OECD's principles on financial education and awareness could be leveraged to structure a sound National Financial Literacy Strategy (OECD, 2005[82]; OECD/INFE, 2012[67]). International conferences, leaflets, television shows and other marketing tools could all prove useful in extending the reach of initiatives by public agencies and private-sector associations.
- To provide practical and project-based entrepreneurial training to equip return migrants with the skills needed to start a business, including through dedicated centres (one-stop-shops). The creation and management of courses tailored to migrant needs should be promoted by public and private training institutions. Support should also continue after the training, with counselling and coaching activities offered at all stages of business creation and development.

Findings of the 2017 monitoring assessment

The Government of Tajikistan has made progress in acting on the OECD recommendations, but much remains to be done to implement them. On the supply side, the NBT is establishing a payment structure to allow remittances and other financial flows to be channelled into the official financial system. However, the impact of these measures will depend critically on the authorities' success in dealing with the banking system's troubles and re-establishing a measure of confidence in the soundness of banks and other financial institutions. On the demand side, financial literacy has become a priority for the government, and the NBT drafted a National Strategy for Consumer Protection and Financial Literacy with the support of the World Bank, to provide a framework for the many different initiatives currently carried out with the support of international organisations (IOs).

Monitoring of Recommendation 1 finds efforts to improve the banking of remittances but access to finance for entrepreneurs remains challenging

Recommendation 1: On the supply side, facilitate the banking of remittances

The banking of remittances has partly improved thanks to new regulation

The NBT, with the support of the World Bank's Payment System Modernization project, set up a national payment system policy framework in October 2014, "that prioritises legal, regulatory, institutional and infrastructural reforms required for the promotion of electronic payments in the country" (FIRST, 2015[83]). The National Processing Centre is now handling 80% of debit card transactions in Tajikistan, reducing the country's dependence on other countries' payment systems. The inefficiency of having all card payments cleared outside the country (mainly in Kazakhstan and Russia) was pushing local banks to invest in their own systems and thus creating additional fragmentation. Moreover, reducing additional costs and promoting the safety of payments increases trust in the financial sector, which is particularly relevant to supporting deposit mobilisation, especially in the current crisis.

In 2016 the NBT also started working with the Russian authorities to connect the country's payment system to the Russian one, to support the transfer of remittances through the official financial system. The resulting reduced costs and greater reliability encouraged many migrants to modify their behaviour. Data from the Central Bank of Russia show that in 2016, remittances from Russia to Tajikistan totalled USD 1.9 billion and that no more than 30% of this (USD 579 million) was transferred through MTOs. This is a considerable shift, as MTOs transferred close to 100% of remittances in the preceding years (Figure 2.7).

Figure 2.7. Remittances from Russia to Tajikistan

USD mn

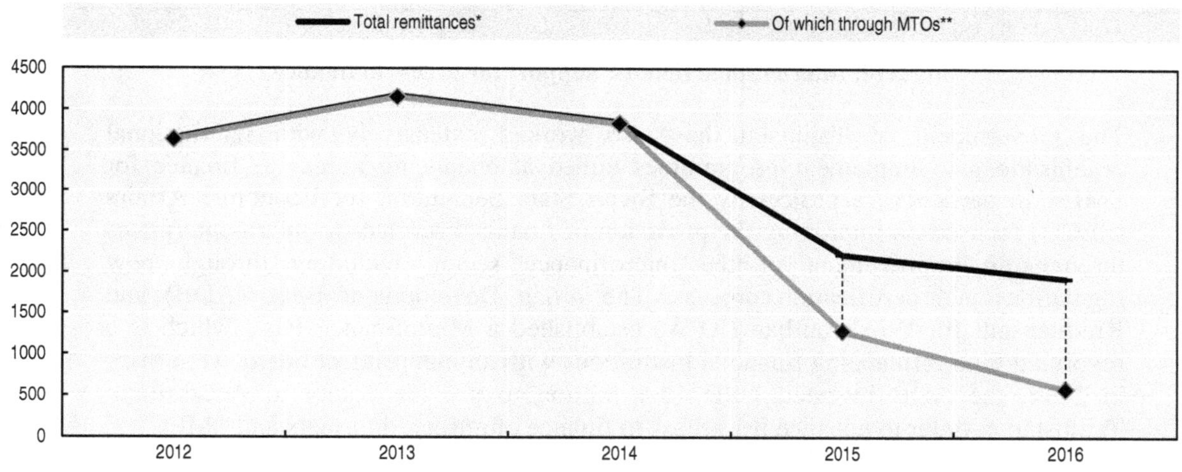

1. Includes cross-border wire transfers of income from physical persons resident and physical persons non-resident to physical persons resident and physical persons non-resident carried out with and without accounts in credit institutions. It includes also remittances via money transfer systems.
2. Includes payment made through ANELIK, BLIZKO, CONTACT, InterExpress Western Union, Zolotaya Korona, Sberbank (Hummingbird), International Money Transfers LEADER, UNISTREAM, and the Russian post.
Source: (Central Bank of the Russian Federation, 2017[84]).

The NBT has also taken additional supply-side measures to increase the penetration of financial products in rural areas, where most migrants and their families comes from. A new NBT regulation[19] led to the opening of an estimated 1 420 Banking Service Units (BSUs), which are smaller than bank branches but provide a range of basic banking services, all around the country. MTOs now often operate through the BSUs around the country, with their staff working in the same buildings. Moreover, the regulation requires that all remittances in RUB must be converted into TJS for withdrawal by citizens at an official rate and that half of the foreign currency must be resold immediately to the NBT.[20]

Several banks have started offering deposit-related savings products tailored to migrants' needs. A bank account can be opened before the migrant departs and the migrant's family has access to it. There have only been limited information campaigns promoting these products, a fact that contributes to their limited use, and their precise impact has not yet been evaluated. Recent turbulence in the banking sector has certainly slowed their uptake.

The National Bank of Tajikistan has triggered a consolidation in the microfinance sector

To encourage consolidation and strengthen the financial stability of MFIs, the NBT introduced higher capital ratios in 2016, raising them from TJS 1 million to TJS 4 million for MFIs (from USD 125 000 to USD 500 000) and from TJS 4 million to TJS 6 million (USD 500 000 to USD 750 000) for micro deposit organisations (MDOs). This measure has put some of the smallest and least active MFIs out of business, reducing their number by 15% to 91, of which 38 were MDOs. The sector, initially supported by IOs (Box 2.14), needed consolidation. The number of microfinance borrowers fell from 561 000 in 2014 to 480 000 in 2015 and 366 000 in 2016, showing that the lack of trust in the banking sector might have spread to the microfinance sector.

Box 2.14. International donors' support for access to finance

The Government of Tajikistan has also worked extensively with international organisations to implement programmes aimed at enhancing access to finance for SMEs. In particular, a project by the Swiss State Secretariat for Economic Affairs (SECO) focused on improving the provision of financial services to micro-enterprises through an improvement of the microfinance sector, including through new regulations and certification process. The Asian Development Bank (ADB) and Kreditanstalt für Wiederaufbau (KFW) established a Microfinance Fund which is a revolving fund refinancing financial institutions with an independent board. Moreover, in 2014, the ADB invested USD 14.4 million to provide equity to AccessBank Tajikistan in order to enhance the access to finance of unserved farmers and SMEs.

Source: (ADB, 2014$_{[85]}$)

However, according to the AMFOT (Microfinance Association of Tajikistan), the technical difficulties involved in integrating the operations and records of small players into bigger systems, and the lack of reliable accounts of past operations, have hindered consolidation attempts. Since 2015, only a few MDOs have obtained banking licences from the NBT, partly due to the current difficult banking market conditions. The only example in 2016 was the MDO Standard Malia, which became the CJSC Bonki Beynalmilal Toimiston (the International Bank of Tajikistan).

The Entrepreneurship Support Fund was established to improve access to finance for SMEs but its governance hinders its effective operation

The State Committee for Investment and State Property Management (SCISPM) established the Entrepreneurship Support Fund (ESF) in 2015,[21] which provides subsidised loans at low interest rates (around 7% against the average market rate of 23%) to SMEs engaged in strategic sectors. The management of the fund has been moved under the Cabinet of Ministers. To date, the fund has supported 132 projects totalling TJS 120.3 million (USD 15.2 million).

International experience shows that transparent, well-managed public credit institutions can support the development of SMEs (OECD, 2016[86]). However, Tajikistan's business associations are not involved in the management of the fund and their levels of trust in it are low, according to interviews carried out by the OECD, both in bilateral meetings and during the open discussion in the Public Private Working Group organised in Dushanbe. They report a lack of consistency and transparency in decision making on loans, and an unclear process for the selection of projects. They also find it difficult to reach the fund, which still lacks a website and a widely available phone number. Moreover, while no official figures are available, the percentage of loan repayments is reported to be very low (less than 50%), which would imply an inadequate risk management system and possible mismanagement of funds.

The opaque decision-making process of the ESF limits its role as a key player in the development of access to finance for SMEs in Tajikistan. The OECD's experience with similar public financial vehicles in other countries in the region suggests that reforming the fund could bring significant improvements for SMEs (OECD, 2016[86]). Involving the private sector more in the management of the fund, making its selection process more transparent and strengthening its risk-management policies could have a big impact on its efficiency and ultimately on the access to finance of SMEs. The PARE 1+1 programme in Moldova shows how the state might co-finance projects in strategic sectors or areas, matching private investments with public funds (OECD, 2015[80]).

Monitoring of Recommendation 2 highlights major efforts to enhance financial literacy and business skills

> *Recommendation 2: On the demand side support business creation and create a one-stop shop for migrants*

The government and the NBT have started to develop some initiatives to promote financial literacy with the support of international organisations

Ministries and government agencies, supported by IOs, have been active in promoting financial literacy through some initiatives. At the beginning of 2017, the NBT elaborated a National Consumer Protection and Financial Literacy strategy with the support of the World Bank, and it is now working on the Action Plan to implement it. This is a particularly welcome initiative, as multiple ministries, government agencies and IOs are currently working on separate projects with similar objectives.

The NBT and the Ministry of Education have been active since 2014, with the support of international organisations. For example, the International Organization for Migration (IOM) is promoting increased productivity of remittances through education and investment. The project offered financial education to 1 500 migrants' families, with 65 to 70 households receiving basic training in business development. Resource Centres in 15 communities also received training to provide better information about labour migration and 15 migrant household associations were set up under each Resource Centre to serve as a link between labour migrants and their communities of origin in order to facilitate the flow of remittances. The private sector has also been active, with financial education training offered by AMFOT, by the Banking Association and by business associations (Box 2.15).

In 2017, the government joined a project run by the OECD and its International Network on Financial Education (OECD/INFE), with financial support from the Ministry of Finance of the Russian Federation. Building on the OECD/INFE's internationally recognised expertise, the project seeks to support the development, implementation and evaluation of evidence-based national strategies for financial education in six Commonwealth of Independent States (CIS) countries, to measure the level of adult financial literacy in each country, and to address the financial education needs of specific target audiences, including migrants and their families.

Box 2.15. Main projects to promote financial literacy in Tajikistan

Projects to promote financial literacy, by improving the financial literacy of the population in general, are expected to also improve the financial literacy of migrants and their capacity to set up a business. During the monitoring programme, the main such projects were:

- The NBT drafted a National Consumer Protection and Financial Literacy Strategy at the beginning of 2017 with the support of the World Bank. The World Bank's support also extends to the production of information material and videos posted on the NBT website, and helping credit institutions to offer financial literacy courses around the country.
- The Ministry of Education and Science and the NBT, with the support of the German Society for International Co-operation (GIZ), organised events aimed at high school teachers in August 2016. The programme developed draft guidelines on financial education on the subject of the "Basis of Economics" in secondary schools, and provided training to 24 trainers, who should in turn prepare 3 000 secondary school teachers to teach this course.
- The NBT, together with credit organisations, the association of banks and the microfinance association (AMFOT) organised the International Week of Financial Literacy in March 2016, with the aim of increasing public confidence in the banking system and expanding awareness of possible financial solutions in the country. In 2015, the previous edition reportedly included 689 students in secondary and high schools of Dushanbe and Khujand, as well as in 8 districts of Khatlon province. The event held in Dushanbe is part of a global initiative called the Global Money Week organised by Child and Youth Finance International. The event engaged an estimated 5.6 million schoolchildren in 2015.

In addition, the State Committee on Investments and State Property Management (SCISPM) created Tajinvest. One of its main of functions is to develop business skills among the population, including returning migrants. In 2016 the SCISPM held 10 business forums and roundtables, inviting young entrepreneurs. The SCISPM also worked with the World Bank on a project to offer capacity building among young entrepreneurs, which consisted of 150 days of training for 3 838 young people in 66 cities and villages in Khatlon, Sughd Regions, RRS and Dushanbe.

The Ministry of Labour, Migration and Employment is updating and has started implementing the country's migration strategy but training centres could offer better entrepreneurship support

The Ministry of Migration, Labour and Employment of the Population (MoLME) is now updating the National Strategy on Labour Migration of Tajik Citizens Abroad for 2016-2020.[22]

To support migrant entrepreneurship, the ministry is offering free and paid-for training to new and returning migrants and their families. The courses offer training in 96 different professions, through a network of 73 training centres all around the country, including Dushanbe, Khorog, Khujand and Kurgantyube. The vocational training offered is usually short term, lasting 1, 3 or 6 months. During the monitoring period a total of 373 098 job-seekers and returning migrants were trained in institutions of primary vocational education (101 117 in 2014, 101 209 in 2015, 105 815 in 2016 and 64 957 in the first half of 2017). The data shared by the MoLME show that in the first 6 months of 2017, 12 259 people were trained in the vocational training centers, and it is interesting to note that 75% of them were women. The certificates attainable at the end of the training are recognised in all CIS countries, but business associations argue[23] that the quality of the courses could still be improved. Moldova offers a good example of how this could be done effectively.

Moreover, entrepreneurship training programmes could be targeted more specifically for women, as they are the predominant group of remittance recipients. To achieve this goal, a more extensive local network would be useful – maybe with the support of local community leaders, who could also be incentivised in connecting and share experience among themselves. More use could be made of the experience of non-governmental organisations (NGOs) working at community level, with the goal of increasing the accessibility of the training.

The way forward

Financing options for SMEs remain tight and the financial crisis in Tajikistan has not helped improve the situation. Rebuilding trust in the financial system must be a core priority for policy makers. The government should focus on rebuilding the population's trust in the banking system as an essential precondition to enhanced financial inclusion. Moreover, a new regulation proposed by the NBT could, if implemented, improve the payment system in the country by permitting new players to enter the market, particularly mobile operators. In any case it would be useful to adopt a systematic mechanism for the transfer and delivery of remittances and expand the range of financial services available (such as "account-to-account" systems, PC banking, mobile banking or ATM banking) increasing competitiveness and reducing costs.

The microfinance sector could be strengthened by pushing the application of the Microfinance Financial Reporting Standards (MFRS) elaborated by the Small Enterprise Education and Promotion Network (SEEP), particularly among small MFIs, to make them more transparent and thus open the door to their possible consolidation and entrance into the formal economy. This framework includes a core set of ratios to measure and analyse financial performance and risk management, and is used by NGOs, non-bank financial institutions or companies, credit unions and co-operatives (SEEP Network, 2010[87]). Banks and MFIs should increasingly focus on creating value for customers by launching new transparent credit products and schemes for migrants, with special packages including preferential rates and benefits related to productive investments in entrepreneurial activities.

The government and the NBT should push forward their efforts on financial literacy, especially by implementing the National Strategy for Consumer Protection and Financial Literacy, specifically addressing migrants and their needs (the inclusion of remittances in the formal financial system and their productive use, including by creating new businesses), and by monitoring and evaluating the impact of current and future financial education and business skills initiatives. Participation in the technical assistance project co-ordinated by the OECD/INFE would be a way of addressing some of these issues.

Box 2.16. Promoting entrepreneurial training: The case of Moldova

The government of Tajikistan could consider the development and promotion of entrepreneurial training programmes and disciplines both in school and through training centres. In the Republic of Moldova, the Fundamentals of Entrepreneurship course is taught in the vocational, specialised and higher secondary education system in order to give students the skills, values and attitudes needed to meet to the challenges and demands of the contemporary labour market and financial system.

Entrepreneurship education is one of the policy directions included in the Consolidated Strategy for the Development of Education for 2011-15 as set out in the Bruges Communiqué on Promoting Entrepreneurship. As a course of study, Fundamentals of Entrepreneurship is a component of the national curriculum as an optional course recommended by the Ministry of Education. The implementation of the given course in pre-university education is carried out through the Junior Achievement Moldova Association (JA Moldova) in co-ordination with the Ministry of Education.

According to the Framework Plan for Primary, Secondary and High School Education for the academic year 2016/17, approved by the Order of the Minister of Education no. 242 of March 25, 2016, Economic and Entrepreneurial Education was included in the list of optional courses recommended for grades I-IV, V-IX and X-XII in high school and contains the following courses: Business Ethics, Consumer Protection, Entrepreneurship, Economic ABC, My Finances, School Company, School Ministries, Entrepreneurship, Economic Education, Applied Economics and Key to Success.

Throughout 2016, Basics of Entrepreneurship was taught in all technical vocational education institutions in the country: 120 hours (96 hours of theory / practice and 24 hours of consultations) in secondary vocational technical education institutions and 90 hours in post-secondary technical vocational institutions.

Source: (Ministry of Education of the Republic of Moldova, 2017[88]; Government of the Republic of Moldova, 2010[89])

The MoLME could further develop its training centres to offer returning migrants business development services. These could include finding possible investors, matching with mentors, sharing knowledge with other businesses and returning migrants, creating links with business associations such as the Chamber of Commerce and expanding the list of public services delivered in the current training centres such as business registration, taxation and licensing, so that the centres would act as well-rounded one-stop shops for returning migrants willing to embark on entrepreneurship initiatives. A good example is the Repat initiative in Armenia (Box 2.17).

Box 2.17. RepatArmenia initiative

The Repat Armenia Foundation is an NGO, established in August 2012 and based in Yerevan. The organisation aims to inform, initiate and actively support the return of high-impact (professional, entrepreneurial) individuals and families to Armenia, leveraging a worldwide network of supporters. The three key principles behind its actions are:

- to promote the concept of repatriation
- to provide individual repatriation support
- to influence government policies for repatriation.

The foundation manages a website, RepatArmenia.org, which provides information about business regulation, education, healthcare and real estate in Armenia. For those who are considering a move to Armenia, the RepatArmenia Foundation also offers one-on-one consultations, networking opportunities during informal monthly events and connection with the Armenian Repatriates Network. It also assists potential repatriates by introducing them to professional service providers that can help them with employment, setting up a business or other aspects of integration.

Source: (Repat Armenia, 2016[90])

Kyrgyzstan: Improving supply-chain financing in agriculture

Agriculture is one of the main sectors in Kyrgyzstan economy and small firms represent the bulk of companies in the sector. Access to finance has been reported as a major obstacle to their development. The OECD made policy recommendations in 2013 to enhance access to finance for SMEs in agriculture that focused on the development of warehouse receipt financing (WRF). The OECD monitored the implementation of the recommendations in 2016. This sub-chapter analyses progress since 2013. It provides additional policy options and actions to further implement the recommendations, including finalising the law and bylaws on WRF, and further promoting this new tool and the storage business.

Context: Obstacles to agricultural SMEs' access to finance

Agriculture in Kyrgyzstan accounted for over 30% of employment and 17% of its gross domestic product (GDP) in 2014 (National Statistical Committee of the Kyrgyz Republic, 2016[91]; World Bank, 2016[92]). The sector is also socially important, being the main source of employment for most of the country's poorest people (Dubashov, Ismailakhunova and Kruse, 2015[93]). Output and productivity increases in agriculture could therefore have a strong impact on Kyrgyzstan's poverty rate.

Access to finance was a key barrier to SMEs in Kyrgyzstan in 2013, as most SMEs had to rely on internal funds as well as credit provided by families and friends. Farmers and agricultural SMEs were particularly credit-constrained. Overall, only 18% of companies in the sector were using bank finance; 79% of respondents to an OECD sector survey reported using internal funds to finance their working capital (OECD, 2014[94]). In addition to high interest rates, ranging from 18% to 24%, one of the sector's key challenges was the difficulty of providing adequate collateral when seeking a bank loan (OECD, 2014[94]). In 2013, 80% of agricultural companies seeking credit were asked to provide collateral equivalent to 120% or more of the total loan amount, usually in the form of real estate. Warehouse receipt financing (WRF) was selected as a financial tool with the potential to alleviate part of the collateral constraints and thus facilitate access to finance in the sector.

Overview of 2013 recommendations

WRF can increase access to finance as it allows farmers to pledge movable assets and inventory to obtain financing for working capital. In addition, WRF allows the farmer to pledge fixed assets for long-term financing for capital expenditures and investments (OECD, 2014[94]). The basic operation of a WRF scheme is described in Figure 2.8.

The benefits associated with WRF extend beyond bridging the collateral gap. By providing the infrastructure to easily store, aggregate, and – over the long term, also package – goods, it can enable farmers to overcome seasonal price fluctuations and thus sell their produce at higher prices. It can also increase the integration of the agribusiness supply chain as a whole, facilitating co-ordination between farmers, traders, input suppliers, and processors.

Figure 2.8. The framework of warehouse receipt financing

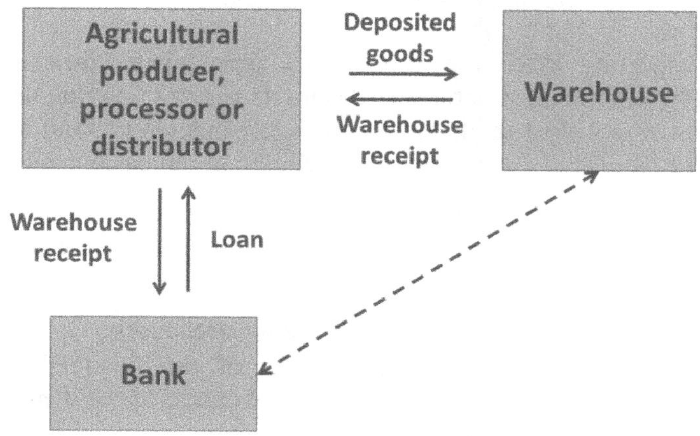

Source: (OECD, 2014[94])

The OECD review in 2013 made three recommendations for introducing WRF to Kyrgyzstan (OECD, 2014[94]):

Recommendation 1: Set up a pilot WRF scheme

A pilot WRF scheme at the local level was proposed to allow for a viable assessment of WRF in practice, as well as to gain the support of farmers and banks. The pilot was thought to be useful to build trust between different stakeholders, such as farmers, warehouse operators, traders and banks.

Recommendation 2: Establish a regulatory framework for WRF

In 2013 Kyrgyzstan had a law on collateral that regulated moveable assets, as well as a central collateral registration system. Some other elements of a regulatory environment for warehouse receipts were also already in place. For example, the civil code contains basic legal norms that characterise warehouse certificates and warehouse receipts (Legislative Assembly of the Kyrgyz Republic, 1998[95]). However, there were no provisions for the use of warehouse receipts as collateral for credit. Therefore, there was a need to develop a legal framework for WRF to allow it to be streamlined at a national level. Setting up the legal background for the registration, certification and inspection of warehouses not only involved adopting the relevant legislation, it also required an agency to oversee these tasks and ensure compliance with financial and technical standards (Box 2.18).

A sustainable system for collecting and disseminating agricultural information and prices was also needed, and existing insurance products needed to be standardised to protect producers and banks from large swings in agricultural prices. Finally, an indemnity fund was expected to help protect banks from warehouse defaults (OECD, 2014[94]).

Box 2.18. Agencies implementing the regulatory framework: Bulgaria

While laws supporting WRF are a necessary prerequisite, they also need to be complemented by additional structures to ensure its smooth functioning. The Bulgarian Government has established public warehouses, an indemnity fund and a specialised agency under the Ministry of Agriculture, in addition to the basic legal framework.

The newly created agency, the National Grain Service of Bulgaria, organises, implements and controls the licensing process for public grain warehouses. Its functions also consist of:

- maintaining public registers of public grain warehouses
- carrying out initial and periodic checks of the financial, operational and technical conditions of public grain warehouses, as well as the quality and quantity of the stored grain
- collecting orders for printing warehouse receipts.

By effectively controlling the public warehouses and their performance, the National Grain Service helps to build trust among stakeholders, and is a key enabler of WRF in Bulgaria.

Source: (Winn, Miller and Gegenbauer, 2009[96])

Recommendation 3: Promote the storage business to attract potential investors

Storage capacity in Kyrgyzstan was unevenly distributed around the country, and few warehouses had more than basic equipment. The WRF solution requires sound and modern storage facilities. Achieving this meant further promoting the storage business and attracting investment. The 2013 review suggested that investment promotion for the storage business could be added to the national investment promotion strategy (OECD, 2014[94]). One way to support the development of storage businesses would be through public-private partnerships, for example to provide land or facilities.

Findings of the 2016 monitoring assessment

The Government of Kyrgyzstan, with the support of the German Society for International Co-operation (GIZ) and the Asian Development Bank (ADB), has made substantial progress in preparing the appropriate regulatory framework for WRF. A pilot has been conducted and has demonstrated the potential of WRF. The expansion of the scheme is threatened, however, by the poor state of warehouse infrastructure in the country.

Monitoring of Recommendation 1 shows a successful pilot WRF scheme

Recommendation 1: Set up a pilot WRF scheme at sub-national level

The launch of a pilot WRF was supported by the GIZ, which held meetings and interviews with 32 warehouse owners in 2 oblasts (Chui and Issyk-Kul) to identify possible pilot warehouses. As no comprehensive register of warehouses existed, warehouses were identified based on information from local authorities, bank branches, and existing donor projects involving warehouses. Twenty of the warehouse owners interviewed agreed to co-operate in pilot credits (Abakirov, 2014[97]).

Three banks – the Commercial Bank of Kyrgyzstan, Bank Asia and OJSC Aiyl Bank – agreed to participate in pilot activities. Local branch managers of these banks were briefed on the functioning and benefits of WRF. Co-operation was established between these local banks and ADB's project on women entrepreneurship in Kyrgyzstan (ADB, 2013[98]). The project channels funds for innovative financial solutions to women entrepreneurs through intermediary financial institutions. Aiyl Bank identified WRF as an innovative financial solution and was therefore able to provide loans through WRF at an interest rate of 12%. Nine loans were agreed during the pilot phase (the harvest season of 2014-15) worth a total of KGS 3 million (Kyrgistani som; USD 55 000).

The pilot also included the creation of initial warehouse certificates modelled on good practices by other countries. Receipts were signed by all parties and contained key information such as the type of produce, quality, price of storage, dates, parties responsible, etc. Other pilot activities included awareness-raising events, initially to inform the financial institutions of the potential benefits of WRF.

The successful implementation of the pilot, although limited in scope, demonstrates the potential of WRF to help agricultural SMEs access finance.

Participants in the pilot mentioned the following challenges and lessons:

- The lack of a legal basis for WRF. This was the main stumbling block as it increased the level of risk for banks, forcing them to set aside additional reserves and decreasing profit margins.[24]
- The lack of a clear system for warehouse licensing.
- The fact that the majority of warehouses were poorly equipped for WRF.
- The lack of a risk insurance system for warehouses, banks and farmers.

The key lessons learnt from the pilot phase were used to inform the discussions and to develop a regulatory framework for WRF in Kyrgyzstan (see next section).

Monitoring of Recommendation 2 reveals the development of a draft regulatory framework

> *Recommendation 2: Establish the legal and regulatory framework for WRF*

The regulatory framework for WRF was developed by a working group (WG) under the leadership of the Ministry of Economy, supported by the OECD and GIZ. The WG was established during the peer review of Kyrgyzstan in 2013, and had helped to develop the original policy recommendations. It outlined the aspects which needed to be covered by the new legislation:

- standards for the warehouses to be included in the register, as well as procedures in case of a violation of the standards;
- the creation of a registry of warehouses and an agency to implement the regulatory framework;

- the rights and obligations of all parties involved, including warehouse owners, bankers and farmers;
- specification of the content and information provided in the different types of warehouse receipts and
- the transfer of rights, and the termination of warehouse receipts and certificates.

The work of the WG was supported by policy practitioners from Ukraine and Bulgaria, based on good practices and key lessons learnt in these countries (Box 2.18). The WG's efforts led to the drafting of a new law that closely resembles the Bulgarian system.

Business associations, especially the Union of Bankers, participated in and supported the drafting of the law. The draft law was subject to public discussions during a roundtable organised in Bishkek on 23 May 2016. It was also circulated for discussion by stakeholders in other cities in Kyrgyzstan (Osh, Jalal-Abad and Naryn). This public-private dialogue approach is expected to help the new policy instrument be broadly accepted and to decrease potential risks associated with WRF.

While Kyrgyzstan's progress in developing the legislation for WRF is commendable, its progress in establishing an environment conducive to the development of WRF is lagging. The most critical gap is the lack of widespread information on market prices for agricultural produce, which are crucial for a well-functioning WRF system. Although government websites provide general information on agriculture, the level of detail is limited. Exact and current prices as well as forecasts are necessary to assess the value of collateral and to decide the optimal date for selling produce.

Similarly, there are no standard insurance products for WRF at this stage. To build confidence in the system, insurance products need to be expanded to protect against bankruptcy and fraud. Insurance companies were contacted to participate in the initial phase of the pilot. While they signalled general interest, in the absence of a regulatory framework they preferred not to insure WRF or to create appropriate products. They also expressed doubts about the quality of the warehouses.

Finally, the government should consider establishing an indemnity fund, which would work like a credit guarantee fund (CGF) tailored to WRF. This would provide an additional level of protection for the banks involved in WRF by providing an additional guarantee. This fund would be complementary to other insurance products, as it would fully reimburse damages and cover cases of default instead of insuring against large price swings.

Monitoring of Recommendation 3 highlights poor investment in warehouses

Recommendation 3: Promote the storage business

The quality and quantity of warehouses that are fit for WRF appear to be limited. Suitable warehouses need to be found and modernised if this financial tool is to fulfil its potential. However, information on warehouses in Kyrgyzstan is outdated: the 2003 agricultural census provides the latest reliable nationwide data. It identified 1 476 facilities in Kyrgyzstan each with a capacity of more than 500 tonnes.

To obtain more accurate information and to assess the readiness of warehouses for WRF, a survey was undertaken with the support of GIZ. The survey did not aim to cover all warehouses nationwide, but rather to obtain reliable, detailed and accurate data on the condition of warehouses that could be eligible for WRF. This identified 50 warehouses with a storage capacity of more than 500 tonnes. These were contacted for interviews.

Initial interviews revealed that 20 of the 50 warehouses did not meet the basic infrastructure requirements for WRF. Besides the technical issues, the survey also identified a number of challenges:

- The warehouses require substantial investments and renovation, as most of them were built during the 1970s.
- Most lack additional services that would add value (e.g. sorting, consolidation, splitting of goods and produce, or transportation services).
- Some warehouses lack minimal security, such as fences.
- Several warehouses were not equipped with refrigerators, thus increasing the risk of losses due to decay.
- Written contracts between owners of warehouses and owners of produce were rare – trust-based oral agreements were more usual.

Due to a lack of warehouse capacity, a number of producers and traders reported that they are building new warehouses with refrigeration equipment (Abakirov, 2014[97]). For example, in the Kochkor region the authorities have allocated 17 hectares of land for warehouse construction. In addition, several banks have shown interest in investing in warehouses and providing credit for their construction once there is an established WRF regulatory framework. Warehouse owners who were interviewed by the OECD argued that investments in warehouses paid off. Several of them have further invested in modernising equipment by purchasing cooling and security technology.

The way forward

The finalisation of the law on WRF is the necessary next step for the full roll out of WRF. Once adopted, the government will need to implement the Law on Warehouses and Storage Certificates, adopt a number of regulations, and monitor the development and impact of WRF and warehouses. It will be crucial to ensure the safety and quality of the first warehouses selected. After a few years following the initial harvest seasons, further support and adjustments might be needed to effectively roll out the instrument to the whole country. Turkey has lessons to share on the continuous efforts needed to improve a WRF system (Box 2.19).

Once the legal framework has been established, further work should also include the creation of a proper insurance product for WRF. Such products can help prevent losses from inappropriate storage and thus improve the solvency of the overall WRF system. In the long term, such efforts can be further facilitated through the creation of a specialised credit guarantee fund for WRF.

Special training needs to be conducted, particularly for staff of the Ministry of Agriculture and Land Reclamation, the body which will keep the register and monitor the warehouses. Carrying out promotional and information activities for the operators of warehouses and agricultural producers is equally important to increase knowledge of and interest in this new product.

Box 2.19. Improvements to Turkey's WRF system

In Turkey, banks have traditionally been large users of warehouse-receipt financing to support the country's important tobacco exports. Many Turkish banks have set up their own warehousing subsidiaries to store the goods that they are financing. Nevertheless, in the large domestic grain market, which was heavily regulated until the late 1990s, warehouse receipt financing was rare.

To support policy liberalisation, a warehouse receipt system was developed as part of the World Bank-funded Agricultural Reform Implementation Project. The programme aimed to reduce distorted incentives and government subsidies, and substitute them with a support system to provide agricultural producers with incentives to increase productivity in response to real comparative advantage. Warehouse receipts presented an alternative approach to costly government price support. Turkey developed proper licensing and inspection procedures, and built institutional capacities in this area. A Law on Licenced Warehousing adopted in 2005 defined the procedure for the authorization and oversight of warehouses (including ministry-issued licences and insurance schemes for stored goods) and gave legal content to the warehouse receipt, which could then be pledged as a guarantee.

This legal framework has been improved through subsequent regulations: the 2011 Regulation on Electronic Warehouse Receipt facilitates the issuing of e-warehouse receipts, and the 2013 Regulation of Agricultural Products Licensed Warehousing consolidates the legal framework for commodity-specific exchange. These organised markets (most of which already owned warehousing infrastructure) received financial and technical support to improve their capacity and use of warehouse receipts in their daily transactions. Large exchanges also invested in building more storage facilities, which provided potential opportunities for growth of the warehouse receipt system.

Source: (FAO/EBRD, $2015_{[99]}$)

Current efforts and investments to improve the quality and quantity of storage facilities in Kyrgyzstan appear insufficient. In the short term, and once the legislative framework is in place, banks might be willing to provide loans for creating storage areas and use them for providing WRF. This could mitigate the problems of non-existent insurance products for WRF and limited trust in the system. In the long term, the newly created Investment Promotion Agency and increased efforts to implement public-private partnerships could attract investment in storage infrastructure.

Notes

[1] Here defined as Kazakhstan, Kyrgyzstan, Mongolia, Tajikistan and Uzbekistan.

[2] Other constraints (such as the informal sector and tax) were perceived as more important by SMEs surveyed by the Business Environment and Enterprise Performance Survey (BEEPS).

[3] Government policies to facilitate diversification and quality upgrading include many areas than other access to finance, such as infrastructure, accumulation of human capital, establishment of trade networks, functioning of factor markets etc.

[4] Rising inequality due to fast economic growth is fuelling social tension, even if poverty is being reduced (World Bank, 2015[365]; Theunissen, 2014[330]).

[5] Mongolia ranked 72nd out of 168 countries in Transparency International's Corruption Perception Index in 2015 (Transparency International, 2016[47]). Mongolia is part of the OECD Anti-Corruption Network for Eastern Europe and Central Asia. The country has started a number of important reforms including in the anti-corruption area, but they are still far from producing sustainable results (OECD, 2015[360]).

[6] The PSP aimed to decrease supply-driven inflationary pressure, especially for the main consumer goods such as meat, flour, retail gas and apartment construction. It did so by directly financing SMEs operating in the sectors. The outstanding programme loans amounted to MNT 714.1 billion at the end of 2013, MNT 633.8 billion at the end of 2014, MNT 232.3 billion at the end of 2015 and are forecast to be down to MNT 27.3 billion at the end of 2016 (Bank of Mongolia, 2015[106]).

[7] Mongolia's experience with microfinance has a long history, being developed in the late 1990s with the support of international organisations. In 2002 the Mongolian Parliament enacted laws to define the roles and responsibilities of non-bank financial institutions and legalising savings and loan co-operatives. In 2001, a consortium of these institutions became XacBank They also created the specialised division XacLeasing, which is introducing the practice of leasing in the SME market. The penetration percentage for leasing as a means of financing in the equipment sector is still low. The EBRD's SME Leasing Policy Initiative has been designed and implemented to support the development of the practice in the country (UNDP, 2016[86]).

[8] In the literature, there are other more direct measures of bank competition, such as the Panzar and Rosse H-Statistic, the Lerner index and the so-called Boone indicator. These indicators try to represent actual player behaviour in the market, but their fragility resides in the necessity for very reliable firm-level statistics that can allow the researcher to calculate input costs precisely. This leads to very restrictive assumptions about banks' cost functions.

[9] According to the US Department of Justice and Federal Trade Commission 2010 Horizontal Merger Guidelines, the agencies will regard a market in which the post-merger HHI is below 1 500 as "unconcentrated", between 1 500 and 2 500 as "moderately concentrated", and above 2 500 as "highly concentrated".

[10] The EPCRC analysis focused on four dimensions: access to finance for MSMEs; institutional and regulatory framework for SME development; skills for SME development; and SME internationalisation tools.

[11] This takes into account the time, cost and outcome of the most common insolvency proceedings and their regulation.

[12] In particular, Mongolia was ranked 59th out of 182 countries in the "Getting Credit" ranking and 89th in the "Resolving Insolvency" ranking, scoring 11 out of 16 for the "Strength of the Insolvency Framework" index.

[13] Gathering information to assess the credit worthiness of MSMEs is challenging and costly for banks, and this leads to strong uncertainty when calculating the expected rate of returns from the loan. Stemming from this imperfect information, the interest rate a bank charges may itself affect the riskiness of the pool of loans by sorting potential borrowers (adverse selection effect) and affecting the action of borrowers (incentive effect; (Stiglitz and Weiss, 1981[329])).

[14] These data refer in particular to the construction sector.

[15] This fee can be calculated as a percentage of the loan or of the guarantee. It can be either paid directly by the MSME to the MCGF, or paid upfront by the lender (OECD/INFE, 2012$_{[140]}$).

[16] These "switching arrangements" can reduce the administrative burden on the customer as the banks perform a considerable part of it. These arrangements typically stem from a self-regulatory code between banks (OECD, 2011$_{[30]}$).

[17] See also the OECD/INFE Guidelines for Private and Not-for-profit Stakeholders in Financial Education (OECD and INFE, 2014$_{[328]}$) regarding conflicts of interest of private stakeholders in the provision of financial education.

[18] The payment system is the interconnected system of technologies, procedures, rules and money transfer systems, providing the circulation of money in the country. Its main function is the realisation of money transfers between credit organisations through correspondent accounts, opened within the National Bank.

[19] Instruction No. 221 in October 2015

[20] This measure is part of the monetary policy aim of building up foreign reserves to stabilise the exchange rate. To sterilise the effect on inflation the NBT has increased its sales of central bank securities and treasury bills from 3.7% of GDP in 2015 to 7.9% of GDP in 2016 (ADB, 2017$_{[144]}$).

[21] The fund was established with the Order of the Government of the Republic of Tajikistan N.34 of February 5 2013, but operations started with the approval of the regulation for the fund, Order N.62 of February 14, 2015.

[22] The previous one was approved in 2000.

[23] Statement based on OECD interviews and discussion during the Public-Private Working Groups in Dushanbe in May and July 2017.

[24] National Bank of the Kyrgyz Republic regulations limit the maximum loan amount granted in the scope of WRF to KGS 100 000 (USD 1 800). More specifically, the lack of a dedicated regulatory framework forced the National Bank to treat WRF credits as unsecured credits, thus limiting the amount of credit awarded. WRF were applied as collateral of up to KGS 100 000; any amounts in excess of this threshold were secured with "regular" forms of collateral.

References

Abakirov, M. (2014), *"О проделанной работе по внедрению пилотного проекта «Финансирование под складские расписки» Май-август 2014" [On the progress of the implementation of the pilot project 'Warehouse receipts financing' May-August 2014].* [97]

ADB (2013), *Grant Assistance - Kyrgyz Republic: Women's Entrepreneurship Development Project.*, http://strategy2050.kz/en/news/19887 (accessed on 6 June 2017). [17]

ADB (2013), *Women's Entrepreneurship Development Project*, http://www.adb.org/projects/documents/womens-entrepreneurship-development-project-gar. [98]

ADB (2014), *Asian Development Bank*, https://www.adb.org/news/adb-s-1st-private-investment-tajikistan-supports-small-business-finance-through-accessbank. [85]

ADB (2015), *Asia SME finance monitor 2014*, http://www.nbkr.kg/newsout.jsp?item=31&lang=RUS&material=76778 (accessed on 6 June 2017). [18]

ADB (2017), *Asian Development Outlook 2017: Transcending the Middle-Income Challenge*, Asian Develp[pment Bank, http://www.adb.org/publications/asian-development-outlook-2017-middle-income-challenge.. [71]

Aggarwal, R., A. Demirguç-Kunt and M. Martinez Pería (2010), "Do remittances promote financial development", *Journal of Development Economics*, pp. 255-264. [74]

AMFI (2017), *Offical website of the Association of Microfinance Institutions of Kyrgyzstan*, http://amfi.kg/ob-assotsiatsii/. [9]

AMFOK (2017), *Official Website of the Association of Microfinance Organizations of Kazakhstan*, http://www.amfok.kz/sections/about_as. [10]

ASIC (2016), *Australian Securities & Investment Commission website.*, http://www.asic.gov.au (accessed on May 2016). [69]

ASIC (2016), *MoneySmart – Financial Guide You Can Trust.*, https://www.moneysmart.gov.au (accessed on May 2016). [70]

Bank of Mongolia (2015), *SME Survey Result 2015*, unpublished. [31]

Bank of Mongolia (2015), *Annual report 2014.* [32]

Bank of Mongolia (2015), *Individual and SME loan report.* [33]

Bank of Mongolia (2016), *Statistical database*, https://www.mongolbank.mn/eng/news.aspx?id=1270. [41]

Bank of Mongolia, Financial Regulatory Commission and Ministry of Finance (2016), *National Program for Financial Literacy 2016-2021*, official government document, unpublished, Mongolbank. [55]

Beck (2010), *The typology of partial credit guarantee funds around the world*, Policy Research Working Paper 4774, The World Bank. [57]

Beck, T., P. Honohan and A. Demnirguç-Kunt (2007), *Finance for all?: Policies and pitfalls in expanding access*, The World Bank. [3]

Beck, T., L. Klapper and J. Mendoza (2008), *The typology of partial credit guarantee funds around the world*, The World Bank. [46]

Business World (2017), *Uzbekistan: Guarantee Fund for small business development established*, http://smiraponitke.com/20/02/2017/uzbekistan-guarantee-fund-for-small-business-development-established.html (accessed on 6 June 2017). [19]

Central Bank of the Russian Federation (2017), *Money Transfer from Russia to Tajikistan (database)*, http://www.cbr.ru/eng/. [84]

Central Bank of Uzbekistan (2016), *Official Website of the Central Bank of Uzbekistan*, http://cbu.uz/en/press-tsentr/press-relizy/2016/05/62457/?INVERT=N. [8]

Central Bank of Uzbekistan (2017), *The Central Bank of the Republic of Uzbekistan, official website*, http://m.cbu.uz/ru/press-tsentr/press-relizy/2017/04/81836/ (accessed on 6 June 2017). [20]

CGFT (2017), *Credit Guarantee Fund of Tajikistan, official website*, http://www.cgft.com/about-cgft/credit-guarantee-fund-tajikistan/ (accessed on 6 June 2017). [21]

DAMU (2014), *Development strategy of "DAMU Entrepreneurship Development Fund" JSC for 2014-2023 years.*, DAMU, http://www.damu.kz/content/files/Presentation_FundDamuStrategy2014_2023.pptx. [59]

DAMU (2014), *Report on the status of development of small and medium enterprises in Kazakhstan and its regions.*, http://www.damu.kz/20664. [60]

DAMU (2016), *History and key milestones.*, http://www.damu.kz/239 (accessed on 17 October 2016). [61]

De la Torre, A., J. Gozzi and S. Schmukler (2008), *Innovative experiences in access to finance: Market friendly roles for the visible hand?*, http://dx.doi.org/10.1596/1813-9450-4326. [45]

Dubashov, B., S. Ismailakhunova and A. Kruse (2015), *Kyrgyz Republic - Biannual economic update: resilience amid turbulence - special focus : meeting the jobs challenge*, http://documents.worldbank.org/curated/en/2015/11/25256017/kyrgyz-republic-biannual-economic-update-resilience-amid-turbulence-special-focus-meeting-jobs-challenge. [93]

Earnshaw, G. (1987), *Mongolia considers trade with west, but how to get goods out?*, http://www.earnshaw.com/other-writings/mongolia-considers-trade-west-how-get-goods-out. [27]

EBRD and World Bank (2015), *Business Environment and Enterprise Performance Survey (BEEPS) V Country Profile: Mongolia*, http://ebrd-beeps.com/countries/mongolia/. [34]

EBRD (2017), *Business Environment and Enterprise Performance Survey (BEEPS) data base*, http://ebrd-beeps.com (accessed on 15 March 2017). [14]

EPCRC (2016), *Mongolia: Banking Sector Overview*, Economic Policy and Competitiveness Research Center. [37]

FAO/EBRD (2015), *Designing warehouse receipt legislation: Regulatory options and recent trends.*, http://www.fao.org/3/a-i4318e.pdf. [99]

FIRST (2015), *FIRST initiative*, http://www.firstinitiative.org/stories/tajikistan-promoting-reforms-payments-systems. [83]

G20/OECD (2015), *High-level Principles on SME Financing*, https://www.oecd.org/finance/G20-OECD-High-Level-%20Principles-on-SME-Financing.pdf. [56]

Government of Georgia (2016), *Public Service Hall website*, http://psh.gov.ge. [65]

Government of the Republic of Moldova (2010), *2011-2015 Consolidated Strategy for Education Development*, Ministry of Education of Mongolia. [89]

Grigorian, D. and M. Kryshko (2017), *Deposit insurance, Remittances, and Dollarization: Survey-Based Evidence from a Top Remittance-Receiving Country*, IMF Working Paper. [75]

ILO (2016), *A one-stop shop for a accessible, transparent and efficient public service delivery: Mongolia*, http://www.social-protection.org/gimi/gess/RessourcePDF.action?ressource.ressourceId=53460. [50]

IMF (2016), *World Economic Outlook: too slow for too long*, https://www.imf.org/external/pubs/ft/weo/2016/01/pdf/text.pdf. [28]

Investment and Export Promotion Agency Kyrygzstan (2017), *The Official Website of the State Agency for Investment and Export Promotion of Kyrgyzstan*, http://www.invest.gov.kg/ru/informatciia-dlia-investorov/regulirovanie-otdelnykh-otraslei/mikrofinansovye-organizatcii/. [13]

KMF (2017), *KMF, official website*, https://www.kmf.kz/en/financial-literacy/ (accessed on 6 June 2017). [22]

Legislative Assembly of the Kyrgyz Republic (1998), *Civil Code (Part II) of the Republic of* [95]

Kyrgyzstan of 5 January 1998, as amended, Legislative Assembly of the Kyrgyz Republic.

Levitsky, J. (1997), *Credit guarantee schemes for SMEs an international review*, http://dx.doi.org/10.3362/0957-1329.1997.013. [44]

Mesnard, A. and M. Ravallion (2006), "The wealth effect on new business startups in a developing economy", *Economica*, pp. 367-392. [79]

Ministry of Education of the Republic of Moldova (2017), . [88]

Ministry of Industry (2016), *Decree by the Minister of Industry No.48, March 22 2016*, Ministry of Industry of Mongolia. [49]

National Bank of Kazakhstan (2017), *Current State of Microfinance Institutions of Kazakhstan*, http://www.nationalbank.kz/cont/. [11]

National Bank of Tajikistan (2017), *Стратегические приоритеты и план действий по развитию механизма защиты прав потребителей финансовых услуг Республики Таджикистан на 2017 - 2019гг.* [24]

National Bank of Tajikistan (2017), https://rus.ozodi.org/a/28500574.html. [76]

National Statistical Committee of the Kyrgyz Republic (2016), *National Statistical Committee of the Kyrgyz Republic*, http://www.stat.kg/en. [91]

National Statistical Office of Mongolia (2015), *Mongolia Monthly Statistical Bulletin*, National Statistical Office of Mongolia. [52]

National Statistical Office of Mongolia (2016), http://www.1212.mn/en. [30]

OECD/INFE (2012), *High-Level Principles on National Strategies for Financial Education*, OECD Publishing. [67]

OECD/INFE (2015), *National Strategies for Financial Education: OECD/INFE Policy Handbook.*, http://www.oecd.org/daf/fin/financial-education/National-Strategies-Financial-Education-Policy-Handbook.pdf. [68]

OECD (2004), *Financing Innovative SMEs in a Global Economy*, OECD Conference for Ministers Responsible of SMEs. [6]

OECD (2005), *REcommendation on Principles and Good Practices for Financial Education and Awareness*, OECD Publishing. [82]

OECD (2006), *The SME Financing Gap (Vol. I)*, Organisation for Economic Co-operation and Development, http://www.oecd-ilibrary.org/content/book/9789264029415-en. [4]

OECD (2008), *Competition and Regulation in Retail Banking 2006; Policy Roundtable of the OECD Competition Committee.*, OECD Publishing, http://www.oecd.org/regreform/sectors/39753683.pdf. [39]

OECD (2010), *One Stop Shops: An Overview of Best Practices related to Three Key Issues*, https://www.oecd.org/mena/competitiveness/privatesectorinitiatives/44795978.pdf. [63]

OECD (2011), *Competitiveness and Private Sector Development: Eastern Europe and South Caucasus*, OECD. [15]

OECD (2011), *Bank Competition and Financial Stability*, http://dx.doi.org/10.1787/9789264120563-en. [38]

OECD (2013), *SME and Entrepreneurship Financing: the role of credit guarantee schemes and* [58] *mutual guarantee societies in supporting finance for small and medium-sized enterprises*, OECD.

OECD (2013), *OECD Seminar on One Stop Shops in Hungary.* [62]

OECD and ADB (2014), *ADB–OECD Study on Enhancing Financial Accessibility for SMEs: Lessons from Recent Crises.*, International Publications, http://digitalcommons.ilr.cornell.edu/intl/368. [16]

OECD (2014), *Regulatory Policy in Kazakhstan: Towards Improved Implementation*, OECD Publishing. [64]

OECD (2014), *Improving supply chain financing in The Kyrgyz Republic: the case of agriculture*, http://www.oecd.org/globalrelations/SupplyChainFinancing.pdf. [94]

OECD (2015), *G20 OECD High Level Principles on SME Financing.* [1]

OECD et al. (2015), *SME Policy Index: Eastern Partner Countries 2016: Assessing the Implementation of the Small Business Act for Europe.*, http://dx.doi.org/10.1787/9789264246249-en. [66]

OECD (2015), *Enhancing Access to Finance for SME Development in Tajikistan*, OECD Publishing. [80]

OECD (2016), *Financing SMEs and Entrepreneurs 2016: An OECD Scoreboard*, http://dx.doi.org/10.1787/fin_sme_ent-2016-en. [7]

OECD (2016), *SME Development Fund and Mongolian Credit Guarantee Fund (direct interviews, 2016)..* [42]

OECD (2016), *OECD interviews with Mongolian banks.*, http://smefund.gov.mn/32.html (accessed on 27 June 2016). [48]

OECD (2016), *Enhancing Access to Finance for MSMEs in Mongolia*, http://www.oecd.org/globalrelations/eurasia-week-roundtable.htm#prs_2016. [86]

OECD (2017), *Small, Medium, Strong. Trends in SME Performance and Business Conditions*, Organisation for Economic Co-operation and Development, http://www.oecd-ilibrary.org/content/book/9789264275683-en. [5]

Petersen, M. and R. Rajan (1995), *The effect of credit competition on lending relationships.*, pp. 407-443. [40]

Pressreader (2017), *Justice Ministry to boost SME financing with new registry (from The UB post)*, https://www.pressreader.com/mongolia/the-ub-post/20170222/281552290625964 (accessed on 6 June 2017). [23]

Repat Armenia (2016), *Repat Armenia website*, http://repatarmenia.org. [90]

SDC (2015), *Annual Report 2014*, Swiss Agency for Development and Cooperation in Mongolia. [51]

SEEP Network (2010), *Microfinance Financial Reporting Standards*, http://www.seepnetwork.org/. [87]

Sultanov, M. (2017), *Secured transactions & collateral registry reforms – Recent developments in Africa, Middle East, Eastern Europe, Central & South Asia.* [25]

UNDP (2016), *Microfinance in Mongolia*, http://www.mn.undp.org/content/mongolia/en/home/ourwork/povertyreduction/successstories/MicrofinanceinMongolia.html. [12]

UNESCO (2013), *UNESCO Institute for Statistics, database.*, http://www.uis.unesco.org/DataCentre/Pages/default.aspx (accessed on 7 July 2016). [54]

United Nations (2015), *Trends in International Migrant Stock: the 2015 revision*, United Nations. [73]

Winn, Miller and Gegenbauer (2009), *The Use of Structured Finance Instruments in Agriculture in Eastern Europe and Central Asia.*. [96]

Woodruff, C. (2007), "MExican microenterprise investment and employment: the role of remittances", *Integration and Trade Journal*, pp. 185-209. [78]

World Bank (2012), *Financial Sector Assessment Program - Mongolia: access to finance*, http://lnweb90.worldbank.org/FPS/fsapcountrydb.nsf/(attachmentwebSI)/Mongolia_DevelopmentModule_TN-AccesstoFinance_Public.pdf/$FILE/Mongolia_DevelopmentModule_TN-AccesstoFinance_Public.pdf. [43]

World Bank (2013), *Paving the Road to Better Financial Decision-Making in Mongolia*, http://responsiblefinance.worldbank.org/~/media/GIAWB/FL/Documents/Surveys/mongolia.pdf. [53]

World Bank (2015), *Principles for Public Credit Guarantee Schemes for SMEs*, http://www.worldbank.org/en/topic/financialsector/publication/principles-for-public-credit-guarantee-schemes-cgss-for-smes. [47]

World Bank (2016), *World Bank – Kazakhstan Partnership Program Snapshot – April 2016.* [26]

World Bank (2016), *Doing Business Indicators*, http://www.doingbusiness.org/rankings. [35]

World Bank (2016), *Global Financial Development database*, http://data.worldbank.org/data-catalog/global-financial-development. [36]

World Bank (2016), *Doing Business 2017 - Equal opportunity for all*, World Bank. [92]

World Bank (2017), *Enterprise Surveys*, The World Bank, http://www.enterprisesurveys.org/. [2]

World Bank (2017), *World Development Indicators (Data)*, http://data.worldbank.org/data-catalog/world-development-indicators (accessed on 9 March 2017). [29]

World Bank (2017), *World Development Indicators*, http://data.worldbank.org/data-catalog/world-development-indicators. [72]

World Bank (2017), *World Development Indicators*, http://data.worldbank.org/indicator. [77]

World Bank (2017), http://datatopics.worldbank.org/financialinclusion/country/tajikistan. [81]

Chapter 3. Business environment in Central Asia: Firms' internationalisation

This chapter focuses on business internationalisation strategies for countries in Central Asia. The OECD has provided policy recommendations in Uzbekistan, Kyrgyzstan and Tajikistan, aiming to improve export and investment promotion policies and strengthen the internationalisation of SMEs. The OECD's work suggests that Central Asian governments should formulate clear value propositions, improve export promotion and monitor the impact of policies, whilst ensuring a continuous public-private dialogue.

Setting the stage

Central Asian firms need to deepen their international integration

Business internationalisation is defined as the process by which firms "initiate, develop, or sustain business operations in overseas markets" (OECD, 2008[1]) and participate in international trade. This includes exporting, opening offices and managing operations in other countries; building linkages with foreign investors and clients; and integrating into global value chains (OECD, 2008[1]).

Business internationalisation can contribute to long-term competitiveness, knowledge transfer and innovation, particularly for small and medium-sized enterprises (SMEs). They are important direct and indirect contributors to global value chains, either as direct exporters or as suppliers to multinational companies (MNCs) that engage in export activities. SMEs thus generate more than half of the value added in international trade in OECD countries (OECD, 2017[2]). Internationalisation can also help SMEs access foreign technology, expand their revenue and production base, and improve their productivity (OECD, 2013[3]).

The internationalisation of businesses in Central Asia remains limited overall. The region generated 0.6% of global exports in 2012 decreasing to 0.38% in 2015 (EIU, 2017[4]; World Bank, 2017[5]).[1] The predominance of hydrocarbons and metals in Central Asia's exports means that SMEs' share of exports is particularly low, and the potential for such export activities to generate knowledge spillovers or productivity increases is limited. The export of natural resources is mostly channelled through large state-owned enterprises (SOEs), leaving little space for SMEs to increase their export activity. The share of directly exporting SMEs is limited in most countries in the region and nowhere exceeds 7.5% (Figure 3.1). This compares to shares of 23% in Poland, 27% in France and 28% in Germany (UPS, 2016[6]). On average, domestic sales represent 90% of the value of SME sales in the region, which shows limited internationalisation in terms of revenues (EBRD, 2017[7]). SMEs are most active in low value-added sectors including agriculture, manufacturing, local services and retail.

As noted, the region's exports are heavily concentrated in natural resources, where large international companies and state holdings predominate and where SMEs play a very limited role, including as suppliers. The export baskets of the Central Asian states are also highly concentrated, with the top three export products in each country representing more than 60% of total exports (Figure 3.2). Export markets are also highly concentrated, with most products exported to the same destinations (World Bank, 2017[5]).

In addition, SMEs are on average more constrained than large companies when trading across borders due to their limited resources to comply with customs procedures, find foreign partners, and overcome logistical and infrastructure barriers (OECD, 2008[1]). In particular in Central Asia, SMEs face long distances to markets, outdated infrastructure, and complex trade documents and border controls as measured by the OECD Trade Facilitation Indicators (OECD, 2017[8]).

SMEs can sidestep the difficulties of exporting directly by integrating into global value chains – supplying larger domestic or multinational companies that are exporters, thus contributing to indirect exports. If indirect exports are taken into account, the share of SMEs exporting in the region roughly doubles. Even so, the share still remains limited, between 2% and 16% of companies depending on the country (Figure 3.1).

Figure 3.1. SMEs' participation in exports in Central Asia

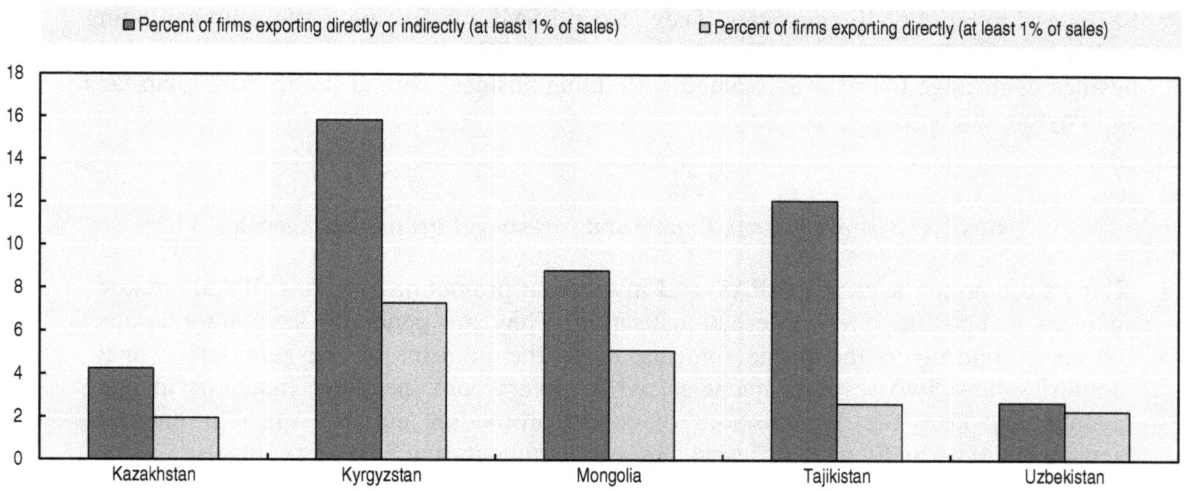

Source: OECD analysis based on (EBRD, 2017[9])

Figure 3.2. Export baskets in Central Asian economies

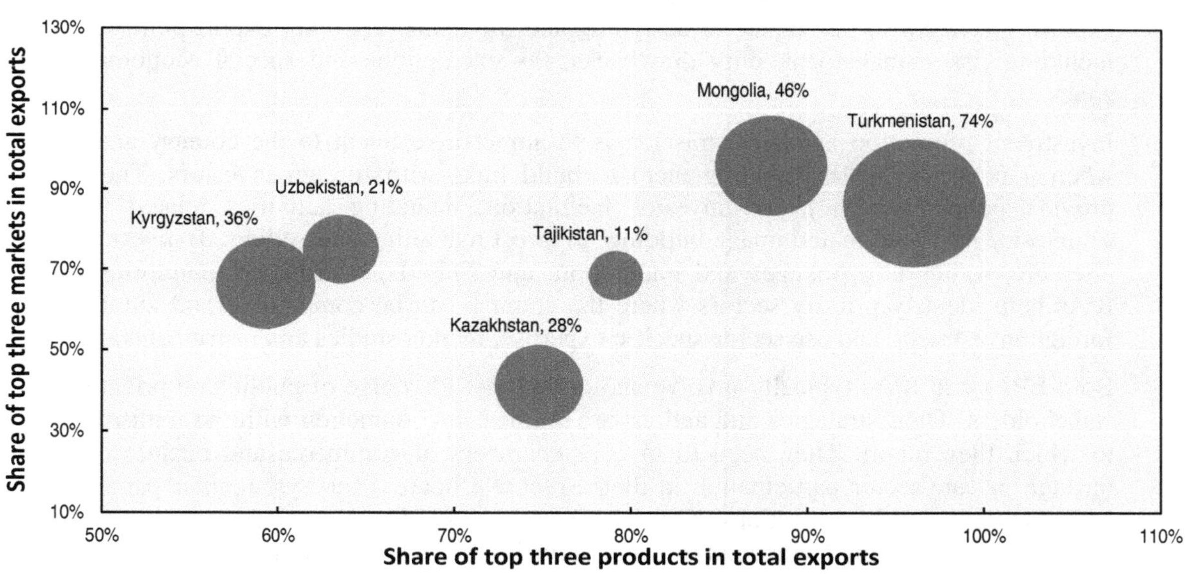

Source: (World Bank, 2017[5]).

The OECD's SME Policy Index framework helps identify policies to support exports, benefit from FDI and better integrate into global value-chains

In order to boost SME internationalisation, governments need to facilitate exports and access to markets, while linking SMEs with foreign investors better (OECD, 2017[2]). Some of the general factors influencing these efforts have been discussed in Chapter 1 of this report, including hard and soft infrastructures for trade policy and trade facilitation.

Policy interventions to address information and knowledge barriers, such as the creation of investment and export agencies, can have a significant positive impact on SME exports (Box 3.1). They help to build links between domestic and foreign companies, to advise SMEs and to build SME capacities. They also aid SMEs in finding a relevant positioning and image for their products. Export finance and risk management programmes help businesses manage the risks associated with doing business abroad (Lederman, Olarreaga and Payton, 2006[10]).

Box 3.1. Best practices in Export and Investment Promotion Agencies

Export promotion agencies (EPAs) and investment promotion agencies (IPAs) are key players in boosting SME internationalisation. They are generally semi-autonomous entities reporting to the prime minister or to the minister of the economy. Some countries have two separate agencies, while others combine these functions in one agency, but keep the two missions of export promotion and investment promotion separate. They usually have different targets, instruments and business contacts.

Export promotion agencies' mission is to support companies seeking to export, including SMEs. A study carried out across 88 EPAs around the world found that EPAs have a positive impact on national exports with an estimated 12% increase in exports on average. They usually have four main tasks: 1) country image building); 2) consulting and export support services; 3) marketing; and 4) market research and publications. Their services are targeted at SMEs, both exporters and those not yet exporting. They also participate in designing and implementing other export policies, including risk management, duty drawbacks, tax exemptions and special economic zones.

Investment promotion agencies' mission is to attract investment to the country and, when it comes to SMEs, helping them to build links with foreign investors. They provide policy advocacy and investor facilitation, including activities related to 1) investor information and image building; 2) direct marketing and selling; 3) investor aftercare; 4) building linkages and integration; and 5) FDI performance monitoring. IPAs help identify priority sectors where the country can be competitive and attract foreign investment, and use sector-specific expertise, market studies and instruments.

Both EPAs and IPAs typically involve and consult a wide range of public and private stakeholders. Their strategies and actions are defined in conjunction with the ministry to which they report. They need to involve chambers of commerce and businesses through private-sector participation in their executive boards, surveys, regular panels and roundtables and joint actions. They also have regional branches in the country (or co-operate with regional agencies) to better serve investors and domestic companies in different regions and to maintain strong relationships with local authorities. They co-operate with other public institutions such as public and private banks to finance exports.

Sources: OECD Analysis based on (Lederman, Olarreaga and Payton, 2006[10]; ISPAT, 2016[11]; Business France, 2017[12]; Byrne, 2016[13])

The OECD's SME Policy Index analyses two dimensions of SME internationalisation – export promotion and integration of SMEs into global value chains. This has been complemented by a dimension on investment promotion (Figure 3.3). This framework helps governments identify policies and tools that will help SMEs to boost exports, benefit from FDI and better integrate into global value chains (OECD, 2015[14]).

Figure 3.3. SME internationalisation framework

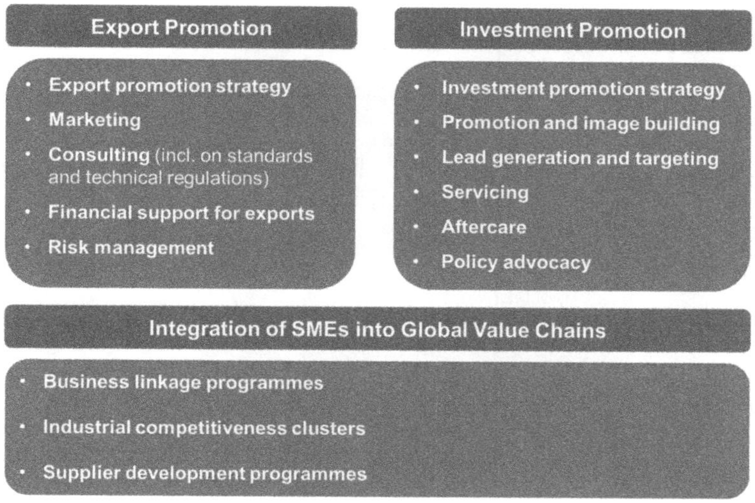

Source: (OECD, 2015[14])

OECD work in Central Asia highlights the potential benefits of investment in support services, promotion activities abroad and private-sector involvement

Most Central Asian countries have set up export and investment promotion agencies and strategies, started to create networks abroad to facilitate trade and information flows between domestic companies and buyers or investors abroad, and created public export banks and financial programmes. However, there is much that can be done to expand and upgrade these efforts.

The OECD studied export- and investment-promotion efforts in Uzbekistan, Kyrgyzstan and Tajikistan, which were peer-reviewed and monitored in the OECD Eurasia Competitiveness Roundtable during 2013-17. Kyrgyzstan has created the building blocks of an effective investment promotion system, building an IPA and by drafting an investment promotion strategy. Tajikistan has focused on reforms to facilitate agribusiness exports and make the most out of its accession to the World Trade Organization (WTO). Uzbekistan has recently focused on creating institutions and policies to support the growth of SME exports. Drawing on their experiences, the OECD recommends further development of policy instruments targeting SME internationalisation in Central Asia (Table 3.1). Common challenges include the need to:

- **Invest in support services by expanding advisory services and training capacities for exporters,** including on certification and knowledge of customs procedures, and by helping match SMEs and MNCs. Support service staff should be knowledgeable about global and regional trends, assessing local competitive advantages, carrying out studies of target markets, and approaching key international investors on a bilateral basis.

- **Develop and co-ordinate export promotion activities abroad** with embassies, consulates, chambers of commerce and other institutions, **and develop a network of agency offices in target countries**.
- **Consult companies regarding their needs** and adjust activities accordingly, for example through independent exporter and investor surveys.

Table 3.1. Overview of selected instruments for business internationalisation in Central Asia

	Kazakhstan	Kyrgyzstan	Mongolia	Tajikistan	Uzbekistan
Investment promotion activities	· Kazakhstan has developed a national investment strategy. · Kazakh Invest (under the Ministry of Investment and Development) is Kazakhstan's IPA	· Kyrgyzstan is drafting an investment promotion strategy with sector focus. · It created the State Agency for Investment and Export Promotion (SAEIP) under the Ministry of Economy of the Kyrgyz Republic in 2014.	· The Foreign Investment and Foreign Trade Agency of Mongolia (FIFTA) plays the role of an IPA.	· Tajinvest is the Tajik IPA. · The Chamber of Commerce and Industry of Tajikistan and other players participate in investment promotion in the country. · The Ministry of Labour, Migration and Employment works to increase remittances.	· The State Committee on Investments has been created to design and support policies to attract investment. · Uzinfoinvest is the Uzbek IPA · The Chamber of Commerce and industry participate in IP efforts.
Export promotion activities	· KazakhExport is the Kazakh EPA. · The activity of KazakhExport is carried out under the State Program for Industrial-Innovative Development of Kazakhstan 2015-2019. · Additional support organisations for Kazakhstan's export development, include DAMU, the Development Bank of Kazakhstan, Atameken and the Centre for Trade Policy Development.	· Kyrgyzstan has launched the National Export Strategy of the Kyrgyz Republic for 2013 2017. · The SAEIP has recently expanded its activities into export promotion.	· The Government of Mongolia has approved the implementation of the Export Promotion Programme. · The FIFTA is also the EPA for Mongolia.	· A national programme has been designed, the Programme for Export Promotion and Import Substitution 2017-2020 that includes the creation of an export bank and an export credit guarantee scheme. · Tajinvest officially participates in export promotion efforts, but no official institution has been designed as an EPA. · In 2014 the Centre for Trade Promotion was founded by the Tajik Chamber of Commerce and the United Nations Development Programme (UNDP).	· A national strategy for export growth has been designed. · The National Bank of Uzbekistan financially supports companies to export. · The Export Promotion Fund (EPF) mostly supports SMEs to export. · The Chamber of Commerce and Industry of Uzbekistan carries out export promotion activities in and outside Uzbekistan. · Sector-specific JSCs are involved in export activities, such as Uzagroexport in agriculture and Uztelsanoat in home appliances.
Integration into global value vhains	· Kazakhstan has developed a Business Linkage Programme for SMEs under the guidance of DAMU Fund as part of its "Business Road Map 2020".	· No formal business linkage programme has been established yet. · Various international organisations support projects to better integrate companies into global value chains, especially in agriculture.	• No formal business linkage programmes are established yet Mongolia maintains a database on foreign investors and local companies interested in participating in business linkage.	· No BLP identified or in place. International organisations support the integration of local SMEs and farmers into global value chains.	· BLPs in place

Source: OECD Analysis based on (DAMU, 2017[15]; FITA, 2017[16]; Kyrgyzstan, 2017[17]; Office of the Prime Minister of Kazakhstan, 2017[18]; OECD, 2017[19])

Uzbekistan: Boosting the export promotion system

Trade is concentrated in a few natural resources in Uzbekistan. Boosting SME exports can support export diversification and development. The government has engaged reform efforts in favour of economic openness, most notably with respect to currency convertibility. In 2017, the OECD provided policy recommendations to enhance the export promotion system in the country. They focus on: consulting services and market intelligence for SMEs, clear value proposition and export promotion networks abroad, as well as monitoring and evaluating the impact of export promotion activities.

Context: Uzbekistan has taken a cautious path to reform

In the years since independence in 1991, Uzbekistan's approach to economic liberalisation has been cautious but nevertheless based on the recognition of the need for reform. The government committed to a gradual series of reforms, which aimed to minimise their negative or disruptive effects. This approach has proven relatively successful. In 2001, Uzbekistan became the first post-Soviet country to regain pre-independence levels of GDP (World Bank, 2017[5]). By then, it had achieved self-sufficiency in oil, increased natural gas exports, and boosted its food self-sufficiency by shifting from farming cotton to wheat (Pomfret, 2006[20]).

Uzbekistan's endowments of easily exportable primary commodities, namely cotton and gold, helped sustain the economy through the initial years of independence. Subsequently, strong public investment became the key source of growth until the late 1990s. Falling cotton prices in the middle of the decade affected the balance of payments, and a lack of macroeconomic flexibility due to delayed structural reforms led the government to establish strict exchange controls in 1996. It did this in order to promote import-substituting industries, protect foreign exchange reserves and subsidise basic food imports. However, this decision generated welfare losses estimated by the International Monetary Fund (IMF) to be somewhere between 2% and 8% of GDP, with exporters suffering particular losses (Rosenberg and de Zeeuw, 2000[21]).

In the early 2000s, as the country faced an economic slowdown, the government enacted a number of economic reforms, with positive effects on economic growth. From 2005 to 2015 average annual GDP growth exceeded of more than 7%, driven by net exports, state-led investments and remittances (Figure 3.4) (World Bank, 2017[5]). However, GDP per capita remains below that of neighbouring countries and below the average of low- and middle-income economies overall (World Bank, 2017[5]).

Figure 3.4. Uzbekistan's exports as a share of GDP, and annual GDP growth

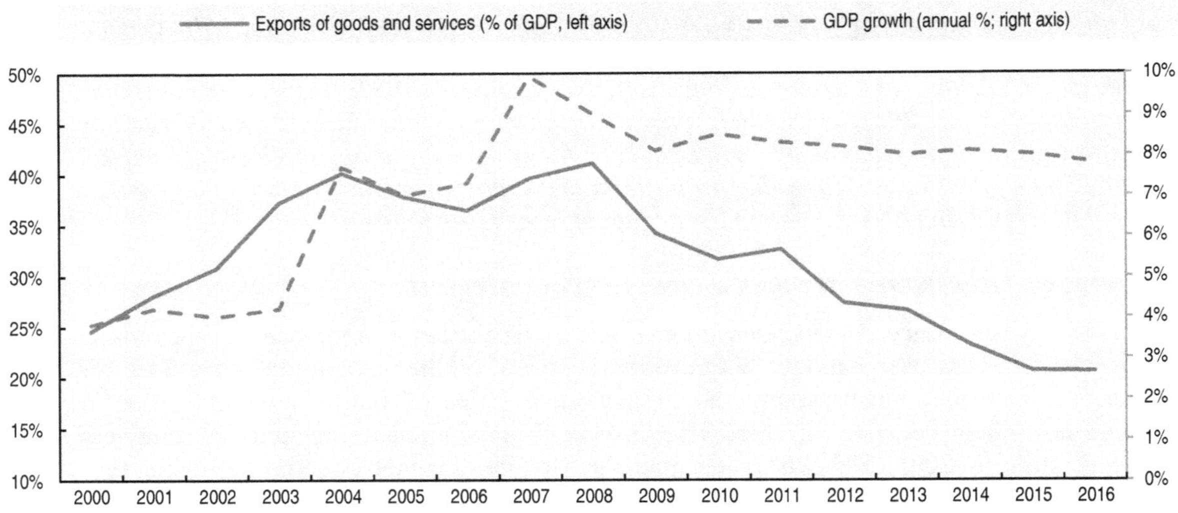

Source: World Bank (2017), *World Development Indicators*, http://data.worldbank.org/indicator.

The role of SMEs in the economy has significantly expanded

The development of private small and medium-sized enterprises (SMEs) and entrepreneurship has been consistently identified as a priority by the government since independence. Several government strategies, programmes and decrees have aimed at supporting the development of SMEs, notably by improving access to finance for small businesses, developing ICT infrastructure, streamlining and eliminating administrative procedures, and simplifying and reducing the tax burden. The government's aims include enhancing the overall business environment, and reducing the interference of the state in the economic activities of SMEs, ultimately generating jobs and income through SME growth and entrepreneurship (Uzbekistan, 2013). In 2017, the government stepped up its reform efforts to these ends. As a result, Uzbekistan moved up 13 positions in the World Bank's 2018 Doing Business Report. The country ranks 74th and was among the top ten economies worldwide in terms of reform progress, with the most notable improvements coming from doing business reforms (World Bank, 2016[22]) (Government of Uzbekistan, 2011[23]).

The role of SMEs in the economy has significantly increased since 2000 in terms of employment, GDP and exports. This trend has further accelerated since 2010, following a new set of presidential decrees and government programmes initiated after the financial crisis.[2] In Uzbekistan, according to official data, SMEs are the biggest source of employment, as they now provide 78% of jobs, compared to 74.3% in 2010 and just below 50% in 2000. This is more than the 70% provided by SMEs on average in OECD countries (OECD, 2017[24]).

Their contribution to GDP has also increased substantially. While SMEs contributed only 31% of GDP in 2000, their share had almost doubled to 56.9% by 2016 (Figure 3.5). They represent more than 45% of industrial production, 61.4% of services, and 98.2% of agriculture production (UzStat, 2017[25]). Tax reduction, simplified business registration and licensing, and easier access to finance are often cited by official sources as the main reforms driving SME development in the country (Government of Uzbekistan, 2011[23]; President of Uzbekistan, 2016[26]).

Figure 3.5. SMEs' contribution to exports, GDP and employment in Uzbekistan

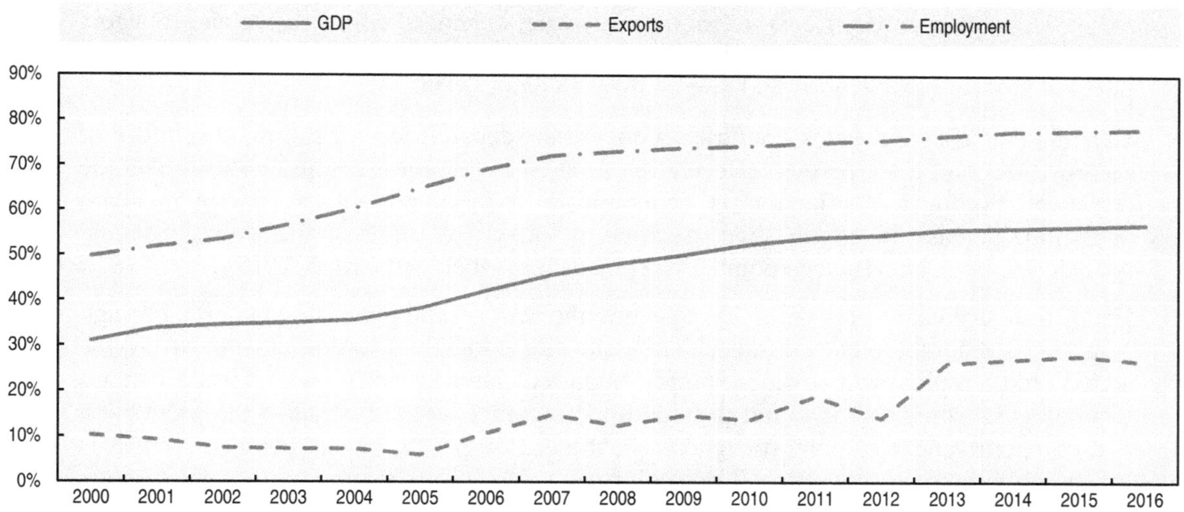

Source: UzStat (2017a), Госкомстат - Развитие Малого Предпринимательства (Бизнеса) В Узбекистане.

SME exports have also significantly increased since 2000, and further accelerated since 2010, with their share of total exports rising from 10.2% in 2000 to 13.7% in 2010 and 26.5% in 2016, according to official data. The government's stated priorities have been focused on simplifying customs procedures, supporting SME export financing, and boosting export promotion.

SMEs' contribution to exports remains relatively limited however (Figure 3.5). Although their share has been growing, SMEs generated less than 30% of Uzbekistan's exports in 2015. This meant that SME exports amounted to less than 6% of GDP, compared to around 15% on average in EU member countries. The weakness of SME exports is in turn reflected in Uzbekistan's comparatively low overall ratio of exports to GDP, which, at 21%, is far below the EU average of 39%. In addition, Uzbekistan's main exports, namely gold, radioactive materials and refined copper, are not the sectors in which SMEs predominantly operate.

SMEs represent more than 76% of exporting organisations on the official data. However, a significant share of exports, particularly in the agricultural sector, is still channelled through state holding companies such as Uzagroexport, which aggregate products from SMEs. SMEs often have sales commission contracts with these specialised foreign trade companies, and will directly export through them. In OECD countries, the contribution of SMEs to exports as upstream producers accounts for more than half of the domestic value added of total exports (OECD and World Bank, 2015[27]). This indirect contribution has yet to be assessed for SMEs in Uzbekistan and should increase the figures for their contribution to exports.

Yet Uzbekistan's economy needs to internationalise further

Boosting exports can have an impact on economic growth. Trade, and particularly exports, can be critical drivers of growth, learning and competitiveness (OECD, 2010[28]). The benefits of trade include, but are not limited to, the effects of specialisation and more efficient allocation of resources; the availability of a greater variety of intermediate goods or services, often at lower cost; economies of scale; enhanced competition; and transfers of skills and technology (Kowalski and Büge, 2013[29]). Research has also identified a positive link between exports and employment (Kiyota, 2014[30]).

Export diversification helps countries reduce their dependence on a limited number of commodities and trade partners. Recent research on low-income countries shows that the effect of export diversification is economically very important, as a one standard deviation increase in export diversification is shown to increase the average annual growth rate by 0.8 percentage points (Makhmadshoev, Ibeh and Crone, 2015[31]).

Imports are critical to both diversifying economic activity and increasing exports. Foreign sourcing is a complement to, rather than a substitute for, the creation of domestic value added and employment from exports. Imported inputs can reduce costs, increase technological sophistication, and provide unique components to enhance the production and competitiveness of domestic goods. In the era of GVCs, export competitiveness is inextricably linked to importing (Lopez Gonzalez, 2016[32]). Creating barriers for imports thus also hinders exports.

Uzbekistan's growth in the past decade was partly driven by trade, as rising prices for primary commodities helped sustain a trade surplus (Mazhikeyev, Edwards and Rizov, 2015[33]). However, the trade surplus is also due to tariff and non-tariff barriers to imports, bolstered by policies to encourage import substitution. More recently, export earnings have fallen sharply due to the drop in commodity prices and the slowdown in the Russian Federation; Uzbekistan's positive foreign trade balance decreased and the current account surplus narrowed to 0.3% of GDP (ADB, 2016[34]). Exports of goods and services represented only 18.8% of Uzbekistan's GDP in 2016, compared to 28.5% in Kazakhstan and 28.5% on average among OECD countries (World Bank, 2017[5]).

Box 3.2. Uzbekistan's export structure by product and partner country

Uzbekistan's exports are currently concentrated in raw materials, especially in three sectors: gas and metals, cotton, and fruits and vegetables. As well as being concentrated in terms of products exported, Uzbekistan's diversification is also limited in terms of its export markets. The top five countries for Uzbek exports – Switzerland, China, Kazakhstan, Turkey and Russia – take 86% of its overall exports (OEC, 2017a).

The country's trade structure remains concentrated, although it is significantly more diversified than it was during the initial years of independence. In particular, the share of exports to the Russian Federation – which stood at 55%of exports in 1992 – had fallen to 9.7% in 2015, while the share of other CIS countries grew (Carneiro & Trushin, 2013). Uzbekistan has also significantly diversified the products it exports since 1992, due to an increase in exports of food products and manufactured goods. For instance, cotton fibre fell from 65% of total exports in 1992 to 9% in 2012 (Carneiro & Trushin, 2013).

Sources: OECD (2017) "What does Uzbekistan export? (2015)"; Carneiro and Trushin (2013), "Changing for the better: The path to upper-middle-income status in Uzbekistan"; ITC (2017), "Uzbekistan".

The need for internationalisation has increasingly been recognised by the government. Its priorities for industrial development and the business environment for SMEs have been set out in several decrees and government strategies. Government efforts have in particular intensified since 2010 and the State Programme that declared 2011 the *Year of Small Business and Private Entrepreneurship* (Government of Uzbekistan, 2011[23]).

More recently, the Development Strategy for 2017-2021 identifies goals such as the "liberalisation and facilitation of export activities, diversification of the export structure and geography, and the expansion and mobilisation of the export potential of economic sectors and territories". The government also aims at full liberalisation of foreign economic activities in the field of exports and the removal of existing obstacles for exporting firms. It has suggested a stronger role for economic counsellors abroad in strengthening exports.

Trade regime, currency convertibility and trade facilitation remain reform priorities

Trade regime

The comparatively limited role of exports in Uzbekistan's economy might stem in part from its trade regime. Uzbekistan is not a member of the WTO and its trade regime was until recently defined by a high level of protection for import-substituting industries and restrictions on exports of food and other products. Its localisation programme provides tax and customs privileges for import-substituting industries and exporters of manufactured products (Ganiev and Yusupov, 2012[35]).

Currency convertibility

Firms complained for many years that currency convertibility issues, such as long and complex procedures for conversion, currency controls and repatriation requirements, increased the cost of exports and impeded the transfer of profits and the sourcing of supplies abroad. This made business transactions and trade more costly, complicated and time-consuming both for imports of inputs used for domestic production and for exports. Although Uzbekistan legally introduced full convertibility of the Uzbek sum for current international transactions in 2003, importers and exporters have faced difficulties in obtaining foreign exchange. According to recent IMF research, Uzbekistan in 2016 was still applying seven out of eight possible capital flow management measures (Horton et al., 2016$_{[36]}$).[3]

These stringent currency controls had an adverse effect on the ability of businesses to carry out their export/import-related operations (EBRD, 2016$_{[37]}$). For all legal entities, including those with foreign investments, access to foreign currency previously required special permission from the Central Bank. Applicants had to open a special foreign currency account in an authorised bank and needed to go through an administrative process established by the Republican Commission for Monetary Policy that required time and effort (Export.gov, 2017$_{[38]}$). This constituted a major barrier for imports but also for exports, because equipment, raw materials, spare parts and other goods often need to be imported to produce exportable goods (Ganiev and Yusupov, 2012$_{[35]}$). This in turn limited the integration of local SMEs into GVCs, as imports play a crucial role by making available advanced inputs, and by providing technology, knowledge and capital (OECD and World Bank, 2015$_{[27]}$).

However, in 2017, consistent with the desire to strengthen export activities, the government took some important steps in the direction of full currency convertibility. In September 2017, a presidential decree abolished the requirement to convert foreign currency export earnings for all types of businesses. The exchange rate is now determined on the basis of market mechanisms, free currency exchange is allowed and restrictive measures have been lifted. Due to these changes, the Uzbek sum immediately dropped to 8100 per USD from 4,200 a day before the introduction of the new exchange rate regime. Liberalisation has been detrimental for the black market (Eurasianet, 2017$_{[39]}$). Currency convertibility and the new exchange rate have been positively received by the international community and by investors (IMF, 2017$_{[40]}$). They could contribute to making the economy more open, expanding export opportunities, and encouraging foreign investors to operate in the country.

Trade facilitation

Another barrier to engaging in foreign trade in Uzbekistan is the impermeability of its borders. Uzbekistan has undertaken reforms to facilitate trade and the flow of goods across its borders, but further work is required. According to the OECD's trade facilitation indicators (TFIs), Uzbekistan matches or exceeds the average performance of lower-middle income countries in the involvement of the trade community, advance rulings, appeal procedures and fees and charges (Figure 3.6). However, its performance in the areas of information availability, formalities (documents, automation and procedures), and governance and impartiality is well below that of other countries in its income group. Its performance is also slightly below average on border agency co-operation (internal and external).

Figure 3.6. Uzbekistan in the OECD trade facilitation indicators

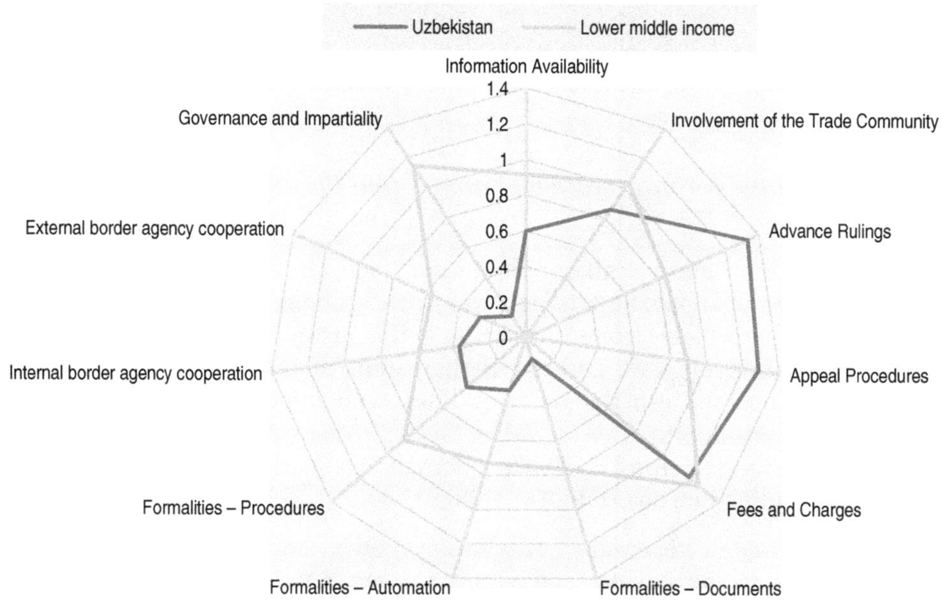

Source: OECD (2017a), "Trade facilitation indicators", www.oecd.org/trade/facilitation/indicators.htm.

Uzbekistan should therefore build on recent efforts, like the "single window" system, as well as further digitisation of formalities to speed up export-related clearance processes (OECD, 2017[41]). Single window systems allow for data exchange by using the latest communication and technology techniques as well as simplified, harmonised and remodelled information systems, leading to greater efficiencies in licensing and customs processes, increased revenue collection and overall trade expansion (ESCWA, 2011[42]). In November 2017, the government of Uzbekistan was preparing the launch of a new "single window" system that would allow online applications for over 20 types of permits, including compliance, environmental, and veterinary certificates. Since 2011, exporters have been able to use a one-stop -shop mechanism, which provides a single customs clearance procedure.

The government of Uzbekistan is currently working on several initiatives to enhance trade facilitation, including the simplification and removal of formalities and documents to exports, and the authorisation for business entities to open bank accounts abroad (Ministry of Economy of Uzbekistan, 2017[43]). In June 2017, the government launched a "green corridor", the goal of which is to provide a simplified procedure for customs and phytosanitary clearance for fruits and vegetables that are supplied to Russia.

To further internationalise its economy, Uzbekistan needs to reform its trade framework, improve the convertibility of its currency and facilitate the cross-border flow of goods. The government is well aware of these challenges and has started addressing them, for instance by eliminating declarations and developing electronic procedures at customs, by easing foreign currency exchange, and by building programmes to support exports through the NBU and the EPF. The next sections of this report focus on how to support small and medium firms' exports, since SMEs can be an engine for internationalisation.

In parallel with trade facilitation, transport and logistical hard infrastructure could be further developed in Uzbekistan. This would enable the country to become a transport and logistics hub, strengthening north-south and east-west links across the Eurasian landmass.

Overall recommendation: Enhance SME export promotion policies and institutions

SMEs can be an engine for internationalisation – but they need specialised support

Given further progress in the overall conditions for trade discussed above, SMEs could play an important role in supporting the government's ambition to increase exports as a source of growth. Due to their strong innovation and adjustment capabilities, SMEs can drive internationalisation in new markets. Participation in international trade through global value chains and the establishment of links with large companies and foreign affiliates, offers further opportunities to SMEs. Such linkages can help SMEs overcome key barriers to exporting, such as access to international markets, finance, technology, management skills and knowledge (OECD, 2008[44]).

SMEs often have limited resources, negotiation power and internal knowledge to overcome difficulties in the business climate, however. SMEs face particular barriers when exporting. They have fewer staff than large companies and hence lack the time, expertise and knowledge to do marketing, sales and distribution abroad. Moreover, they are not always aware of the quality standards or certification requirements in target markets. SMEs consistently identify lack of knowledge of foreign markets and difficulties in reaching them as major impediments to exporting, thus calling for enhanced export promotion policies.

Export promotion policies are "the set of policies and practices aimed at affecting directly or indirectly export from a given country". They typically include a wide set of measures such as: developing export infrastructure, introducing consulting activities to improve knowledge of foreign markets, expanding the network of export promotion abroad and monitoring the impact of export institutions (Belloc and Di Maio, 2011[45]). Such policies help SMEs to 1) address asymmetric information and market failures when exporting; 2) foster spillovers, technology sharing and learning-by-doing for exporters; and 3) identify and leverage competitive advantages (Lederman, Olarreaga and Payton, 2006[10]; Hausmann and Rodrik, 2003[46]).

SMEs in Uzbekistan report that they lack knowledge of foreign markets, and they suffer from limited access to consulting and export support services. Existing agencies carry out selected export promotion actions, including fairs, country visits and market studies, but the outcomes of these actions for SMEs are sometimes unclear, and their impact is not assessed, reported or shared with businesses. To improve competitiveness and facilitate SME exports, the government should work on establishing and expanding its export promotion system in line with OECD recommended practices. Key steps include expanding the network of export promotion agencies abroad, especially in target markets; developing export services and consulting activities for SMEs, including on certification; and streamlining and enhancing the systems for monitoring the country's export promotion system.

Uzbekistan's export promotion system has been recently established. Figure 3.7 provides a high-level overview of the institutions currently in place. The government, through the

Ministry of Foreign Trade and the Ministry of Economy, provides strategic oversight. The core players involved in export promotion are the SME Export Promotion Fund (EPF) and the Chamber of Commerce and Industry of Uzbekistan (CCIU), which represents the voice and interest of businesses in this process. Uzbekistan's economic counsellors provide further support through embassies abroad. Uzstandart and the State Committee for Assistance to Privatised Companies and Development of Competition also undertake activities that support, or are part of, export promotion.

The system as a whole is still taking shape – the EPF (described in Box 3.3) was created in 2013 and Uzstandart's Bureau for the Promotion of Exports was created in 2011.

Figure 3.7. Schematic view of SME export promotion institutions in Uzbekistan

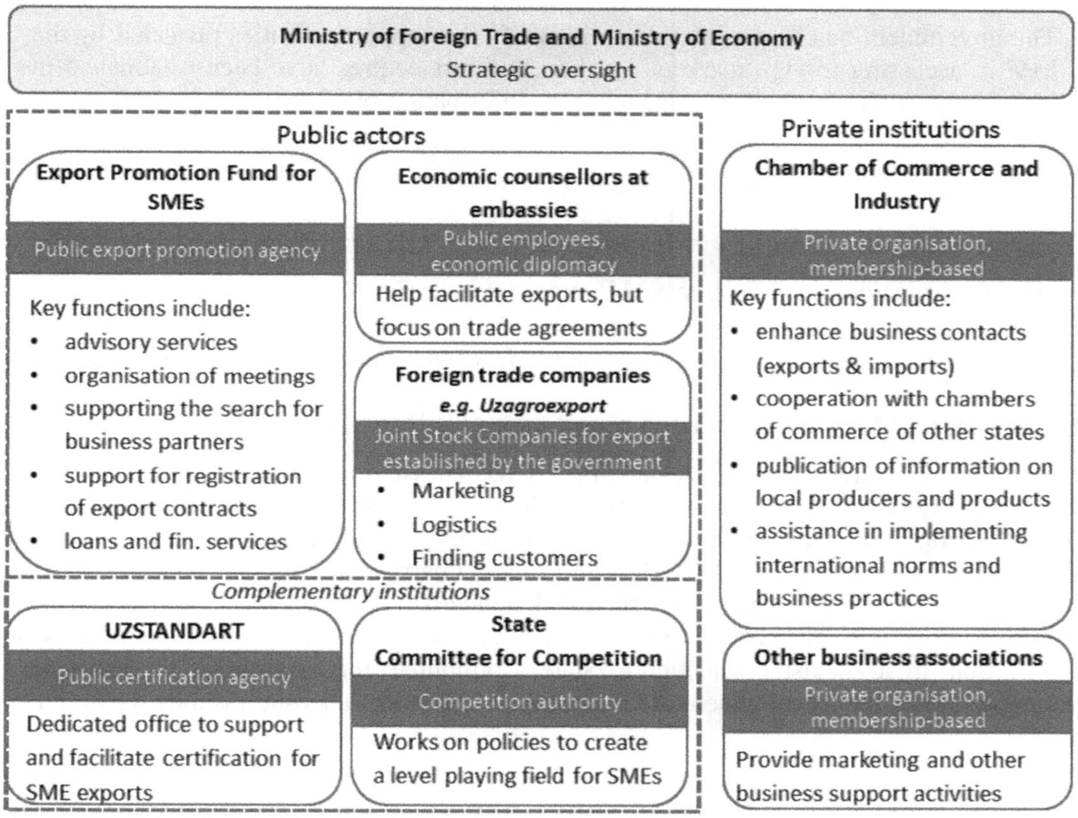

Source: OECD Analysis, 2017.

Box 3.3. Uzbekistan's export promotion fund

In an effort to boost SME exports the government of Uzbekistan created the Export Promotion Fund for Small Business and Private Entrepreneurship (EPF) under the National Bank of Uzbekistan (NBU) in 2013. The EPF provides the following services: organisation of meetings, seminars, providing advisory services, supporting the search for business partners, support for the registration of export contracts with Uzbekistan's authorities, research on standards in target markets, legal services, and loans and financial services. The fund provides 80% of these services free of charge. At the time of writing, the EPF employs 122 staff. It has seven offices abroad, with plans to open more. It is also represented in each of the 14 regions of Uzbekistan.

The government has begun reforms to intensify the support activities provided by the EPF in accessing foreign markets. Further, business centres have been established in Uzbekistan, which provide a single advisory information platform, including on export activities.

Source: OECD interviews and questionnaire, EPF presentation.

Recommendations to enhance SME export promotion

Develop consulting activities to improve SMEs' knowledge of foreign markets

Challenge: SMEs in Uzbekistan report lack of information as a key barrier

The OECD interviewed companies and the CCIU. They reported that lack of information was a key barrier to doing business abroad. Such information gaps typically include lack of knowledge about market trends and competitors, and about entry barriers such as customs duties or certificates (Box 3.4). Information barriers also include a lack of sector-specific expertise, including on international standards and operations. This assessment by businesses is confirmed by public institutions and think tanks involved in export promotion in Uzbekistan, including State Committee for Assistance to Privatised Companies and the Development of Competition, and think tanks surveyed by the OECD.

Box 3.4. Information barriers to SME exports in OECD and non-OECD economies

Information barriers are frequently identified as critical barriers to exporting by SMEs in OECD and non-OECD countries. For example, two of the three top non-financial barriers to SME exports identified by the OECD (2008) were:

- Limited information to locate/analyse markets. This factor was the most cited internationalisation barrier among the responding firms, suggesting that information gaps remain a critical challenge to SMEs even in the current era of extensive information availability.
- Lack of managerial time, skills and knowledge. Difficulties arising from limited managerial knowledge emerged as a top barrier to SME internationalisation in several surveys. Managerial risk perceptions and lack of knowledge about international markets were major reasons for not engaging in international trade. Limitations in managers' internationalisation knowledge similarly emerged as a leading obstacle to export initiation.

Similarly, a more recent review (WTO, 2016) found that critical issues for SMEs were limited information about the working of foreign markets and difficulties in accessing export distribution channels and contacting overseas customers. Other issues include costly product standards and certification procedures, and, in particular, a lack of information about requirements in foreign markets.

Sources: OECD (2009), Top Barriers and Drivers to SME Internationalisation, http://www.oecd.org/cfe/smes/43357832.pdf; WTO (2016), World Trade Report: Levelling the Trading Field for SMEs

Export promotion institutions and policies can provide tools to overcome such knowledge and export skills barriers (see Box 3.7). Targeted and sector-specific market studies can help build knowledge of target markets and identify niches which Uzbekistan's SMEs could occupy. Similarly, advisory services can provide SMEs with the skills they need or help them to outsource some activities. Helping SMEs to gain export skills and knowledge is particularly relevant when it comes to helping them integrate into global value chains.

Export promotion capacities

Uzbekistan is building up its export promotion capacities and staffing in the public and private sectors. The EPF has a staff of 122, and 54 employees work in the field of export promotion at the CCIU, of whom 12 are based abroad. However, critical sector-specific expertise still seems to be lacking. Few of the staff in Uzbekistan's export promotion institutions have an industry background, and there are no dedicated teams for specific sectors (OECD interviews).

The experiences of OECD countries suggest that sector-specific expertise is extremely useful and effective in helping companies overcome the many barriers to exports that they encounter. The lack of sector-specific expertise is linked to a lack of clearly defined strategic sectors and niches that Uzbekistan can target. For example, Germany's export promotion efforts gained a lot of momentum once the country decided to focus on the renewables sector and structured its efforts around this (Berg, 2016[47]). France has also built teams of industry experts on priority sectors, including agribusiness, culture, health and urban services.

Certification

Certificates confirming the quality of products are critical barriers to entry for many potential export markets. Companies cite issues with certification as one of the main barriers they face, and report difficulties in finding certification companies in Uzbekistan. A lack of knowledge of EU certification and the lack of availability of such certificates hinders exports to EU markets, particularly in agriculture. The number of certification companies in Uzbekistan remains limited despite the country's substantial efforts to increase its capacity to certify products. The certification body Uzstandart is increasingly working to facilitate and support exports. A bureau for the promotion of exports has been created within Uzstandart charged with the provision of information and free consulting services regarding international and country-specific requirements for standards, the promotion of products overseas and other parameters (certification, labelling, packaging, etc.) and developing proposals for achieving compliance with international standards.

Action 1: Identify target markets and sectors through public-private dialogue

To target efforts, the public and private sectors should work together to identify markets and sectors where Uzbekistan has or is developing a competitive advantage. Uzbekistan could use several steps to identify such markets based on expected supply and demand. On the supply side these include assessing its revealed comparative advantages; identifying domestic and international competitors, their market presence and investment plans; and analysing the positioning of Uzbek products on the market compared to competitors. On the demand side, Uzbekistan should analyse local and international consumption trends, the expected growth in sectors where Uzbekistan aims to export, consumer preferences and purchasing power, and possible distribution channels. This work should take into account existing logistical centres, transport routes, tariff conditions, customs regulations and the overall trade environment in the target market. It could also encompass the analysis of specific aspects of the market such as product regulations and standards. The International Trade Centre has developed tools to facilitate such analysis (ITC, 2017[48]). Public-private working groups and consultations can be useful when defining such a strategy. They should be inclusive and bring together the Ministry of Foreign Trade, the Ministry of Economy, the EPF, the CCIU, the Centre for Economic Research (CER), and other key actors involved in the definition of export policy, as well as the agencies executing export promotion and private businesses, including those that would like to export but have not yet done so.

Based on the sectors and markets selected, the EPF should then develop a strong knowledge base by hiring or training the experts needed. Ideally, such experts should be providing basic market- and sector-specific analysis free of charge, while providing more tailored market studies at the request of individual companies for a fee. Uzbekistan should create an easily accessible database of such reports, bringing together the work of all the public institutions involved.

Action 2: Expand advisory and training capacities and support preferential access for SMEs

In interviews with the OECD and during Working Group meetings, companies repeatedly raised the issue of lack of skills for exporting and business internationalisation. These results were supported by a questionnaire the OECD sent out to policy makers and organisations active in the area of SME export promotion in Uzbekistan. Local private and public organisations organise regular roundtables and events related to export issues. However, there has been no accurate business survey on the exact skills needed and barriers experienced. Uzbekistan, either through the ministries in charge or via the EPF and CCIU, should regularly and formally survey businesses to identify key barriers to exporting and build a better understanding of companies' needs. Based on such a survey and the above-mentioned identification of priority markets and sectors, the EPF should build and extend its specialised training and advisory capacity.

In OECD countries, such surveys are usually carried out by the export promotion agency with the support of an independent survey company. For instance, the French national export agency Business France asked exporting companies about the major difficulties they faced in exporting and their knowledge of the services offered by Business France and other actors in the French export promotion system, as well as their impact. This helped Business France refine its export service offer (Business France, 2016[49]).

The EPF and the CCIU should further develop their advisory services for SMEs in line with the needs they have expressed. Studies highlight the financially positive effect of export promotion advisory services: in a study of the impact of export promotion agencies (EPAs) and their strategies covering 104 advanced and developing countries, Lederman, Olarreaga and Payton (2006) found that, on average, each dollar spent on export promotion yielded a USD 300 increase in exports for the median EPA. However, they also found a great deal of variation across regions, levels of development and types of instruments, which points to the need for careful design and implementation, as well as rigorous monitoring and evaluation of EPA efforts. Furthermore, they find strongly diminishing returns, which suggest that, "as far as EPAs are concerned, small is beautiful".

These advisory services, market studies and training need to be advertised both to SMEs which are already exporting and those not yet exporting. Export institutions in Uzbekistan can use the EPF, the Chamber of Commerce and Industry and local authorities to inform firms about their existing programmes and services and expand the regional reach of services. This can also be achieved by creating an online or offline "single information window" for SMEs (Lee, 2017[50]).

Initially, training and advisory services should be provided either free of charge or at a subsidised rate, since SMEs often find it difficult to obtain the funding needed. For example, Australia reimburses companies for 50% of their eligible export promotion expenses (Austrade, 2017[51]). Trust in the quality of the services provided might also be limited in the beginning. Vouchers or tax breaks for SMEs can also serve to help create a private market of advisory services and help limit market distortions. However, assistance should be designed in such a way as to help firms transition either towards more paid services or to become less reliant on the public system of export promotion as their exporting activities mature.

The EPF and the CCIU should study the profile of trainers (either full-time staff or external consultants) providing advice to SMEs and find a balance between external or internal offers. The experience of SMEs which are already exporting could be leveraged in order to create networks of good export practices and export expertise. For instance, Korea has created SME export academies run by export promotion institutions to train entrepreneurs and SMEs on export processes, and encourage them to consider export opportunities. They aim not only to develop exporting skills, but also to build an internationalisation mindset among SMEs (Lee, 2017[50]).

Action 3: Attract more certification companies to the country

In addition to knowledge and skills programmes, the government needs to provide more support for companies seeking to obtain certification. Companies mention the cost of certification as a barrier, but even more important is the limited access to certification services, as Uzbekistan has very few certifying companies. More international certifiers need to be attracted to Uzbekistan. Easier access to certification services, as well as higher standards of certification might also help raise overall product quality levels up to international standards and provide a clear benchmark and indicator of the quality of Uzbekistan's products. Certification companies interviewed by the OECD reported challenges related to the general business environment, such as currency convertibility and profit repatriation, as well as specific challenges on certification, including the distance between international standards and current local standards. However, they did not exclude expanding operations in the country.

Uzbekistan could target several international certification companies, starting with those that already operate in other countries of the region, such as Bureau Veritas, SGS or Tüv Süd. Concerted efforts could be organised with the investment promotion agency UZINFOINVEST to help them understand local needs, identify clients, comply with local regulations and standards, and benefit from tax and investment incentives. The current set of reforms in the country, especially regarding currency, should also be promoted to these companies. Competitive neutrality with existing agencies and certification companies is also crucial to foster their development. The first investment promotion steps could be to directly contact the companies' headquarters in the region, promote doing business in Uzbekistan in the certification sector during a presentation at the headquarters or remotely, and organise a study visit of business representatives to Uzbekistan, including meetings with potential clients.

Certification and its quality implications are particularly relevant for the agricultural sector. For example, it is not possible to obtain organic product certification in Uzbekistan. Uzbekistan should therefore further increase its work on building certification capacities at Uzstandart. This includes organising specific workshops with international experts both for Uzstandart staff, and directly for SMEs, but also funding vouchers for SMEs to participate to training, and to hire consultants and support staff to implement standards in their daily operations.

Expand the export promotion network abroad and provide a clear value proposition in target markets

Challenge: SMEs in Uzbekistan lack connections to target markets

Marketing activities to promote exports are extensively used in OECD countries and developing economies alike. Export promotion agencies abroad were found to have a significant effect on increasing exports for both developed and developing countries (Lederman, Olarreaga and Payton, 2006[10]; Lederman, Olarreaga and Payton, 2010[52]; Martincus et al., 2010[53]; Martincus and Carballo, 2012[54]). The effects were found to be particularly relevant for SMEs (Wilkinson and Brouthers, 2006[55]; Alvarez, 2004[56]; Durmuşoğlu and et al, 2012[57]). Marketing and export promotion activities abroad are also needed by businesses looking for international clients. For example, the OECD

(2009) identified the inability to contact potential overseas customers as another key barrier to exporting. Recent surveys also highlight the difficulty of obtaining adequate representation in target export markets, while other studies found that a key impediment to internationalisation for SMEs was difficulties finding an appropriate foreign market partner. A further difficulty mentioned by businesses is gaining access to suitable distribution channels in international markets.

Uzbekistan's SMEs are no exception to this overall pattern. During focused interviews with SMEs and business associations, the lack of knowledge that they mentioned was clearly linked to a lack of connections to target markets and potential business partners abroad. Companies also mentioned potential buyers' lack of awareness of Uzbek products. The EPF and the CCIU are expanding their international networks of representatives in an effort to meet this challenge, but they remain limited in comparison with those of OECD countries. Uzbekistan's main export promotion agency, the EPF, has opened offices in Bulgaria, Italy, South Korea, Germany, China, Kazakhstan and Latvia, as well as two offices in the Russian Federation and Switzerland. To facilitate the supply of Uzbek goods abroad, trade houses have been established in Russia, Latvia, India, Tajikistan, and the United States (New York). Most of these offices were opened during the past year. They are operated on a part-time basis by business partners or in co-operation with the economic counsellors in Uzbekistan's embassies. Plans are underway to create 15 more offices in Europe and the Middle East. The criteria for selecting these countries have not yet been specified.

The CCIU has 12 representatives abroad, two in the Russian Federation, two in Switzerland and one each in the Czech Republic, Kuwait, Italy, Spain, the United Kingdom, Portugal and Korea. Like those of the EPF, the CCIU's offices abroad are operated on a part-time basis by business partners with experience of doing business in Uzbekistan (CCIU, 2017$_{[58]}$).

Uzbekistan's diplomatic missions also support the internationalisation of businesses. In early 2017, Uzbekistan committed itself to increasing the role of the economic counsellors based at its embassies. As of March 2017, 19 economic counsellors were based at embassies in 12 countries.[4] However, these counsellors are concerned with a broad set of tasks, and trade or export promotion is only one of them. According to Martincus et al. (2010), foreign missions may stimulate exports but usually these are exports of products with less severe informational impediments (products that are often already being exported) and which accordingly require fewer specific skills to deal with them. Trade counsellors are thus important in promoting exports but they are probably not the most efficient tool for *diversifying* the export structure, especially if SMEs are the focus of such efforts.

While the CCIU's trade representatives are local in the sense that they are natives of the target market and are well acquainted with the business community there, most of the trade staff are posted from Uzbekistan. Almost all economic counsellors are seconded from the Ministry of Foreign Trade. Similarly, few of the staff in the EPF's offices have genuine sector expertise. Box 3.5 describes Germany's structured network of public and private organisations as an example Uzbekistan might want to consider.

Box 3.5. Germany's network of export promotion agencies abroad

Export promotion in Germany is characterised by the division of labour between the public and private sectors. The federal government directly promotes exports through Germany Trade and Invest (GTAI) and its network of 220 embassies and consulates, and also co-finances the activities of the Chambers of Commerce Abroad (AHK). Regional and local governments and business associations are also engaged in export promotion. The Federal Ministry of the Economy and Technology co-ordinates the federal and regional actors. The GTAI and the AHK closely co-operate in promoting Germany as a business location.

The GTAI aims to support export-oriented companies based in Germany and to promote Germany as a location for industrial and technological investments in order to attract investors who create or secure jobs. The GTAI has 2 offices in Germany and its own network of 46 offices abroad. These offices are staffed by industry analysts who perform research on site and gather data about foreign markets. This network has approximately 60 specialists distributed in the main export markets. The services provided include comprehensive and client-oriented data and information (e.g. macroeconomic analyses and forecasts, country and industry analyses for over 125 countries, and business contacts) and information about calls for proposals in foreign countries; investment and development projects; and legal, tax, and customs regulations. In gathering these data, the GTAI targets countries, sectors, sectors within countries and countries within sectors. The main users of these services are SMEs displaying the whole range of export experience (from non-exporters to potential exporters). The GTAI charges a below-market price for specialised reports requested by individual companies.

Exporting companies are also supported by 120 overseas chambers of commerce in more than 80 countries. This support includes the provision of market and sector information; legal, tax, and custom advice; assistance in finding business partners and arranging business meetings; and representation and accompaniment at fairs. Within Germany, the 81 German chambers of commerce and industries provide access to this network. By law, all companies must be a member of one chamber. The federal government provides funding to these foreign trade chambers to perform export promotion activities. In 2008, resources amounted to USD 62.4 million, including spending on attracting investment.

To ensure the efficiency of this international network, Germany relies on strong monitoring and evaluation capacities, and a tailor-made approach, taking into account companies' individual needs to assess the effectiveness of the system.

Sources: (Berg, 2016[471]); Jordana, Volpe Martincus and Gallo (2010), Export promotion organizations in Latin America and the Caribbean: An institutional portrait, http://publications.iadb.org/handle/11319/3183

Uzbekistan's export promotion network faces another barrier – the country currently offers an unclear value proposition. Its export promotion lacks focus on particular sectors and target markets, and Uzbekistan has no substantial national branding strategy. Creating a country brand is an efficient marketing instrument, especially for agribusiness products where producers are typically small companies with very limited marketing budgets and products, providing fewer opportunities for differentiation. The development of a country brand should always be tied to strong and objective quality certification. Box 3.6 describes the experience of Trentino province in Italy, which recently developed the "Trentino" and "Qualità Trentino" brands to promote its agribusiness products.

Box 3.6. Branding in Trentino, Italy

National and regional branding is increasingly important, especially in agribusiness. The Trentino province in Italy has created the "Trentino" and "Qualità Trentino" brands to provide marketing instruments for the promotion of its agri-food products. Trentino's branding strategy focuses on increasing the quality of its agri-food production and strengthening the products' link to their region of origin. The brands are specifically designed to identify agribusiness producers that respect quality, typically local and sustainability standards. The benefits linked to this kind of branding are the following:

- better communication of the values associated with Trentino
- opportunity for producers to gain visibility
- promoting a unified image of Trentino in national and international markets
- synergy with other forms of promotion, such as tourism promotion.

In practice, firms can apply to use the brand online. Registration is free of charge, and firms can use the brand for three years if they meet the defined criteria. These include the territoriality of the firm (i.e. firms must be based in Trentino), the firm's capabilities to contribute to local socio-economic development and the preservation of the environment, as well as the promotion of Trentino's image within the markets where firms operate. The use of the brand is managed by the Tourism and Promotion Division of the Trentino Development Agency.

Source: OECD analysis; Marchio Trentino (n.d.), Marchio Trentino website, www.marchiotrentino.it.

Uzbekistan should expand its export promotion network abroad, both in quantitative terms and in terms of the geographical and sectoral priorities set. This includes action in two areas.

Action 4: Expand the number of representation offices abroad with local staff

Uzbekistan should focus on expanding its network of representative offices abroad. This should first and foremost happen in markets that are considered promising. For example, China is a key export partner for Uzbekistan, but neither the EPF nor the CCIU have a representative there. The same is true for the United Arab Emirates (UAE). In order to most effectively expand its network of offices abroad, the government should develop a clear strategy on priority markets for exports, in co-operation and consultation with the private sector. As a purely public organisation, the EPF should be the core institution responsible for expanding the network. Uzbekistan could consider widening the EPF's mandate to include export marketing overall, instead of confining it to SMEs as it is now.

Staff working in these offices should be familiar with both Uzbekistan's export potential and the sectors and countries of interest. Ideally, the EPF should staff the offices in key markets with both Uzbek and local staff, as already done in South Korea, Switzerland and Russia. Hiring should be competitive and transparent and aim to recruit multilingual staff with a strong experience in the sectors of interest. New staff should have business skills, experience in negotiating and a strong business background. Staff should have clear objectives in terms of contacts established, meetings facilitated and business contracts concluded. Similarly, economic counsellors can best support exports if they have prior business experience, as there is evidence of a strong link between their prior business experience and the success of commercial diplomacy (Naray, 2011[59]).

Action 5: Work on a clear value proposition in co-operation with the business community

In order to make its export promotion efforts most useful and effective, Uzbekistan should formulate clear value propositions for each of the target markets identified. This includes establishing a well-publicised branding and marketing strategy. Public-private consultations can help identify the export positioning and value-added message that Uzbekistan wants to adopt when addressing foreign markets, in particular beyond Central Asia. Establishing an Uzbekistan-specific brand that reaches Central Asian markets can help; it could be sector-specific and also be adjusted according to the region. Specialised companies can help find out how Uzbekistan's producers and their products are perceived in the markets of interest. Based on this information, Uzbekistan can then build its value proposition, for example in reliable but affordable industrial products, or fresh agricultural foods, leveraging the country's association with the Silk Road.

Uzbekistan can then use existing outreach channels to communicate a coherent and cross-cutting message across all trade and export promotion entities involved. Messaging should be cross-cutting. Uzbekistan could also work on building networks of successful exporters, as these can be very useful for leveraging existing exports and showcasing success stories to foreign business partners. Promotion activities could and should take place in areas frequented by potential future business partners, such as international airports or sector-specific business fairs. Synergies with Uzinfoinvest and other agencies concerned with promoting Uzbekistan abroad should be identified and exploited.

Monitor the work and impact of export institutions

Challenge: The current monitoring system is more focused on inputs than on impact

As Uzbekistan strengthens its export promotion system, it should closely monitor whether the resources devoted to export promotion activities are being used efficiently. Understanding a programmes' effectiveness and realigning its priorities if needed requires a clearly defined assessment of the activities undertaken and the funds spent (Jordana, Volpe Martincus and Gallo, 2010[60]). Evaluations can take place at different levels, from analyses of export performance at the macroeconomic level to individual interviews with enterprises that have benefitted from public programmes or received support from the EPF or CCIU (De Wulf, 2001[61]).

The ministries and the economic counsellors concerned with exports and export promotion in Uzbekistan already engage in extensive monitoring and reporting activities. This includes quarterly and yearly reports of programmes implemented, activities undertaken and actual exports. Currently, reporting seems to be largely focused on the inputs provided, such as the number of companies assisted or the number of outreach activities undertaken (letters written etc.); participation at fairs supported; or the number of reports provided. Focused interviews found that such reporting activities are burdensome and time-consuming. In addition, it remains unclear how the results of such reporting are used to realign priorities.

Despite the strong focus on reporting, no client surveys appear to be undertaken after the provision of support. Client surveys have been used in several OECD countries and are a useful tool for obtaining clear estimates of the impact of activities, as opposed to merely assessing the volume of activities. Better quantitative and qualitative evaluation of the effects of export promotion policies and activities will make it possible to gain a clearer understanding of such critical issues as the cost-effectiveness of operations, the rate of return on services provided or the need for realignment of priorities. More generally, exporter surveys can give the authorities a better understanding of the priorities and needs of businesses when it comes to exporting.

Action 6: Develop and implement a set of actionable key performance indicators

Uzbekistan should work on improving its monitoring and evaluation efforts while making sure that the time burden involved remains reasonable. This is best achieved by developing a set of clearly defined key performance indicators (KPIs). Box 3.7 provides an overview of the KPIs used in assessing France's export promotion agency Business France, which range from macroeconomic indicators on SME exports to firm-level data using exporter surveys.

In Australia post-support evaluation is performed using telephone surveys on a random sample of firms which are asked about their satisfaction with the services provided by the export promotion agency (Belloc and Di Maio, 2011[45]). In other countries, evaluation is based on the direct measurement of the impact of export promotion programmes on the export volumes conducted by external entities, such as survey companies.

Focusing on actionable KPIs will enable Uzbekistan to adjust its export promotion programmes and regularly review the progress achieved. It could help the government prioritise, expand or decrease activities depending on their use and impact. The authorities should regularly review the functioning and effectiveness of the export promotion programmes in place and take action to realign priorities if needed.

The country should also develop the use of exporter surveys. The EPF could launch formal surveys of businesses at various stages of the export cycle (exporters, non-exporters, new exporters), in collaboration with the CCIU and an independent survey agency. This would help identify their main difficulties and readjust the EPF's actions and programmes accordingly. Uzbekistan could also develop feedback loops with its offices abroad to report on business contacts and needs.

Box 3.7. Monitoring and evaluation of export promotion services in France

Business France is the French agency in charge of export promotion. Created in 2015 as a result of a merger of the French export and investment promotion agencies, Business France places a strong focus on providing its service in the most effective way possible. Business France aims at making public support for internationalisation more visible, easier understandable and more accessible for businesses. It also provides long-term support to high-potential enterprises on all aspects of the internationalisation value chain with the goal of increasing knowledge of local economic networks and developing technology partnerships with foreign enterprises.

To this end, a number of key performance indicators were established and are monitored, including:

- macroeconomic indicators: total SME exports, and share of SMEs in total exports
- number of SMEs with export contracts
- number of SMEs and entrepreneurs accompanied by Business France through collective events or individual support (outputs)
- outcomes: number of new business contracts after one year and two years (following the first business contact facilitated by Business France), number of different markets, average additional turnover.

Business France also gathers a number of external KPIs using a survey company to assess and monitor its performance according to businesses, and to understand their difficulties when exporting:

- knowledge of Business France (and other export institutions) among businesses
- issues faced by businesses when exporting
- awareness of the specific services provided by Business France (credit exports, Labelfrance, specific events)
- the relevance of these offers according to users.

The KPIs have evolved from quantitative and input/output-focused indicators to be more focused on outcomes and on the needs of users. They relate to a direct result orientation from Business France and allow it to focus on the actual use and efficiency of services.

Sources: BusinessFrance (2016), Companies and Exports; Cour des Comptes (2011)

Sector focus: Promoting exports in the agriculture and home appliance sectors

The government and Working Group members considered two sectors to be key areas of interest for export promotion efforts:

- **The home appliances sector**. This nascent sector is supported by several industrial policy instruments. While the initial strategy focused mainly on import substitution, the government is now putting more focus on exporting home appliances.

- **The agricultural sector**. Historically, Uzbekistan's exports have been dominated by cotton fibre exports. The country has now diversified its agricultural production away from cotton and exports fresh and processed fruits and vegetables. However, several barriers limit agricultural exports, including lack of infrastructure and certification.

Home appliances: A nascent sector for export

The government has put in place wide-ranging policies in order to boost the development of manufacturing in general and particularly the home appliance industry. It has established special economic zones to attract foreign and local investment, through exemptions from a series of taxes and customs payments and the simplification of bureaucratic procedures for business entities. Uzbekistan's Localisation Programme is intended to increase the production of import-substituting and export-oriented products through fiscal incentives for companies which produce in Uzbekistan (Government of Uzbekistan, 2015[62]).

These policies have the stated goal of increasing the level of exports and the internationalisation of Uzbekistan's manufacturing industry. However, localisation programmes can affect export-oriented industries by constraining the imports of needed inputs and undermine the competitiveness of industries that benefit from them. Strong industrial policy measures and local content requirements can increase production costs, distort prices and reduce access to technology, with ultimately detrimental effects on industrial competitiveness (OECD, 2016[63]; Warwick, 2013[64]). According to one recent assessment, the Localisation Programme, in particular, actually brought about an *outflow* of capital and labour from export-oriented sectors to those targeting the domestic market. Between 2008 and 2013, the volume of locally-manufactured products for the domestic market increased 3.6 times faster than the volume of locally-manufactured export-oriented products (Azamatov, 2016[65]).

Uzbekistan remains a net importer of home appliances, but the country's exports to a growing number of destinations have increased over the last two years as production capacities have grown. In 2015 Uzbekistan mainly imported finished domestic appliances from China (58% of the total), Turkey (10%) and the Russian Federation (9%), while its trade balance in this product category featured a deficit of around USD 88.9 million (UN Comtrade, 2017[66]). Nevertheless, exports are growing. Between 2011 and 2015 the monetary value of home appliance exports rose by 471%, mainly consisting of washing machines, air conditioners, refrigerators and freezers (UN Comtrade, 2017[66]). In 2015, the largest markets for Uzbekistan's home appliances were Kazakhstan and Kyrgyzstan, while in 2016, Uzbekistan started supplying the Ukrainian market under the Artel brand as well as exporting to South Caucasus countries and the Middle East, according to interviews with manufacturing companies.

When interviewed, companies and business associations in the sector cite lack of information and knowledge of target markets as a key barrier to exports. The difficulties faced by the home appliance sector exemplify the need for Uzbekistan to expand its export promotion activities, especially in marketing and consulting activities.

Marketing

Considering Uzbekistan's proximity to several large markets, the EPF and sector associations could better target and understand these markets and segments. Uzbekistan has a privileged access to the Central Asian market, and is already exporting to

Kazakhstan and Kyrgyzstan. The country needs to sustain its competitive advantage by deepening its knowledge of these markets. New markets being explored include the Middle East, and in particular the UAE. According to industry experts interviewed by the OECD, one potential niche in these markets is for reliable, very competitively priced, basic products for large, middle-income families. Uzbekistan could aim to meet this growing demand. Iran and India are two more markets that are both rapidly growing and accessible from Uzbekistan, but the specific requirements and the competition in those markets need to be carefully studied. Market studies would need to look at industry and product trends, client profiles, competitors, sales forecasts, and distribution channels. These studies could be jointly commissioned from market research companies established in target countries or prepared by a pool of industry experts within the EPF or in collaboration with local partners, including economic counsellors at the embassies, consulting companies and business networks. Clear positioning of Uzbek products sold under their own brands will also be critical, supported by a communication campaign and promotion actions, for example in airports, business fairs and the media.

Consulting

The EPF and industry associations could help to enhance the knowledge and standards of the sector. They could invite foreign experts and organisations familiar with the target markets to help them expand their knowledge of access and other conditions in those markets. The sector will also need to be able to meet market entry requirements and these capabilities could be built through technical workshops open to all interested companies. These activities could be funded by the industry association, the EPF and large companies, and be offered to SMEs at a discount rate. In order to address the lack of certification opportunities in the country, especially Eurasian Conformity (EAC) and CE certifications, Uzbekistan could identify certification companies operating in the region, especially in Kazakhstan, and establish partnerships with them. It could also fund consulting and capacity-building sessions with visiting certification experts. A similar approach could be used to attract risk insurance companies willing to support Uzbek companies in the sector. These activities need to be widely promoted to national and local business associations. Further needs could be identified by surveying both exporting and non-exporting companies, including SMEs.

In addition to specific export promotion measures, Uzbekistan could benefit from shifting from hard industrial policies towards softer ones. The government should play the role of facilitator in promoting collaboration, knowledge exchange and networking between public and private actors (Warwick, 2013[64]). Some of the "soft" measures include supporting entrepreneurship through advisory services and capacity building for SMEs; the creation of incubators; creating clusters between SMEs involved in the sector (mostly suppliers to large businesses) and large companies, foreign investors and suppliers, research centres and government agencies; maintaining a level playing field in the local market to ensure more efficiency and competitiveness; and attracting more foreign investors into the sector to encourage knowledge transfer and increase economic opportunities.

Agriculture: A strategic sector with export potential

Agriculture represents a strategic economic activity for Uzbekistan. It accounts for about 17% of Uzbekistan's GDP and around 27% of total employment (Pugach and et al, 2016[67]; UzStat, 2017[68]). The sector has historically been dominated by cotton farming but more recently the government has worked to diversify the sector into exportable food products. Raw cotton and textiles have decreased from 77% of total exports in 1995 to 19% in 2015 (OEC, 2017[69]). Exports of food products consist mainly of fresh fruits and vegetables, with processed products still playing a marginal role (Nepomnyashchaya, 2016[70]). In 2015, exports of fresh fruit and vegetables amounted to USD 492 million, 8.4% of total exports, while processed food only accounted for 0.78% of exports and a total value of USD 42.6 million (OEC, 2017[69]).

The government established Uzagroexport, a foreign trading company for fresh and processed fruits and vegetables in 2016. It provides marketing, trade and logistical services to support agricultural SMEs' exports, including market research, linking with foreign clients through trade houses and offices abroad, and logistical centres and warehouses. Uzagroexport exports on the basis of commission contracts concluded with farms, agrofirms, processing organizations, and other economic entities. The company does make a positive contribution to the growth of agrifood product exports by acting as a producer organisation and guaranteeing the quantity and quality of the exported products (Uzagroexport, 2017[71]). However, such a centralised and monopolistic organisation risks depriving SMEs of the opportunity to export and find foreign partners directly. In June 2017, in an attempt to boost production and exports by agribusiness SMEs and entrepreneurs, a presidential decree removed the monopoly of Uzagroexport on the export of fresh fruits and vegetables abroad (Ferghana, 2017[72]). This could improve the access to foreign markets as well as the competition conditions for other firms that wish to export.

However, food exports face several barriers, including complex and time-consuming procedures for customs clearance, the lack of knowledge and capacity to enter foreign markets outside Central Asia, and insufficient storage facilities and refrigerated trucks. Exporters also face limited availability of financing and an incomplete system of export insurance, which, contrary to international practices, does not provide assistance in the case of damage to goods during transport (CER, 2016[73]).

The geographical diversification of agricultural exports remains limited. Kazakhstan represents the largest market for Uzbekistan's fruit and vegetable products, accounting for 67% of total food exports, followed by the Russian Federation (17%) and Afghanistan (5%). Taken together the Eurasian Economic Union member countries account for about 86% of food exports (Olimkhonov, 2017[74]). Only 1.9% of Uzbekistan's total food exports are exported to the European Union, partly because of certification issues. However, the European Union is a trading partner with great potential, as demand for fruits and vegetables has been increasing. Between 2010 and 2014, European imports of peanuts rose by 59% in USD terms, dried fruits by 44%, watermelons and melons by 24%, and grapes by 19% (Olimkhonov, 2017[74]). All of these products are currently produced by Uzbekistan. In order to benefit fully from the opportunity offered by the EU and other export markets, Uzbekistan needs to increase its export promotion activities in agriculture to ensure that Uzbek products can access target markets, and to enhance their image and reputation beyond Central Asia.

Marketing

Uzagroexport has recently launched a single brand for export called UzAgro. This new brand aims to guarantee the high quality and origin of products for buyers (UzReport, 2017[75]). Further, new draft legislation examines the creation of a national "BestinUzbekistan" logo, which would be used to promote the export of domestic products. SMEs would be able to use the logo free of charge under the condition that their products reach a certified level of quality (Ministry of Economy of Uzbekistan, 2017[43]). These are important first steps to develop national or regional brands to better promote in particular agrifood products in Central Asia and in the EU. Uzbek products are known for their quality in neighbouring countries, and formalising and protecting the brand could help sustain and increase the economic opportunities in the sector as France did with the development of the "*Appellation d'Origine Controlée*" (AOC) system (see Box 3.8). The identification and building of brands can be carried out with the support of international experts at the national and at the regional level, and with the contribution of local producers and business associations. This step needs to be followed by other key components of a brand, including the consistent quality of final products sold under the brand, the guarantee on production methods and origins of products, and proper traceability. To maximise the impact of the brand, Uzagroexport could also consider adopting a positioning and a value proposition to be associated with the brand based on the quality or origin of products that will resonate with customers.

Box 3.8. The AOP/AOC geographical labels in France

French agricultural producers benefit from two geographical labels, the *Appellation d'Origine Contrôlée* (AOC) and the *Appellation d'Origine Protégée* (AOP), whose main goal is to protect products that are linked to a particular know-how and a specific geographic region from fraud, while at the same time preserving and promoting the products' images in national and international markets. The AOC was created in France before the Second World War for wines and eau-de-vie (spirits), but since 1990 it has been made available to all types of food products. The AOP label was established in 1992 by the European Union and is the European equivalent of AOC. Both AOC and AOP are intellectual property rights and as such they are protected by the Lisbon Agreement of the World Intellectual Property Organisation (WIPO).

The *Institut National de l'Origine et de la Qualité* (INAO) is a public institution under the French Ministry of Agriculture which is in charge of issuing the AOC and AOP labels. The INAO contributes to local economies by preserving niche markets for small producers when the value-added of their products is the result of the region's specific production methods or historical reputation.

Products under the AOC and AOP labels represent an important slice of the French food system. In 2015, the turnover generated by these products amounted to about EUR 20 billion. France currently features 50 dairy products with the AOC/AOP labels, 44 fresh or processed fruit and vegetable products, and 366 types of wine and eau de vie. The latter, in particular, significantly benefit from AOC and AOP labels in terms of export promotion and penetration of foreign markets.

Sources: INAO (n.d.) Institut National de l'Origine et de la Qualité website, www.inao.gouv.fr; AFD Working Group presentation; Agreste (2016), "AOC, label rouge et CCP peinent à l'exportation"

Considering the importance of food products in Uzbek exports, the EPF could develop the internal capacity to carry out market studies, targeting the EU, Japan, South Korea and the Middle East in the first instance. It could examine market entry conditions and develop training and consulting services accordingly in collaboration with the CCIU and sector associations. For instance, Business France regularly carries out and publishes online focused market studies that correspond to SMEs' needs for information on new markets. These include recent studies such as Regulations on Food Products in Canada, the Fruit and Vegetable Market of Italy in 2016, and the Food and Drink Products Market of the UAE in 2016 (Business France, 2017[76]).

Consulting

Uzbekistan could benefit greatly by upgrading its system for analysing of safety and quality of food products, as well as for certification. At present, the European Union, South Korea and Japan do not recognise the results of the tests performed in Uzbek laboratories and require exporters to send sample products to their national laboratories before issuing certificates and importing the products (CER, 2016[73]). Only 43 enterprises in Uzbekistan hold an ISO 22000 Food Safety Management certificate, and this further hinders exports to many countries (Olimkhonov, 2017[74]). Uzbekistan's government could establish modern laboratories and introduce new certification requirements in line with international standards in order to boost the internationalisation of the agribusiness sector. It could also develop workshops and training to help local SMEs reach the new standards and obtain certificates. These measures, along with strong producers' organisations and well-developed extension services, would contribute to building the international reputation of the quality of Uzbek products, going beyond pure branding.

Uzbekistan could implement sector-specific measures in addition to export promotion activities. In particular, it could consider establishing logistics supply centres in target markets and in Uzbekistan connected with wholesale markets and other trade hubs in EU member countries, such as Rungis and Lyon in France (State Committee on Competition, 2016[77]). Other measures to support the competitiveness of Uzbek food products, and their positioning abroad could include: further improvements in storage capacity across the country, investment in mechanisation with schemes to support farmers (including extension services and support to producers' organisation), attracting foreign food processing companies to stimulate local capacity, and the development of green and environmentally friendly technology.

The way forward

The government has recently initiated major reforms to boost export, support entrepreneurial activities and improve the overall business climate. This includes the adjustment of the legal definition of business entities, support to SME development through new incentives in the tax regime, and the simplification and reduction of licensing and export procedures and regulations in order to better comply with international standards in export markets (Ministry of Economy of Uzbekistan, 2017[43]).

Regarding export promotion policies, Table 3.2 presents an indicative roadmap for implementing these policy recommendations. This roadmap takes into account the expected time needed to establish and implement the policy actions, as well as the need to implement these activities simultaneously. Close public-private consultation will be critical to effective implementation. Key partners in implementing the reform consist not only of Uzbekistan's organisations in charge of export promotion, such as the EPF or the CCIU, but also international partners such as AFD, GIZ or USAID.

Table 3.2. Suggested implementation roadmap for Uzbekistan

Recommendations	Indicative implementation timing		
	Short term < 1 year	Medium term 1-3 years	Long term > 3 years
Develop consulting activities to improve SMEs knowledge of foreign markets			
Action 1: Develop market studies and hire industry experts to further improve knowledge of markets			
Action 2: Expand advisory and training capacities and support preferential access for SMEs			
Action 3: Attract more certification companies to the country			
Expand the network of export promotion abroad and provide a clear value proposition in target markets			
Action 4: Expand the number of representation offices abroad with local staff			
Action 5: Work on clear value proposition in co-operation with the business community			
Monitor work and impact of export institutions			
Action 6: Develop and implement a set of actionable KPIs			

Source: OECD Analysis, 2017.

Kyrgyzstan: Revamping the investment promotion system

Business internationalisation in Kyrgyzstan could be further enhanced by establishing sound investment promotion institutions and activities. The OECD designed policy recommendations in 2013 and monitored their implementation in 2016. This sub-chapter analyses the progress made, and suggests solutions to further improve the investment and export promotion systems. Recommendations include finalising the investment promotion strategy, deepening sector expertise in the investment promotion agency, and developing export promotion activities.

Context: A small open economy

Kyrgyzstan is a relatively open economy: foreign trade represented 125% of the country's gross domestic product (GDP) in 2014 (World Bank, 2016[78]). Its early membership of the World Trade Organization (WTO) and its comparatively liberal trade regime have supported the emergence of an intermediary trade sector that provides employment for low-skilled workers, many of them women. For example, WTO membership has promoted the emergence of a competitive garment export sector in Kyrgyzstan in which women are strongly represented (UNDP, 2015[79]).

Kyrgyzstan's accession to the Eurasian Economic Union (EEU) in August 2015 shifts the context for business internationalisation. While EEU membership will give the country unfettered access to a large market, it might nevertheless have an adverse impact on investment in Kyrgyzstan. In particular, the higher tariffs at EEU external borders, such as between Kyrgyzstan and China, might undermine Kyrgyzstan's foreign trade, in view of the important role of non-EEU inputs (especially in the garment sector) and re-export activities from China, Turkey and other countries in Kyrgyzstan's foreign trade.

Overview of 2013 recommendations

The 2013 review found that Kyrgyzstan's investment promotion policies and institutions were limited in both in scope and quality (OECD, 2014[80]). The country lacked basic investment promotion activities, an active investment promotion agency (IPA) and a dedicated strategy to attract foreign direct investment. The review urged the government, with the support of the OECD and the German Society for International Co-operation (GIZ), to work on policies and tools to strengthen the internationalisation of SMEs. A public-private working group and a policy assessment of investment and export promotion tools identified priority areas for action. Two sets of recommendations were provided to the government:

Recommendation 1: Strengthen investment policies and activities

This recommendation involved starting sector-specific investment promotion activities, establishing business linkage programmes, and creating a new IPA. The first step was for the government to take a systematic approach to assessing sectors, and to designing and implementing investment promotion activities in these sectors. This would involve: (1) identifying priority sectors for the country; (2) analysing global trends; (3) assessing Kyrgyzstan's strengths and weaknesses; (4) finding and addressing target investors; and (5) preparing investment promotion activities. It was recommended that this approach be included in a national investment strategy for the priority sectors selected. Business linkage programmes could then increase business opportunities and positive spill-overs by encouraging contracts between local suppliers and investors. Kyrgyzstan was also urged to create an IPA that adopted best practices from OECD countries, especially Ireland and Turkey. The role of the IPA would be to sustain investment promotion activities, create a point of contact for investors, and facilitate their relations with ministries (OECD, 2014[80]).

Recommendation 2: Use garment and textile manufacturing as a pilot sector for investment promotion

In 2013, garment and textile manufacturing were estimated to represent 5-15% of GDP and 4-12% of employment. The sector consisted primarily of SMEs, mainly owned by women. Garment production increased ten-fold between 2003 and 2013, driven largely by the rise in exports, especially to Russia and Kazakhstan (Choi et al., 2014[81]). This export-driven growth was favoured by Kyrgyzstan's accession to the WTO in 1998, the implementation of an open trade regime, and simplified customs clearance procedures (Choi et al., 2014[81]).

Companies in the garment industry were facing competition challenges driven by the lack of a sector strategy, weak promotion, limited technical capacities, and outdated technology. Overall, the OECD recommended that the sector could be better supported by: 1) investment promotion activities; 2) a coherent sector strategy; 3) investments in mid-level technical skills and modernisation of the vocational education and training (VET) system, for example through the Shvei Profi technical training centre; and 4) the establishment of a garment cluster based around the Technopolis industrial park project (OECD, 2014[80]).

Findings of the 2016 monitoring assessment

The trade environment for Kyrgyzstan's garment sector has changed substantially since 2013. Until 2011 the sector benefited from low tariffs on inputs thanks to Kyrgyzstan's WTO membership. It also benefitted from special trade agreements and tariff-free garment exports to Russia, whereas Russia levied tariffs on garment imports from other countries. The situation changed with Russia's WTO membership in 2012, with significant consequences for the Kyrgyz garment industry. Russia's WTO membership implied the gradual lowering of import tariffs up until 2020. These measures have started to progressively decrease Kyrgyzstan's trade advantage with Russia. In particular, Russia's overall tariffs on textiles and garments were phased out in 2015, the year Kyrgyzstan joined the EEU.

Kyrgyzstan's accession to the EEU has also had an impact on the sector – both positive and negative. On the one hand, the EEU provides Kyrgyzstan with free access to a market of more than 170 million people. On the other hand, the implementation of a common external value-based tariff negatively affects the garment industry, which relies on fabrics imported from countries outside the EEU. Kyrgyzstan's previous simplified tariff regime was replaced by an average EEU *ad valorem* tariff of 8.1% in 2015, which will be lowered to 6.9% in 2020 (Choi et al., 2014[81]). Choi, Perez, Luis and Myburg (2014) estimate that membership of the EEU will increase the cost of imports and thus overall garment production costs by 3.6% to 7.7% (Choi et al., 2014[81]). This uncertain trade environment has delayed domestic and foreign investment in the sector.

Monitoring of Recommendation 1 highlights the creation of an investment promotion agency and a draft strategy

Recommendation 1: Strengthen investment and export-promotion policies and activities

Kyrgyzstan established an IPA in March 2014 under the aegis of the Ministry of Economy. The agency consists of four departments: investment project promotion, investor support, information analysis and development of public-private partnerships. Discussions are currently under way to upgrade the status of the IPA to an autonomous body under the government.

The mission of the IPA is to "Improve the investment climate of Kyrgyzstan and to build confidence through long-term, fruitful partnerships with international investors" (Investment and Export Promotion Agency Kyrygzstan, 2017[82]). To this end, it participates in the development and implementation of measures to stimulate investment activity and to increase the investment attractiveness of the country. It supports interaction among state bodies, local authorities, the business community and the private sector to promote investment through public-private partnerships and private investment. In addition, the IPA participates in developing national infrastructure projects and investment programmes.

The IPA targets specific expertise in the tourism, garment and agro-processing sectors, although the final list of priority sectors is still to be defined in the forthcoming National Investment Promotion Strategy (see below). In terms of geography, the IPA focuses its work on investors from Turkey, China, Korea, Kazakhstan, Russia, the Middle East and India. The National Sustainable Development Strategy for 2013-17 had already identified investment policy as a priority, including the establishment of the IPA. However, it did not include a focus on sectors.

Kyrgyzstan is also developing a National Investment Promotion Strategy in order to develop a targeted, strategic and multi-stakeholder approach to foreign direct investment. Several workshops were held in 2016 to draft the new investment strategy. They involved the private sector, the various ministries and government agencies relevant to foreign direct investment, the IPA and donors. Several international experts participated in the workshops, including two from Ireland and one from Turkey. The workshops focused on methodological aspects and good practices in investment promotion, including the selection of sectors, the identification of competitive advantages, and the creation of a business case for investing in Kyrgyzstan. Following the workshops, three core sectors were initially selected: garments, tourism and agro-processing. The list of sectors is expected to increase to reflect priorities defined by the government.

In 2015 the IPA had a staff of 21 experts selected through open competition. Staff speak English, as well as other relevant languages (Russian, Turkish, Japanese, German, French, etc.). Staff participate in training and study tours in Kyrgyzstan and abroad, for example in Germany. They also organise and attend investment forums abroad and in Kyrgyzstan.

Investment promotion tools have been created by the IPA, especially websites that target potential investors (www.invest.gov.kg, www.ppp.gov.kg). They provide easily accessible and up-to-date information on investment opportunities for external investors.

Similarly, the IPA has published brochures on Kyrgyzstan's business environment, and its Facebook page is regularly updated.

However, many aspects of the IPA's work are still in their infancy. For example, there is no department concerned with the monitoring and evaluation of the IPA's activities. Similarly, although an investors' support division exists, aftercare and post-investment services are not provided in a systematic manner as staff and expertise are limited at this stage of the IPA's development.

Monitoring of Recommendation 2 shows positive impacts on investment in the garment sector

Recommendation 2: Use garment and textile manufacturing as a pilot sector for investment promotion

Horizontal investment and export promotion efforts have already benefited the garment sector. One example of a recent investment facilitated by the IPA consists of a Turkish company constructing a textile factory. This investment marks an important step towards locating a greater share of the textile and garment supply chain in Kyrgyzstan.

An export promotion strategy has been drafted and approved, highlighting the role of exports for the garment sector and its SMEs. The strategy mentions a number of activities, including participation in trade fairs, and the provision of market information, trade facilitation and financial support schemes. In addition, support has already been given to firm-level strategies. With USAID support, the Kyrgyzstan Centre for Textile and Apparel Research is helping companies with activities such as marketing, compliance, human resources, sourcing, and line productivity.

Progress on developing the skills needed for the garment sector's workforce has stalled, however. There is no systematic co-operation between educational institutions and enterprises. The quality and quantity of VET for garment workers have not improved – for example, the Shvei Profi technical training centre is still not working as its teaching licence remains suspended.

The industry-wide organisation of clusters and co-operatives is still as limited as in 2013. For example, work on the Technopolis project, which was intended to host a garment cluster, has stalled. Despite efforts to allocate land for building the Technopolis and to develop a business plan, and numerous study trips to Baku, Ljubljana and Urumqi, the project has yet to materialise, and funding is still not secured.

The way forward

Kyrgyzstan has made significant progress in improving its investment and export promotion climate. However, further success demands greater effort to sustain the progress made.

Kyrgyzstan has identified three priority sectors in its draft investment promotion strategy (agroprocessing, garments, and tourism) based on the government's strategic objectives, as well as their contribution to employment and value added. The government should continue to assess the garment sector in light of EEU accession to identify whether and how its business environment has evolved. It would be important to continue attracting investments to the textile sector to ensure the competitive supply of inputs. This could also be achieved by facilitating collective buying agreements by SMEs in the garment sector or clusters within it. If the future outlook for the garment sector is likely to be negative, the country could consider other industries that require similar skill sets, such as light electronics assembly.

Policy practitioners and experts should be continuously involved in drafting and further developing the strategy. The final investment promotion strategy should incorporate their inputs. Launching and presenting the strategy at a high-level event would serve to increase its reach and signal to potential investors the importance given to foreign direct investment (FDI) by the government.

The strategy should include a concrete action plan with a corresponding timetable and the means to monitor performance. The plan should set specific targets, such as the amount of new FDI investments, SME investments, the regional spread, and the amount of new exports. It should also set agreed outcomes, such as net employment creation, corporate tax revenues earned, and the economic value added.

Building sector-specific expertise and investment promotion capacity within the IPA is a key task. Greater sector-specific expertise would allow for targeted promotional activities. Good practice indicates that sector-specific expertise is a key success factor for IPAs around the world. The example of Turkey is an interesting case in point (Box 3.9). Building this capacity should involve hands-on training from policy practitioners with experience working in other IPAs, as well as study tours and training. Stronger co-operation with Turkey's Investment Support and Promotion Agency (ISPAT) would provide valuable contact with experienced policy practitioners in the field of investment promotion.

Developing the skills and expertise required for aftercare services and supply chain development, such as FDI-SME linkage programmes, is a priority. While investment promotion activities are a key component for attracting investments and ensuring competitiveness, the government should not lose focus on improving the overall investment climate in Kyrgyzstan.

The IPA should also work on supporting companies in the target sectors through tailored export promotion activities, such as export-oriented marketing and consulting. Export costs are often very high for SMEs. Providing good market knowledge of recent trends in target markets, demand shifts and standards can be of great value to ensure the competitiveness of companies in the priority sectors.

Box 3.9. Turkey's Investment Support and Promotion Agency

The Investment Support and Promotion Agency of Turkey (ISPAT) was created in 2007 to boost Turkey's attractiveness among foreign investors. ISPAT operates as an intermediary and facilitator between investors and authorities and strives to decrease the cost, time and number of procedures for investors. It does so by providing sector reports and analysis, offering support for site selection and real estate prospecting, facilitating meetings with local authorities, and providing aftercare services.

Turkey's increasing level of FDI inflows, as well as positive results in international assessments, are testament to the agency's success. The World Bank's Global Investment Promotion Best Practices Survey ranked ISPAT's website as the seventh best investment promotion website in the world.

ISPAT assesses Turkey's investment needs in target sectors, and develops and implements sector-specific promotion strategies to attract investments. First, the assessment of Turkey's investment needs is based on criteria that mirror the country's economic priorities, such as the level of import substitution, technology intensity, employment and export potential. Second, ISPAT assesses how these needs can be targeted by investors through the presence of industry clusters, regional potential, access to raw materials, low cost of entry in the market and a favourable competitive environment. Third, ISPAT prepares sector-specific action plans to promote and generate investments for sectors that are both of interest to investors and in line with Turkey's priorities.

Source: (ISPAT, 2016[11])

Tajikistan: Supporting agricultural exports

Increasing exports in Tajikistan's agricultural sector represents an important factor for the growth of the country's economy. The OECD provided policy recommendations in 2014, which were monitored in 2017. This sub-chapter analyses the achievements and suggests further improvements, such as supporting product certification and implementing the single-window at customs.

Context: Agricultural trade and Tajikistan's growth

Trade in agriculture is crucial for the development of Tajikistan's economy, considering its importance for the country's gross domestic product (GDP) and exports. Fruit and vegetable products made up 6.8% of total exports in 2015, to a value of USD 57.2 million of which 33% came from exports of dried fruits (apricots and nuts), 28% from onions and 7.9% from rice. The value of these exports has fallen from USD 60.7 million in 2014 and USD 66.5 million in 2013. The chief market for these products is Kazakhstan, which imported USD 38.4 million worth of fruit and vegetable products, or 67% of the total.

Growth in exports of these products could support the development of small and medium-sized enterprises (SMEs), which are the main players in these markets. In 2015 there were 39 401 registered companies in Tajikistan in total, of which 1.3% had more than 200 employees (including publicly owned companies). Of the 8 981 formal companies in agriculture, 85% have fewer than 30 employees and 99% fewer than 200 (OEC, 2017[83]; TajStat, 2017[84]).[5]

Export promotion efforts face some important structural challenges. First, Tajikistan's location and topography mean that developing the country's connective infrastructure will be a particular priority if it wishes to expand exports and diversify its export markets. Some 93% of the country is mountainous, the nearest seaport is 3 100 km from the border and the infrastructure on the overland trade routes with neighbouring countries (Afghanistan, China, Kyrgyzstan and Uzbekistan) are inadequate, despite recent developments with China.

Second, institutional export support structures require further improvement. Tajikistan has improved its trade regime, becoming a member of the World Trade Organization (WTO) in 2013 and is currently considering the possibility of joining the Eurasian Economic Union. Yet Tajikistan ranks 144th on the Trading Across Borders category of the World Bank's *Doing Business 2016* report (World Bank, 2016[85]). The "distance penalty" that Tajik exporters face in view of their location is thus compounded by difficult customs procedures and customs regulation, as well as the frequent lack of a recognised certification of compliance for exported products (OECD, 2015[86]).

Overview of 2014 recommendations

The 2014 OECD review focused on boosting agricultural trade, suggesting policy choices that could enhance both the institutional export support structure (e.g. customs, certification and export promotion) and the agriculture sector (e.g. strategy, vertical and horizontal integration and the availability of statistics) (OECD, 2015[86]).

Recommendation 1: Overhaul the export strategy and improve export support institutions

In 2014, the government was advised by the OECD to revise its border procedures to lower the administrative costs for enterprises willing to embark in international trade, which should be particularly beneficial for SMEs. In particular, the review recommended:

- Simplifying border procedures by introducing and adopting a risk-management approach to customs clearance, carrying forward work on establishing a "single window"[6] for export-import and transit operations, and introducing a "trusted trader system" to simplify procedures for importing and exporting companies with a proven track record of impeccable behaviour;
- Increasing the effectiveness of overall export promotion activities by defining responsibilities for national branding, leveraging Tajik diaspora networks in export markets and guiding SMEs through the necessary administrative procedures for trade and
- Investing in modern quality-control and certification policies, including incentives to businesses to meet international standards (OECD, 2015[86]).

Recommendation 2: Improve taxation and financial system for agribusiness exporters

In various surveys, businesses in Tajikistan highlighted problems with the complexity of taxation and the unpredictability of its enforcement by tax inspectors ((World Bank, 2017[87]; EBRD, 2017[88]; IFC, 2011[89]). The OECD recommended the introduction of a simpler model with a uniform tax for SMEs in agriculture, aimed at:

- reducing the number of hours spent filling tax requirements
- reducing the number of agencies to be visited to comply
- guaranteeing transparency throughout the process (OECD, 2015[86]).

The 2014 review also recommended further support for financing agribusiness exports. This could be done by setting up an export finance institution that could provide export guarantees and subsidised loans for companies seeking to export. Setting up public agencies offering technical, financial and administrative support to exporting businesses has proven valuable in other countries in the region, including Kazakhstan (OECD, 2015[86]).

Recommendation 3: Strengthen the agribusiness value chain

To strengthen the supply chain, the OECD review suggested that Tajikistan should:

- Increase horizontal integration of producers by improving the legal framework and promoting service co-operatives.
- Enhance vertical co-operation through the establishment of agricultural clusters, bringing together producers, processors and exporters. A pilot cluster with the participation of banks, government agencies and academic institutions should be considered, for example in Sughd province, which is the region closest to the Silk Road and one of the most productive regions.
- The government should also invest more in the development of agricultural skills, by focusing on offering better extension services and training opportunities (OECD, 2015[86]).

Recommendation 4: Institutions should better implement and monitor agribusiness policies

The OECD suggested that the government should enhance its ability to devise, implement and monitor agribusiness policies. This means:

- Improving co-ordination between the Ministry of Agriculture and the agencies operating in the sector (the National Statistical Institute and the Chamber of Commerce), and involving local businesses and agricultural business associations in the implementation of the strategy for agriculture.
- Defining clear goals and measurable outputs from the start of the strategic planning phase. The key performance indicators (KPIs) should be SMART: specific, measurable, achievable, realistic and time-bound, and they should be objectively monitored throughout the implementation phase (OECD, 2015[86]).

Findings of the 2017 monitoring assessment

Tajikistan has partially implemented the recommendations, but a number of steps remain if they are to be implemented fully and effectively.

Monitoring of Recommendation 1 indicates that effective implementation needs to follow the updating of strategic documents

> *Recommendation 1: Overhaul the export strategy and improve export-support institutions*

New regulations and government strategies have included the key building blocks of a well-functioning export support system, but effective implementation will be critical

The Ministry of Economic Development and Trade (MEDT) has performed a thorough analysis of the main barriers to trade and elaborated a comprehensive strategy to overcome them. In particular, the Action Plan on Improving Investment Climate in the Agricultural Sector and Agricultural Trade Development (APIICA) and the Mid-Term Development Strategy of the Republic of Tajikistan for 2016-2020 explicitly include policy recommendations formulated by the OECD in 2014 (Box 3.10).

Since 2008, Article 399 of the Customs Code has provided for a risk-management approach to customs clearance (Tajikistan, 2008[90]). However, representatives of international organisations working with the customs authority report that the approach has not yet been implemented, a view which is confirmed by the OECD's trade facilitation indicators (TFIs). The TFIs highlight the need to complete the development of risk-management procedures currently under elaboration to enhance automated formalities at the border (OECD, 2017[8]).

No substantial progress has been made towards the creation of a national brand during the monitoring period. A laudable exception was the regional brand for Sughd Oblast, created with the support of the United Nations Development Programme (UNDP) and now widely used to guarantee product quality. The UNDP is now working with Kathlon region to launch its regional brand.

Box 3.10. OECD recommendations in the government's mid-term strategy

The government of Tajikistan elaborated an overarching strategy to guide policy making in the 2016-20 period. The main recommendations it included were:

- "Adopt the necessary changes in the customs code on eliminating the barriers for international trade development by SMEs", arranging the operations in accordance with international standards, and "Improve customs regulation to support the local producers within the WTO norms", in line with the recommendation of simplifying trade procedures including customs.
- "Improved regulatory framework for export development and selected import substitution", in line with the recommendations for the improvement of export promotion institutions and activities.
- Develop and implement the concept of 'reliable market player' to simplify the procedures within the export activities". This corresponds to the concept of a "trusted trader" in the OECD's policy recommendation. [7]

Sources: (OECD, 2015[86]; Government of Tajikistan, 2016[91])

At the moment the diaspora networks are underused, with a few initiatives from the Ministry of Migration and Labour, more aimed at attracting foreign direct investment (FDI) than creating a network to support Tajik exporters in foreign markets.

A single window for customs has been partly implemented and should soon start operations

A customs single window is at an advanced stage of implementation thanks to the support of the EU and the Asian Development Bank (ADB; Box 3.11). The single window for export, import and transit procedures in Tajikistan was approved and established by two successive government resolutions in 2008 and 2010.[8]

Box 3.11. The single window for customs in Tajikistan

The implementation phase started with an EU-funded project in 2012-14 and led to:

- The definition of the detailed specification and requirements of the information system for the single window and the development of the portal to manage applications for the issuance of permits in electronic form by nine "single window centres".
- The completion of tendering for the hardware needed and its delivery to the 52 active offices and 12 servers, and the establishment of a virtual private communications network for the transmission of electronic data.
- A series of training courses in the use of the platform were conducted in all 52 offices.

However, the single window has never been fully implemented due to technical issues with the information technology system that should manage its activity. It remains a priority for the government and is included in the Mid-Term Strategy 2016-2020. Implementation continues with the support of the ADB.

No institutional public structure to support exports has been created, with most of the activities to support businesses carried out by the Chamber of Commerce.

Progress has been made in accreditation but further efforts are needed on product certification

The MEDT has taken several steps to improve product certification in collaboration with Tajikstandart, the government agency in charge of defining and implementing standards, to improve the quality of laboratories and enhance the certification system. Food and agricultural products tested by the agency are accredited by the national system of accreditation of Kazakhstan. Three laboratories and 23 methods of chemical analysis have been accredited since August 2012, with an accreditation period of 5 years up to August 2017 (USAID and GAIN, 2015[92]). In July 2015 the laboratories were audited again by the Kazakhstan National Center for Accreditation and passed the test, thus easing cross-border trade in these products. Specialists from the agency train companies to implement and maintain procedures based on the Hazard Analysis and Critical Control Point (HACCP) procedures.

Since 2014 Tajikstandart and the MEDT have also been developing new methods in accordance with international standards. For example on new accreditation of potential testing laboratories and on planning for the supply of new equipment. The quality of the laboratories should be improved to offer a wider variety of services to assess product quality and to make it easier to export products.

The government has also established a National Centre for Accreditation, to resolve the conflict of interest arising from Tajikstandart managing both certification and accreditation. Since 2007 the International Trade Centre (ITC) has recommended separating the two functions, as keeping accreditation and conformity assessment services in the same organisation is considered unacceptable at international level, as the risk of collusion is too high.[9] This has led to a lack of recognition of Tajik certification by foreign bodies, and in turn increased difficulties for Tajik exporters as exports need to be retested and recertified (ITC, 2007[93]). The Swiss State Secretariat for Economic Affairs (SECO) and the ITC have continued their support and in 2015, by Order No. 626 of the Government of Tajikistan, the independent National Accreditation Centre was established. It should become a member of the mutual recognition arrangements of the International Laboratory Accreditation Cooperation (ILAC) and the International Accreditation Forum (IAF) to gain international recognition of its test reports and certificates. However business associations note[10] that it is not yet fully functioning.

Monitoring of Recommendation 2 shows that tax administration remains an issue, despite efforts to improve tax legislation

Recommendation 2: Improve taxation and financial system for agribusiness exporters

Legislation to simplify tax collection is in place but tax administration is still considered a major barrier by local and foreign businesses

The government has simplified tax compliance for SMEs in agribusiness in recent years but fiscal pressure is still high. A new tax code came into force in January 2013, introducing a special system of payment for agricultural producers which requires taxpayers to pay only one type of tax (uniform tax). The same reform also simplified tax reports. In August 2016 the government presented a draft law[11] that aims to further simplify the tax system and attract foreign investment.

Tajikistan has created a system for the electronic submission of tax returns to simplify tax administration. It introduced this e-filing in 2012 with the support of the World Bank, but by 2014 only 6 000 firms out of a potential 80 500 were using the service. During the monitoring period the number increased steadily, with more than 20 500 taxpayers submitting their declarations electronically in 2016.

Tajikistan has also expanded its electronic system for filing and paying taxes, as recorded in the Paying Taxes category of the World Bank's *Doing Business* rankings. These efforts have led to Tajikistan significantly improving its ranking during the monitoring period, climbing from 178th in 2014 to 140th in 2017. The number of tax payments per year has fallen from 69 to 12, even if the total hours needed to pay taxes remained broadly unchanged. For those without an internet connection, the offices of the tax inspectorates provide accessible terminals for the provision of electronic tax returns. However, business associations report that digitisation is only partial, as the forms have to be downloaded, signed and then sent by post to the tax administration.

Despite these legal and technical improvements, the government still needs to take action in this area, as many private enterprises and international organisations still consider the tax system to be opaque and unpredictable. The "revenue based" tax system gives tax agents incentives to reach revenue targets that may be misaligned with the business reality of companies. At the moment the government, with the support of the World Bank, is devising a reform to the Tax Department to make it more efficient and effective at collecting revenue, enhance the level of voluntary compliance, and improve the quality of taxpayer services. This reform will be concluded by the end of 2019 (World Bank, 2017[94]).

The Ministry of Agriculture, as well as agricultural firms interviewed by the OECD, also report important issues linked to the implementation of the uniform tax. It appears that farmers have to pay additional taxes on top of the uniform tax in several economic sectors, which undermines the purpose of a single unified tax. For instance, first transformation steps of agricultural raw materials such as cotton are subject to additional taxation. Agricultural firms also mention that the tax administration has stopped refunding value-added tax (VAT) on domestic products. VAT refunds for SMEs are a common tax practice in OECD member and non-member countries to ensure that VAT remains neutral for business taxpayers. OECD economies in particular have implemented many different VAT simplification measures, including exemption thresholds and simplified schemes for calculating VAT liability (OECD, 2015[95]). Tajikistan's tax code is also frequently reported to be complex and burdensome, especially for SMEs.

The government strategy includes an export guarantee fund, but it has yet to be implemented

Tajikistan does not yet have a national system to support exports although the government is discussing the possibility of setting up an export guarantee fund that could benefit firms in the agriculture sector. The MEDT and the Ministry of Finance mentioned that the creation of a bank for export promotion is included in the Mid-Term Strategy for 2016-20.[12] This activity has not been funded by the state budget, and no precise implementation timeline has been defined. An inter-ministerial working group is considering the options, but no decision has been made.

OECD member countries have well-integrated export promotion systems, which also offer subsidised finance, to support the international competitiveness of their businesses. These systems share several key features: an active network of public and private players in home and target countries, the close involvement of private sector actors in the system, the creation of a specific agency to support exports, tailor-made services for businesses and SMEs, and funding and risk insurance mechanisms dedicated to exports (Lederman, Olarreaga and Payton, 2006[10]; IGC, 2011[96]). France provides a good example of a structured export system that was reorganised to improve its co-ordination and efficiency (Box 3.12).

Monitoring of Recommendation 3 shows that efforts have been mostly focused on enhancing skills

Recommendation 3: Strengthen the agribusiness value chain

The Ministry of Agriculture, with the help of international organisations (IOs), has supported the strengthening of agribusiness value chains with the Programme for Reforming the Agriculture Sector of the Republic of Tajikistan for 2012-2020.

The Agrarian University of Tajikistan and the development community are focusing on programmes to develop skills in the agribusiness sector

The Agrarian University of Tajikistan, under the Ministry of Education, offers courses and material to contribute to the development of a skilled workforce. IOs have also carried out many important programmes since 2014, focusing on making the agribusiness sector competitive and boosting skills, with the objectives of improving food security, private-sector development and enhanced trade (Box 3.13).

Box 3.12. Good practice in trade promotion: The example of Business France

Business France is a national agency focused on the international development of the French economy. It demonstrates how a country can successfully engage in trade promotion. Business France supports French companies in their international development by operating in multiple trade-related areas as well as co-ordinating with a plethora of institutional partners. The agency is also in charge of attracting foreign direct investment (FDI) to France and promoting France's attractiveness to foreign businesses. Its engagement has thus helped to display the open and diversified nature of the French economy. This is an outcome Tajikistan is still aspiring to.

In particular, Business France has managed to set up a functioning ecosystem based on agreements with shareholders and stakeholders spread all across France. Co-operation works in multiple ways: agreements are established to ease the international development and growth of the French economy. Its stakeholders are:

- The French state: a Performance and Objectives Contract determines the export strategy and the exact resources allocated over a three-year period.
- The French regions: Business France has to deliver optimal trade promotion services to companies spread across France's territory.
- BPIfrance, France's development bank: allowing the provision of joint services to SMEs, particularly with regards to export financing and export promotion services. This facilitates business opportunities for SMEs and mid-size companies abroad.
- The Chamber of Commerce and Industry (CCI): the CCI identifies and trains SMEs, while Business France delivers the trade promotion services. A similar division of labour has been set up with the trade consulting companies which offer downstream business development services.
- MEDEF, the employer's union of France: co-ordinates with the representatives of French businesses.

For example, Business France supplies four types of services to the agribusiness sector: 1) business intelligence (e.g. tailored market studies); 2) trade fairs (e.g. design and management of French pavilions); 3) Business-to-business (e.g. product presentations and events); and 4) tailor-made individual services (e.g. communication services or product market tests).

Business France thus offers services on both the macro and micro level: it co-ordinates on the macro level to support the strategic development of France's international trade, and at the same time it supports businesses on the micro level, creating business and investment opportunities for SMEs and mid-size companies abroad.

Sources: (Business France, 2017[97]; Business France, 2017[98])

Box 3.13. Skill enhancement in the agribusiness sector

The Enhanced Competitiveness of Tajikistan Agribusiness Programme funded by the EU is aimed at the development of Tajik agrifood value chains, the competitiveness of agri-food enterprises and the quality and marketing of their products (European Commission, 2017b). Other projects are playing an important role in sustaining the development of the agribusiness sector, skills and trade, including the German Society for International Co-operation's (GIZ) Support to Regional Trade in Central Asia programme, the United Kingdom's Department for International Development's (DFID) Growth in Rural Economy and Agriculture in Tajikistan programme, the UNDP's Formulation of Trade Development Programmes at National and Oblasts Levels, and SECO's Trade Co-operation Programme.

Horizontal integration has been given some support through co-operatives and extension services

The organisation and development of extension advisory support for farmers is one of the stated priorities of the government's Programme for Reforming the Agriculture Sector of the Republic of Tajikistan for 2012-2020. The Ministry of Agriculture has departments in all districts and regions which work in close collaboration with farmers and include agricultural specialists to advise small-scale farmers. In 2013 the Ministry of Agriculture started participating in a Japanese International Cooperation Agency (JICA) project to train five officials in Japan every year in the most up-to-date techniques which they can then disseminate in Tajikistan.

The non-commercial co-operative Sarob became almost completely financially sustainable in 2015 and has 74 advisory service offices in Khatlon Region. The co-operative plays a major role in the horizontal integration of the sector and was established in 2012 through the technical assistance groups (TAGs) project funded by the EU, DFID and GIZ. Other TAGs are active in the country, working on a "fee for service" basis and providing an effective service to farmers to achieve measurable yield increases, based on regular crop monitoring, crop management advice and effective use of inputs such as fertilisers, water and pesticides (WOCAT, 2017[99]).

Many non-governmental organisations (NGOs) also offer advisory services in Tajikistan, supported by international organisations. For instance, in Soghd Region alone there are 117 advisory service offices; 50 of which were organised with the support of NGOs and the remaining 67 by rural organisations, which collaborate with 65 079 individual farmers (*dekhan* farms).[13]

Monitoring of Recommendation 4 suggests that proper statistics and key performance indicators are still lacking

Recommendation 4: Institutions should better implement and monitor agribusiness policies

The mid-term government strategy includes agricultural policy actions recommended by the OECD

The government has included the OECD's recommendation to increase the focus on reliable data for policy making in the agri-business sector in both the Action Plan on Improving Investment Climate in the Agricultural Sector and Agricultural Trade Development (APIICA) and the Mid-term Development Strategy of the Republic of Tajikistan for 2016-2020. This reflects the government's recognition of the need to increase the effectiveness of its policies.

Business surveys should be institutionalised and focus more on understanding the crucial issues for agribusinesses

The Ministry of Agriculture gathers micro-level data in all regions of Tajikistan through its regional offices, but with a focus on production. These data are subsequently transmitted to the National Statistical Institute for re-elaboration and then published on a quarterly and annual basis. The Chamber of Commerce carries out business surveys[14] with its members and shares the results with the government, but this exercise is not focused enough on agribusiness issues to inform policy decisions.

The experience of OECD countries shows that surveys focusing on relations with supply chains, and barriers to doing business such as skills, access to finance, infrastructure, regulations, environment, and awareness of government's programmes can contribute to effective policy making. The ministry should develop the internal capacity to monitor and analyse the results in order to draw policy conclusions. For example, in Canada, the Ministry of Agriculture surveys farmers through its local agencies and with the support of private contractors. These surveys enable the ministry to gain insights on the use of its services, measure satisfaction, gather feedback and suggestions, and better understand the use of technology by farmers. The ministry can then assess and adjust its advisory, insurance, training, funding and many other programmes accordingly (Government of Canada, 2012[100]).

The Ministry of Agriculture is building internal capacity, but still needs to implement a thorough monitoring system

From 2013 to 2016, over 360 specialists from the Ministry of Agriculture were enrolled in special training on a range of technical issues (Box 3.14).

Box 3.14. Training the staff of the Ministry of Agriculture of Tajikistan

With the support of several development partners and IOs such as JICA, the Turkish International Cooperation Agency, the Thailand International Cooperation Agency and the Food and Agriculture Organization of the United Nations (FAO), specialists of the Ministry of Agriculture took part in study trips to receive short training courses in several topics, including strengthening the indicators of emergency situations for animal diseases, quality control of individual products in agro-industry, establishing information and consulting centres, novel methods of agricultural development, and strengthening farming organisations in Central Asian countries.

Source: (Ministry of Industry, 2016[101])

The Ministry of Agriculture frequently creates monitoring documents and reports. However, it has yet to identify and monitor detailed KPIs focusing on outcomes, create a thorough monitoring system, and understand how monitoring can feed into policy making.

Proper policy design and implementation are crucial. The OECD has learned that, to be effective, agricultural policies should follow a cycle that starts with the formulation of policy objectives and continues with the evaluation of the performance of current policies, the design of the new policies and finally a process to monitor and evaluate the achievements of these policies. In principle, the design of the information systems should go hand-in-hand with the design of the policies so that adequate information is generated from the beginning. Moreover, in-depth studies of this kind allow for consultation with the potential winners and losers from a reform, so that appropriate responses and corrections can be devised (Van Tongeren, 2008[102]). These principles are also reiterated in the latest OECD publication on the specific policies undertaken by OECD member countries and developing economies during the last year (OECD, 2016[103]).

The way forward

One overarching priority is to improve government statistics regarding SMEs. The data currently available through the National Statistical Institute of Tajikistan are limited to general information such as total numbers and numbers of *dekhan* farms. They do not allow policy makers to craft tailored policies taking into account precise numbers, sectors of activity, share of revenues from export, financial situation, productivity and regional peculiarities. The annual Structural Business Statistics (SBS) of the European Union, managed by Eurostat, constitute a best practice example that Tajikistan could consider following (Eurostat, 2017[104]).

On the export side, Tajikistan needs to implement its new strategies and regulations on exports and improve co-ordination between institutions supporting exporters. Export promotion activities are reported to be carried out by the Ministry of Economy. The mandate to conduct these activities could be extended to Tajinvest, which is already in charge of investment promotion, and resources need to be assigned to perform these activities. The experience of OECD member countries and of other Central Asian countries, including Kyrgyzstan (see Box 3.15, shows that having a single agency in charge of export and investment promotion can help find synergies (office sharing, marketing, support functions) and implement joint actions, although the two missions are different.

Box 3.15. Export promotion in Kyrgyzstan

Kyrgyzstan created the Agency of Investment Promotion in 2014 under the Ministry of Economy, and has extended its mandate to include export promotion activities since November 2016. Both activities of the new State Agency for Investment and Export promotion (SAIEP) correspond to different missions and national strategies.

The IPA's mission is to improve the investment climate of Kyrgyzstan and to build confidence through long-term fruitful partnerships with international investors. The agency is drafting a new investment promotion strategy that focuses on priority sectors.

The new export promotion function aims to increase export flows and select the sectors in which the country should specialise by implementing targeted actions. Kyrgyzstan had already launched its Export Promotion Strategy 2015-2017 when it added the functions of an EPA to the existing IPA. The strategy identifies priority sectors, including garment, dairy, agricultural products and tourism, as well as activities such as trade facilitation, information and promotion, access to finance, and quality of infrastructure.

The agency is currently in the process of developing its export promotion activities, and exploring synergies with the investment promotion part. The experience of OECD member countries such as Business France suggest that synergies can be found in marketing activities, joint offices and support functions, among others.

Sources: (OECD, 2017[105]; Business France, 2017[76]; Government of Kyrgyzstan, 2015[106]; State Agency for Investment and Export Promotion of Kyrgyzstan, 2017[107])

Tajikistan should also introduce a more structured approach to "nation branding" to support export promotion and the attractiveness of Tajik products, possibly through Tajinvest. The agency recently took part in a mission to Armenia to study the work carried out in these areas by a partnership of Business France and the Development Foundation of Armenia, Armenia's national authority for investment, export and tourism promotion. To increase its reach, the Agency should further co-operate with the Chamber of Commerce and the network that it has developed with other chambers of commerce in the regions where Tajikistan exports, especially in Russia and China.

Tajikistan should implement its risk-management approach to customs, combined with bringing the single window into full operation in the coming years. The government should also support the operations of the new National Centre for Accreditation, as it will bring the separation Tajikistan needs between its certification and accreditation procedures, which will in turn ease the trading of agricultural products. Moreover, the quality of the laboratories should be improved to offer a wider variety of services to assess product quality and make them exportable to foreign markets (which should themselves be carefully studied to assess the best possible positioning in terms of the price, quality and quantity of Tajik products).

The government should rebuild trust by acting to make the tax system fairer for firms in the agriculture sector. It will need to make important reforms including: reducing areas of ambiguity in the interpretation of the tax code, minimising unnecessary tax audits, and rationalising tax exemptions and systematising the eligibility criteria for them (Strokova and Ajwad, 2017[108]).

On the agriculture side, the government could further improve the legal framework, including tax incentives, and increase technical and financial support for establishing co-operatives in order to further develop co-operation. Kazakhstan has successfully developed its network of co-operatives by educating farmers about them and providing technical assistance (OECD, 2015[109]). The government could invest in the establishment of commodity protocols with existing and new markets and promote an agribusiness council to spearhead/co-ordinate commodity development and provide "soft" infrastructure to facilitate market access for agricultural products.

Finally, to monitor the effective impact of its agricultural policies, the government should build the internal capacity of its agriculture ministry and build reliable surveys among farmers and agribusinesses to have reliable statistics. The government should develop detailed KPIs that focus on outcomes and a thorough monitoring system, while ensuring that monitoring and evaluation feed effectively into policy making. In this area, the government could make use of the business surveys conducted by the Chamber of Commerce to determine the factors impeding the development of export of agricultural products.

Notes

[1] These figures exclude the exports of services in Turkmenistan due to the unavailability of data.

[2] These programmes include but are not limited to: the Industrial Development Programme of Uzbekistan for 2011-2015, the 2011 Presidential Decree on *Additional Measures to create the most favourable Business Environment for the Further Development of Small Business and Private Entrepreneurship,* and the 2011 State Programme *Year of Small business and Private Entrepreneurship.*

[3] There are repatriation requirements in place on: capital and money market instruments, credit operations, direct investment, liquidation of direct investment, real estate transactions and personal capital transactions. Repatriation requirements on derivatives and other instruments were not regulated at the time of writing (Horton et al., 2016[36])

[4] Belgium, China, France, Germany, Kazakhstan, Korea, Malaysia, the Russian Federation, Turkmenistan, Ukraine, the United Arab Emirates and the United States.

[5] To these numbers, we should also add the informal micro-companies which are especially prevalent in agriculture, about which there is very little data. Recent estimates suggest that the number of employees in informal agricultural companies could be double those in formal companies (Strokova and Ajwad, 2017[108]).

[6] A "single window" is a system that allows traders to lodge information with a single body to fulfil all import- or export-related regulatory requirements. The "entrance", either physical or electronic, is managed by an agency that then in turn informs all other appropriate agencies, guaranteeing savings in the time and cost of compliance for traders.

[7] Programmes identifying "reliable market players" or "trusted traders" are also called authorised economic operator (AEO) programmes. They are voluntary trade facilitation initiatives that recognise businesses with a secure supply chain and compliant trade practices, rewarding accredited businesses with a range of trade facilitation benefits (e.g. priority trade services, differentiated examinations, mutual recognition arrangements). To become a "trusted trader", an operator must meet a wide range of criteria, including a positive track record of compliance with trade regulations and co-operation with customs authorities (usually at least two years), financial

solvency, and proven practical standards of competence or professional qualifications (European Commission, 2017a[357]; Government of Australia, 2017[332]).

8 First introduced with Resolution of the Government of Tajikistan No. 659 (2008) and then established with Resolution No. 630 (2010) of the Government of Tajikistan.

9 In an analysis of 2006, none of the 10 laboratories visited, which were accredited, would have passed an assessment in accordance with the ISO/IEC 17025 standards (ITC, 2007[93]).

10 Statement based on OECD interviews and discussion during the Public-Private Working Groups in Dushanbe in May and July 2017.

11 Draft law named "About modification and additions in Tax Code of the Republic of Tajikistan".

12 The Key Direction 3.6.1.2 called Establish the Institutions of Export Promotion includes the specific policy action "Establish the bank for export promotion and import substitution".

13 *Dekhan* is the word used for individual or family farms in Central Asia.

14 Five other business associations carried out business surveys with grant support from the UNDP in 2014-16.

References

ADB (2016), *Asian Development Outlook 2016: Asia's Potential Growth*, Asian Development Bank. [34]

Alvarez, E. (2004), *"Sources of export success in small- and medium-sized enterprises: The impact of public programs"*, http://dx.doi.org/10.1016/j.ibusrev.2004.01.002, pp. 383-400. [56]

Austrade (2017), *"What is EMDG?"*, http://www.austrade.gov.au/Australian/Export/Export-Grants/What-is-EMDG. [51]

Azamatov, A. (2016), "Duty-free expectations", *Economic Review, 2016/10 edition.* [65]

Belloc, M. and M. Di Maio (2011), *"Survey of the literature on successful strategies and practices for export promotion by developing countries"*, International Growth Centre. [45]

Berg, W. (2016), *Business Intelligence & Export Promotion: made in Germany.* [47]

Business France (2016), *Companies and Exports, first study, press file*, Business France and Kantar Public, http://www.businessfrance.fr/communiques-presse/1ere-etude-kantar-public-business-france-les-entreprises-considerent-la-france-comme-un-hub-d. [49]

Business France (2017), *Business France Experience in Trade & Investment Promotion, Presentation to the Ministry of Economy of the Kyrgyz Republic,July 2017.* [12]

Business France (2017), *Business France Experience in Trade & Investment Promotion.* [76]

Business France (2017), *Business France website*, http://en.businessfrance.fr/home (accessed on 2 May 2017). [97]

Business France (2017), *"Business France presentation", OECD Working Group (April 2017).* [98]

Byrne, P. (2016), *Major Structural Components of an Investment Promotion Agency Strategy*, Background paper to an OECD Workshop on Investment Promotion in Bishkek. [13]

CCIU (2017), *"International cooperation"*, http://www.chamber.uz/en/page/914 (accessed on [58]

18 March 2017).

CER (2016), *Повышение производственного и экспортного потенциала плодоовощной отрасли Узбекистана: проблемы и перспективы, [Increase in the production and export potential of the fruit and vegetable industry of Uzbekistan: problems and perspectives]*, Center for Economic Research. [73]

Choi, J. et al. (2014), *Kyrgyz Republic - The garment sector: Impact of joining the customs union and options to increase competitiveness*, http://documents.worldbank.org/curated/en/2014/06/20460187/kyrgyz-garment-sector-impact-joining-customs-union-options-increase-competitiveness. [81]

DAMU (2017), *Institutional website*, https://www.damu.kz/en (accessed on 29 June). [15]

De Wulf, L. (2001), *"Why have trade promotion organizations failed, and how can they be revitalized?"*, World Bank, http://documents.worldbank.org/curated/en/905581468140376821/Why-have-trade-promotion-organizations-failed-and-how-can-they-be-revitalized.. [61]

Durmuşoğlu, S. and et al (2012), *"The effect of government-designed export promotion service use on small and medium-sized enterprise goal achievement: A multidimensional view of export performance"*, http://dx.doi.org/10.1016/j.indmarman.2011.09.016., pp. 680-91. [57]

EBRD (2016), *"Transition report 2016-17: Uzbekistan"*, http://2016.tr-ebrd.com/countries/. [37]

EBRD (2017), *Trade dimension*, http://ebrd-beeps.com (accessed on 26 June 2017). [7]

EBRD (2017), *Business Environment and Enterprise Performance Survey (BEEPS) data base*, http://ebrd-beeps.com (accessed on 15 March 2017). [9]

EBRD (2017), *Tajikistan overview*, http://www.ebrd.com/where-we-are/tajikistan/overview.html. [88]

EIU (2017), *Turkmenistan, Country report*, Economist Intelligence Unit. [4]

ESCWA (2011), *Key Factors In Establishing Single Windows For Handling Import/Export Procedures And Formalities: Trade Facilitation And The Single Window*, Economic and Social Commission for Western Asia. [42]

Eurasianet (2017), *"Uzbekistan Returns to Currency Convertibility, Delivers Blow to Black Market"*, http://www.eurasianet.org/node/84981. [39]

Eurostat (2017), *Small and Medium-sized enterprises. Structural Business Statistics*, http://ec.europa.eu/eurostat/web/structural-business-statistics/structural-business-statistics/sme. [104]

Export.gov (2017), *"Uzbekistan - Foreign exchange controls"*, http://www.export.gov/article?id=Uzbekistan-Foreign-Exchange-Controls. [38]

Ferghana (2017), *"Uzbekistan: Any entrepreneur can sell vegetables and fruits abroad"*, http://enews.fergananews.com/news.php?id=3385&mode=snews. [72]

FITA (2017), *Foreign Investment and Foreign Trade Agency of Mongolia, Invest in Mongolia, Institutional website*, http://investmongolia.gov.mn/en/ (accessed on 26 June 2017). [16]

Ganiev, B. and Y. Yusupov (2012), *"Uzbekistan: Trade regime and recent trade developments"*, Institute of Public Policy and Administration, University of Central Asia. [35]

Government of Canada (2012), *Customer Service and Satisfaction Survey*. [100]

Government of Kyrgyzstan (2015), *Governmental Plan for Export Development of the Kyrgyz Republic for 2015-2017*. [106]

Government of Tajikistan (2016), *"Mid-Term Development Strategy of the Republic of Tajikistan 2016-2020"*, (unpublished). [91]

Government of Uzbekistan (2011), *Year of Small Business and Private Entrepreneurship, State programme*, Government of Uzbekistan. [23]

Government of Uzbekistan (2015), *Program of Localization of the Production of Finished Products, Components and Materials for 2015-2019*, Government of Uzbekistan. [62]

Hausmann, R. and D. Rodrik (2003), *"Economic development as self-discovery"*, http://dx.doi.org/10.1016/S0304-3878(03)00124-X, pp. 603-33. [46]

Horton, M. et al. (2016), *Exchange Rate Developments and Policies in the Caucasus and Central Asia*, International Monetary Fund. [36]

IFC (2011), *Tajikistan country note.* [89]

IGC (2011), *Survey of Literature on Succesful Strategies and Practices for Export Promotion by Developing Countries*, http://www.theigc.org/wp-content/uploads/2011/06/Belloc-Di-Maio-2011-Working-Paper.pdf. [96]

IMF (2017), *Press Release no 17/539*, https://www.imf.org/en/News/Articles/2017/09/19/pr17359-statement-by-imf-managing-director-christine-lagarde-on-uzbekistan. [40]

Investment and Export Promotion Agency Kyrygzstan (2017), *The Official Website of the State Agency for Investment and Export Promotion of Kyrgyzstan*, http://www.invest.gov.kg/ru/informatciia-dlia-investorov/regulirovanie-otdelnykh-otraslei/mikrofinansovye-organizatcii/. [82]

ISPAT (2016), *Experience Sharing: Investment Attraction with Sector Focus, Presentation to the Ministry of Economy of the Kyrgyz Republic, May 2016*, Bishkek. [11]

ITC (2007), *Recommendations for Improving the National Quality of Infrastructure in Tajikistan*, UNCTAD/WTO. [93]

ITC (2017), *"Uzbekistan"*, http://www.intracen.org/layouts/CountryTemplate.aspx?pageid=47244645034&id=47244652817. [48]

Jordana, J., C. Volpe Martincus and A. Gallo (2010), *"Export promotion organizations in Latin America and the Caribbean: An institutional portrait"*, Inter-American Development Bank,, http://publications.iadb.org/handle/11319/318. [60]

Kiyota, K. (2014), *"Exports and Employment in China, Indonesia, Japan and Korea"*, OECD Publishing, http://dx.doi.org/10.1787/5jxzqqw84vmp-en. [30]

Kowalski, P. and M. Büge (2013), *"Assessing the trade-related sources of productivity growth in emerging economies"*, OECD Publishing, http://dx.doi.org/10.1787/5k437p82nxq1-en. [29]

Kyrgyzstan (2017), *Invest in Kyrgyzstan, website*, http://www.invest.gov.kg/en/about-agency (accessed on 29 June 2017). [17]

Lederman, D., M. Olarreaga and L. Payton (2006), "Export promotion agencies: what works and what doesn't", *World Bank Policy Research Working Paper*, p. No. 4044. [10]

Lederman, D., M. Olarreaga and L. Payton (2010), *"Export promotion agencies: Do they work?"*, http://dx.doi.org/10.1016/j.jdeveco.2009.09.003., pp. 257-65. [52]

Lee, J. (2017), *"SME export support policy of Korea and globalization".* [50]

Lopez Gonzalez, J. (2016), ""Using foreign factors to enhance domestic export performance"", *OECD Trade Policy Papers, No. 191*, http://dx.doi.org/10.1787/5jlpq82v1jxw-en. [32]

Makhmadshoev, D., K. Ibeh and M. Crone (2015), *"Institutional influences on SME exporters under divergent transition paths: Comparative insights from Tajikistan and Kyrgyzstan"*, http://dx.doi.org/10.1, pp. 1025-38. [31]

Martincus, C. et al. (2010), *"Information barriers, export promotion institutions, and the extensive margin of trade"*, http://dx.doi.org/10.1007/s10290-009-0043-0, pp. 91-111. [53]

Martincus, C. and J. Carballo (2012), *"Export promotion activities in developing countries: What kind of trade do they promote?"*, http://dx.doi.org/10.1080/09638199.2010.500741, pp. 539-78. [54]

Mazhikeyev, A., T. Edwards and M. Rizov (2015), *"Openness and isolation: The trade performance of the former Soviet Central Asian countries"*, http://dx.doi.org/doi:10.1016/j.ibusrev.2015.03.001, pp. 935-47. [33]

Ministry of Economy of Uzbekistan (2017), *Draft legislation on the measures to improve the infrastructure for the development of entrepreneurship and the improvement of the Business Environment*, https://regulation.gov.uz/ru/documents/1580. [43]

Ministry of Industry (2016), *Decree by the Minister of Industry No.48, March 22 2016*, Ministry of Industry of Mongolia. [101]

Naray, O. (2011), *"Commercial diplomats in the context of international business"*, http://dx.doi.org/10.1163/187119111X557382, pp. 121-48. [59]

Nepomnyashchaya, O. (2016), *"Вопрос пищевой важности" [The issue of the importance of food]*, CER, Tashkent, pp. 69-73. [70]

OEC (2017), *"What does Uzbekistan export? (2015)"*, http://atlas.media.mit.edu/en/visualize/tree_map/hs92/export/uzb/all/show/2015/ (accessed on 22 March 2017). [69]

OEC (2017), http://atlas.media.mit.edu/en/profile/country/tjk/. [83]

OECD and World Bank (2015), *Inclusive Global Value Chains*, G20 Trade Ministers Meeting. [27]

OECD (2008), *Removing Barriers to SME Access to International Markets.* [1]

OECD (2008), *Enhancing the Role of SMEs in Global Value Chains*, OECD Publishing, http://dx.doi.org/10.1787/9789264051034-en. [44]

OECD (2010), *"Trading out of poverty"*, http://dx.doi.org/10.1787/journal_dev-v10-art16-en., pp. pp.7-41. [28]

OECD (2013), *Promoting Investments and Job Creation in Central Asia through Business Linkage Programmes.* [3]

OECD (2014), *Expanding the garment industry in the Kyrgyz Republic*, http://www.oecd.org/globalrelations/ExpandingtheGarmentIndustry.pdf. [80]

OECD (2015), *Policy Framework for Investment*, Organisation for Economic Co-operation and Development, http://www.oecd-ilibrary.org/content/book/9789264208667-en. [14]

OECD (2015), *Increasing Exports in Tajikistan: The Case of Agribusiness*, OECD Publishing. [86]

OECD (2015), *OECD Tax Policies Studies - Taxation of SMEs in OECD and G20 countries*, OECD Publishing. [95]

OECD (2015), *Strengthening Agricultural co-operatives in Kazakhstan*, OECD Publishing. [109]

OECD (2016), *"The economic impact of local content requirements"*, OECD. [63]

OECD (2016), *Agricultural Policy Monitoring and Evaluation 2016*, OECD Publishing, http://dx.doi.org/10.1787/agr_pol-2016-en. [103]

OECD (2017), *Small, Medium, Strong. Trends in SME Performance and Business Conditions*, Organisation for Economic Co-operation and Development, http://www.oecd-ilibrary.org/content/book/9789264275683-en. [2]

OECD (2017), *OECD Trade Facilitation Indicators*, http://www2.compareyourcountry.org/trade-facilitation. [8]

OECD (2017), *Boosting SME Internationalisation in Uzbekistan through better export promotion policies*. [19]

OECD (2017), *"Enhancing the contributions of SMEs in a global and digitalised economy", Meeting of the OECD Council at Ministerial Level, 7-8 June 2017..* [24]

OECD (2017), *OECD Trade Facilitation Indicators*, http://www2.compareyourcountry.org/trade-facilitation. [41]

OECD (2017), *Activities and good practiceces to establish an Export Promotion Agency based on OECD experience*. [105]

Office of the Prime Minister of Kazakhstan (2017), *Office of the Prime Minister of Kazakhstan), Institutional website*, https://primeminister.kz/en/page/view/gpiir (accessed on 26 June 2017). [18]

Olimkhonov, A. (2017), *"Что посеять, как продать?" [What to sow, how to sell it?]*, CER, Tashkent, pp. 76-81. [74]

Pomfret, . (2006), *The Central Asian Economies since Independence*, Princeton University Press. [20]

President of Uzbekistan, K. (2016), *Our Main Goal is to Cardinally Deepen the Reforms and Structural Transformations Carried out in our Economy, Open Up a Broad Path for Private Ownership, Small Business and Entrepreneurship*, Statement at the Expanded Meeting of the Cabinet of Ministers. [26]

Pugach, I. and et al (2016), *"Сельскохозяйственная политика в производстве пшеницы и диверсификации производства сельскохозяйственных культур в Узбекистане" [Agricultural policy in wheat production and diversification of crop production in Uzbekistan]*. [67]

Rosenberg, C. and . de Zeeuw (2000), *"Welfare effects of Uzbekistan's foreign exchange regime", IMF Working Paper, No. 00/61*, International Monetary Fund. [21]

State Agency for Investment and Export Promotion of Kyrgyzstan (2017), *State Agency of Invesment and Export Promotion*, http://www.invest.gov.kg. [107]

State Committee on Competition (2016), *Export Potential and Trade Development: New Challenges and Opportunities in agribusiness*. [77]

Strokova, V. and M. Ajwad (2017), *Jjobs Diagnostic: Tajikistan - Strategic framework for Jobs*, World Bank. [108]

Tajikistan, G. (2008), *Customs Code*. [90]

TajStat (2017), *Employment by Economic Activity 2011-2017*, http://www.stat.tj/en/database/real-sector. [84]

UN Comtrade (2017), *UN Comtrade Database*, https://comtrade.un.org/.. [66]

UNDP (2015), *Labour migration, remittances, and human development in Central Asia*, http://www.undp.org/content/dam/rbec/docs/CA%20M&R%20HD%20paper%20frozen%20ENG%20Layout.pdf. [79]

UPS (2016), *European SME Exporting Insights Study*. [6]

USAID and GAIN (2015), *Report on Assessment of Food Laboratories in Tajikistan*, USAID and Global Alliance for Improved Nutrition. [92]

Uzagroexport (2017), *Uzagroexport website*, http://uzagroexport.uz/en (accessed on 21 June 2017). [71]

UzReport (2017), *"Uzbekistan launches single brand to export fruits"*, https://uzreport.news/economy/uzbekistan-launches-single-brand-to-export-fruits (accessed on 18 August 2017). [75]

UzStat (2017), *ОСНОВНЫЕ ПОКАЗАТЕЛИ социально-экономического развития Республики Узбекистан за 2012-2015гг [Main indicators of the socio-economic development of the Republic of Uzbekistan between 2012 and 2015]*, http://www.stat.uz/ru/statinfo/dinamicheskie-ryady (accessed on 21 March 2017). [68]

UzStat (2017), *Госкомстат - Развитие Малого Предпринимательства (Бизнеса) В Узбекистане, State Committee of the Republic of Uzbekistan on Statistics*. [25]

Van Tongeren, F. (2008), "Agricultural policy design and implementation. A synthesis", *OECD Food and Agriculture and Fisheries Papers*, p. Paris. [102]

Warwick, K. (2013), "Beyond Industrial Policy: Emerging Issues and New Trends", *OECD Science, Technology and Industry Policy Papers*, p. No. 2. [64]

Wilkinson, T. and L. Brouthers (2006), *"Trade promotion and SME export performance"*, http://dx.doi.org/10.1016/j.ibusrev.2006.03.001, pp. 233-52. [55]

WOCAT (2017), *Technical Assitance Groups (TAGs) - Tajikistan*. [99]

World Bank (2016), *Doing Business Indicators*, http://www.doingbusiness.org/rankings. [22]

World Bank (2016), *World Development Indicators, database*, http://data.worldbank.org/indicator. [78]

World Bank (2016), *Doing Business 2016: Measuring Regulatory Quality and Efficiency*, World Bank. [85]

World Bank (2017), *World Development Indicators*, http://data.worldbank.org/data-catalog/world-development-indicators. [5]

World Bank (2017), *Trading across borders: Doing business reforms*, http://www.doingbusiness.org/data/exploretopics/trading-across-borders/reforms. [87]

World Bank (2017), *Tax administration in Tajikistan*, http://projects.worldbank.org/P127807/tax-administration?lang=en. [94]

Chapter 4. Business environment in Central Asia: Skills

This chapter provides an overview of skills challenges facing the private sector in Central Asia. Vocational education and training (VET) can play a crucial role in responding to the needs of the labour market and of the economy. Employers must be involved in VET policy making to ensure it provides the right mix of skills. The OECD has helped design VET instruments in Kazakhstan and Kyrgyzstan. These two case studies suggest a need to strengthen firms' involvement in public-private dialogue on skills, and to support the implementation of key VET instruments for small and medium-sized enterprises.

Setting the stage

Central Asian firms face skills gaps that vocational education and training can help bridge

A well-educated and skilled workforce is a cornerstone of a country's competitiveness, fostering high productivity, growth and innovation. Skills development policies are thus crucial in promoting inclusive growth (OECD, 2015[1]). VET policies are essential in responding to labour market needs, and contribute to economic competitiveness. Policy reforms in this area can be considered a priority, and need to foster the engagement of employers in developing a well-skilled labour force and to meet labour market requirements (OECD, 2010[2]; 2016[3]).

SMEs are usually quite exposed to skills gaps considering their limited capacity to address skill needs internally (OECD, 2016[3]). They have limited resources to identify, hire and train employees, in terms of both time and money. They have small internal training and human resource management capacities to organise training and prepare complicated paperwork, activities which typically involve significant fixed costs and economies of scale. They might have important losses of production during training and retraining periods, even if such training is beneficial on the long term. SMEs are also very sensitive to employee turnover and more dependent on the performance of each employee (G20/OECD, 2015[4]).

VET policies aim to ensure that the competencies provided by the education system match those needed in the workplace and to smooth the transition from education to work (G20/OECD, 2015[5]). VET can provide the labour force with a wide range of trade, technical and professional skills needed by companies. VET institutions typically teach practical occupational skills that are needed in the labour market and that will make graduates immediately employable and more productive. VET programmes also increasingly aim to build cognitive (numeracy, literacy) and social-emotional skills (team working, communication) to allow trainees to be more flexible and to be able to adjust to changing market needs after their courses are completed (OECD, 2010[2]).

One of the main challenges for VET policies is to provide more formal workplace training activities for SMEs, which constitute the great majority of enterprises and provide the bulk of employment in most countries (UNESCO, 2017[6]). At initial VET level, workplace training helps students better understand the world of work, and transition to jobs in SMEs and in large companies. Continuous VET allows workers to broaden their knowledge and skills base, thus helping businesses to increase their productivity and innovate (OECD, 2014[7]). SMEs tend to make less use of formal training and VET programmes. In OECD countries, employees of SMEs have 50% less access to training compared to large firms (OECD, 2016[3]).

These challenges are highly relevant for Central Asian countries. They have achieved virtually universal literacy, but companies in the region regularly report that insufficient human capital development and skills mismatches are key challenges. Almost one-fifth of companies surveyed in the EBRD/World Bank Business Environment and Enterprise Performance Survey (BEEPS) identify an inadequately educated workforce[1] as a major constraint on business development (Figure 4.1). The most recent BEEPS data suggest that this constraint might even be underestimated by companies, compared to access to finance and taxation in the aftermath of the financial crisis (EBRD, 2017[8]).

Figure 4.1. Educational adequacy of the workforce for SMEs in Central Asia

Percentage of SMEs identifying an inadequately educated workforce as a major constraint in Central Asia and in other developing regions

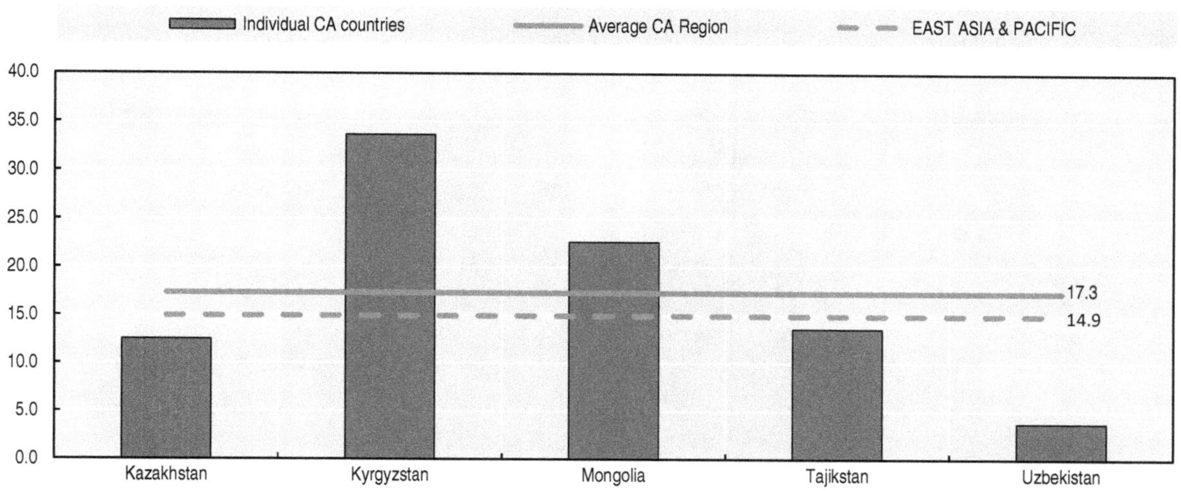

Source: (EBRD, 2017[8])

Identifying skill needs and recruiting are also challenging steps for SMEs in Central Asia. The labour market infrastructure in the region tends to be underdeveloped with few job offer websites, limited access to the Internet to search individual company websites and few places where job offers are physically displayed, such as VET schools and employment centres. This creates high transaction costs for SMEs when it comes to expressing their resource needs and identifying suitable candidates. It also makes things more difficult for job seekers. Geographical distances in the region add to the cost and complexity of the recruitment phase (OECD, 2013[9]; 2014[7]; 2016[3]).

Only 45% of employees of the SMEs surveyed by BEEPS in Central Asia have access to formal training as part of lifelong learning (EBRD, 2017[8]). This is significantly lower than in other regions. For example, the percentage is 67% in East Asia and Pacific. SMEs in the region are less likely than large companies to partner with VET institutions to organise training sessions or to release workers from their daily work to attend training (OECD, 2013[10]). SMEs also underline the lack of incentives to fund and participate in formal training and the limited visibility and targeting of the training offered by VET institutions (OECD, 2016[3]).The lack of skill surveys, including those aimed at SMEs, makes it hard for VET institutions to identify what type of skills are needed by the majority of SMEs, and adjust their training to offer to better target SME needs.

The OECD report on Skills beyond School outlines the characteristics of a well-functioning VET system

The OECD offers a set of tools and recommendations to address key policy challenges and support the development of VET systems (OECD, 2010[2]). Drawing on international experience, it has defined the key characteristics of strong vocational education systems, with its findings covering both initial and continuous VET (OECD, 2014[11]). Three characteristics have an immediate effect on SMEs (Figure 4.2). They are 1) the quality of training, and how it matches employers' needs; 2) the assessment and certification of skills, allowing skills acquired in SMEs to be recognised and transferred; and 3) the supporting conditions for VET policies that enable SMEs to better understand and be involved in VET policy making and implementation (OECD, 2014[12]). This chapter will examine these characteristics more in detail, alongside the specific instruments supporting them.[2]

Figure 4.2. Key characteristics of effective vocational systems

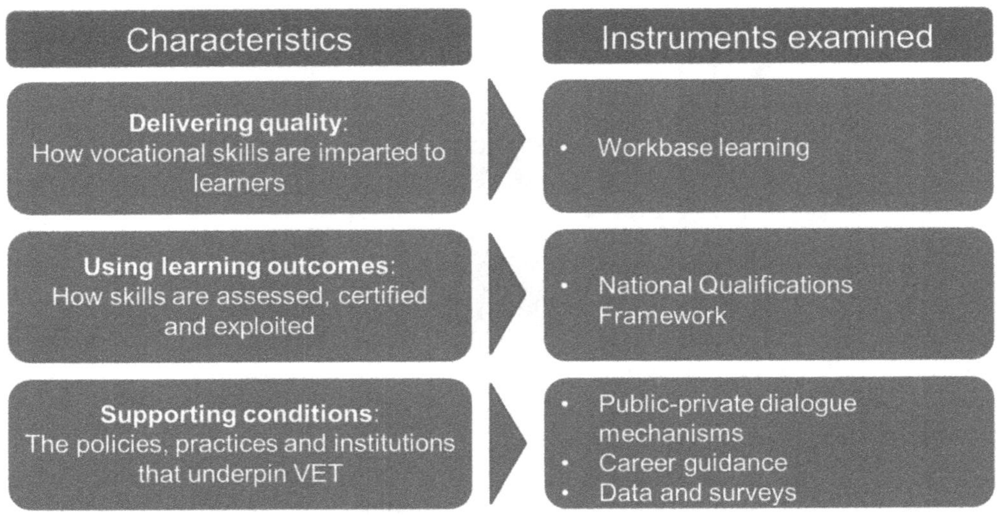

Source: (OECD, 2014[11])

Based on these key characteristics of effective vocational systems, the OECD has recommended the use of the following VET instruments to enhance the efficient of VET in OECD member and non-member countries (OECD, 2014[12]).

Workplace training, such as apprenticeships and internships, provides a strong learning environment for SMEs and for employees. It can help close the skills gap by accelerating the transfer of knowledge between the educational system and firms. Such training can also reduce information asymmetries between SMEs and the workforce and foster the development of on-the-job skills (OECD, 2014[7]).

National qualification frameworks (NQFs) are classification tools aimed at enhancing the quality and relevance of qualifications between the educational institutions and the labour market (European Union and GOPA, 2016[13]). They can increase the transparency of qualifications and make skills assessment easier for SMEs, help secure recognition of skills acquired in SMEs, and help SMEs to identify relevant VET programmes. **Occupational standards** (OSs) are complementary tools that are key to defining common standards of performance, and the knowledge and skills employees need to perform effectively (OECD, 2015[1]).

Public-private dialogue mechanisms such as public-private boards and skill surveys can foster collaboration with SMEs. Formal boards can discuss skill needs and the current VET instruments, and help design policy solutions. Representing the voice of SMEs is a major challenge that could be addressed by involving SME representatives and business associations with a majority of SME members.

Career guidance has become increasingly important and demanding in a rapidly evolving job environment. Students need independent, informed, reliable guidance that will provide them with good knowledge of the labour market and of learning opportunities, and help them make relevant career choices. This requires career centres to develop strong links between VET schools and companies (OECD, 2010[2]).

Strong data on the labour market, skills needs and VET training are crucial to informed policy making. **Skill surveys** are useful tools that governments can use in collaboration with business associations to understand skills needs, training practices, and the relevance of VET programmes for SMEs.

OECD work on VET in Central Asia suggests increasing public-private dialogue, enhancing the legal framework and strengthening institutions

All Central Asian countries have started to adopt, design and implement VET strategies and policy instruments (Table 4.1) (ETF, 2014[14]).

The OECD has studied VET systems in two Central Asian countries, Kazakhstan and Kyrgyzstan. These were peer-reviewed in 2013/2016 and 2014 in the OECD Eurasia Competitiveness Roundtable. Kazakhstan provides an example of a country implementing a NQF and OSs. Kyrgyzstan has designed new measures to develop workplace training for both initial and continuous VET. Key recommendations that could benefit other countries in the region include:

- **Increasing public-private dialogue**: policy makers in Central Asia should further involve private firms – particularly SMEs – in public-private dialogue mechanisms. The private sector is increasingly involved in the making of skills policy and established formal and informal channels to discuss VET policies, including skills councils. The involvement of SMEs in this process can be further enhanced by ensuring that business associations represent the voice of SMEs, by involving incubators and entrepreneurs' associations, and by organising specific sessions for SMEs within the existing national skills councils. Other forms of consultations, like skill surveys and field interviews, can also be used to gather information from firms.
- **Enhancing the legal framework and building institutions**: for example, the OECD has recommended that Kazakhstan empower an institution in charge of the NQF and OS and design incentives targeting SMEs. In Kyrgyzstan, the implementation of workplace training has demonstrated the need to revise the legal framework – including the labour code – and to design incentives targeted at SMEs that could raise their interest in offering workplace training.

Table 4.1. Overview of selected VET development in Central Asia

Country	Kazakhstan	Kyrgyzstan	Mongolia	Tajikistan	Uzbekistan
Workplace training	Workplace training required by law in VET programmes, but limited evidence of their use	New legal framework and (tax and financial) incentives for workplace training under approval	Limited evidence of the use of workplace training	Limited evidence of the use of workplace training Predominance of informal employment	Active partnerships between VET institutions and companies on workplace training Financial and tax incentives for SMEs when hiring VET graduates
National qualification framework	Establishment of an NQF OS under development	Principle of an NQF approved by the government	NQF under development	NQF mentioned in the national strategy but still at a conceptual level	NQF not yet established
Public-private dialogue mechanism	Existing national, regional and sector VET councils, with irregular meetings Creation of state holding Kasipkor in charge of modernising VET Key role played by the National Chamber of Entrepreneurs (Atameken)	Creation of National Skills Council and sector councils High levels of involvement by business associations in policy dialogue, including the CCI Creation of a dedicated VET agency	Quarterly meetings of the National Council on VET Strong involvement of the CCI and of the Mongolian Employers' Federation (MONEF) Creation of a network of centers for employment service	Creating of a National Advisory Board for VET 73 public training centres offering training for SMEs	Sector skills councils being developed SME voice represented by the CCI
Career guidance	Creation of career centres in the most recent education institutions	Recent development of career centres in several VET and tertiary institutions	Public-private cooperation and career advice supported by Social Partnership Officers in VET schools	Career centres not developed in VET institutions	N.a.
Data and surveys	Data collected by the Ministries of Labour and of Education and by the National Statistical Institute, no comprehensive set of data No skill survey	Data mainly based on the national household survey Limited data on employers and VET students No specific skill survey	Development of a labour market information system No skill survey	No labour market information system No skill survey	Existing set of data on VET Limited dataset on key education indicators No skill survey
What can be done	Further involve SMEs in policy dialogue and skill councils Complete implementation of VET tools, including OS and workplace training	Increase the use of data and business inputs into policy-making Strengthen the links between business and VET institutions Implement new regulations on VET instruments	Develop sector councils e.g. textile agriculture, construction - Further involve businesses in implementing VET instruments, including the NQF and workplace training	Further involve companies in VET policy dialogue and implementation Further use donor support for education and skills Promote the use of VET instruments to companies	Continue to involve SMEs and the business community in the implementation of VET instruments adapted to SMEs, including NQF and skill surveys

Source: OECD analysis based on (ADB, 2016[15]; Álvarez-Galván, 2014[16]; Ashurov, 2015[17]; ETF, 2014[14]; ETF, 2014[18]; ETF, 2015[19]; ETF, 2015[20]; ETF, 2016[21]; European Union and GOPA, 2016[13]; Ministry of Labour and Social Protection of Mongolia, 2016[22]); (OECD, 2013[9]; OECD, 2013[10]; OECD, 2015[1]; OECD, 2016[3])

Kazakhstan: Designing occupational standards

Bridging skills gaps is a key concern for Kazakhstan's businesses. In 2016, the OECD advised the government to make more use VET instruments, especially national qualifications frameworks (NQFs) and occupational standards (OSs). Its recommendations included further involving the private sector, building appropriate local institutions and expertise on these instruments, and developing education curricula based on them. This work was applied to a promising sector for Kazakhstan's economic diversification, the petrochemical and chemical industry.

Context: Vocational education and training in Kazakhstan's petrochemical and chemical industry

Kazakhstan is well positioned to develop its domestic petrochemical and chemical industry as part of its overall diversification efforts because of growing internal and external demand, proximity to substantial markets, and its rich natural resource endowments. Worldwide, global competition is driving a trend of continuous up-skilling, re-skilling and multi-skilling of the current workforce, producing better-qualified new entrants. Skills upgrading in turn can encourage cluster development in the sector and attract foreign investment (OECD, 2009[23]). The sector is thus a meaningful case study on how the improvement of skill policies could help the country develop higher value added industries.

Kazakhstan's petrochemical and chemical industry lacks qualified staff. The United Chemical Company (UCC), the institute responsible for bolstering Kazakhstan's chemical industry, has identified staff needs to be almost 6 000 people for the projects that it is overseeing (plant operators, mechanics, dedicated experts etc.) (United Chemical Company, 2015[24]). According to a survey by the European Bank for Reconstruction and Development (EBRD), inadequate workforce skills constitute one of the biggest problems faced by Kazakhstan's firms, especially the larger ones (EBRD, 2015[25]).

Vocational education and training (VET) is essential for growing the petrochemical and chemical industry, which involves complex industrial processes, equipment and working methods requiring highly specialised technicians (Box 4.1). Semi-skilled and skilled workers (technicians) make up a large portion of the workforce in the petrochemical and chemical sector, with jobs such as process operators, maintenance technicians, laboratory technicians and mechanical testing technicians. As an example, in Germany, which has the most developed chemical industry in Europe, 56% of workers employed in the chemical industry in 2011 were skilled workers with vocational education and training (56% skilled workers, 16% graduates, 13% technicians, 10% unskilled workers and 5% trainees) (CEFIC, 2013[26]; Union of Chemical Industries of Lyon, 2015[27]; ILO, 2011[28]). In the United States, which produces 15% of the world's chemicals, production occupations made up about 42% of total employment in the sector in 2009. Installation, maintenance and repair specialists accounted for 10% of the total (American Chemistry Council, 2015[29]).

Within the VET system, occupational standards (OSs) in particular, are an essential link between workplace employment requirements and human capital development (i.e. education and training programmes), and affect individuals throughout their lives. Kazakhstan currently lacks any occupational standards for petrochemistry. A few standards have been developed for the chemical sector, but employers were not sufficiently involved in the process.

Box 4.1. Vocational education and training in petrochemistry in Atyrau

Kazakhstan's Atyrau region in the west of the country has great potential for petrochemical production. In 2013, Atyrau accounted for 46% of Kazakhstan's total oil and gas production. The region is near to some of Kazakhstan's major oil fields, as 90% of explored fields are in western Kazakhstan (Dzekunov and et al., n.d.[30]). The Programme for Industrial-Innovative Development of Kazakhstan for 2015-2019 identified petrochemistry and the production of chemicals for industry as priority sectors for Atyrau. The Integrated Petrochemical Complex located in the region is targeting polypropylene production of 500 000 tonnes per year and polyethelene production of 800 000 tonnes per year. The Atyrau refinery is being upgraded to construct an aromatic hydrocarbon facility, which will enable it to begin production of benzene and paraxylene – basic products for Kazakhstan's petrochemical industry. To do so, the region would require staff with strong vocational education and training to satisfy the demands of the industry.

However, in spite of this context, Atyrau's colleges do not yet offer specialised courses in petrochemistry. Some institutions are considering creating programmes in this field (for example, Atyrau Polytechnic College and the Atyrau Petroleum Education Centre – Atyrau Petrotechnic). Atyrau Petrotechnic conducts training in oil and gas, and is establishing links with oil and gas companies in the region. It is planning to introduce a few chemistry programmes in the short term. The United Chemical Company is also considering creating a competence centre to train staff for the Atyrau petrochemical complex. The existence of occupational standards in petrochemistry and chemistry would facilitate these endeavours, and align companies and education institutions around a common understanding of occupations in this industry.

Source: OECD interviews 2013-2015; (Dzekunov and et al., n.d.[30]; United Chemical Company, 2015[24]; KPI Inc., 2015[31]; Polytechnic College, 2015[32]; Business Monitor Kazakhstan, 2013[33]; KazMunaiGas, 2015[34])

Focusing on occupational standards will facilitate dialogue between the government, business and education institutions (Box 4.2). In addition, it will standardise the definition of occupations in the sector and will make it easier for companies to forecast their short, medium and long-term skills needs. Finally, it will improve the responsiveness of study programmes to business requirements by basing them on a common understanding of what students must be able to learn and be able to do by the end of their studies. Ultimately, occupational standards will increase the competitiveness of the petrochemical and chemical industry.

Box 4.2. Occupational standards

Occupational standards (OSs), sometimes also called professional or competency standards, are standards of performance that people are expected to achieve in their work, as well as the knowledge and skills they need to perform effectively. A standard for an occupation (e.g. carrying out maintenance in downstream operations) is usually a document that lists:

- the tasks and activities to be carried out (e.g. check status of all relevant utilities, such as steam, water, electrical, pneumatic systems)
- the knowledge and skills required (e.g. how to use the company's Safe Systems of Work processes to identify hazards and mitigate or reduce risks to as low as reasonably practicable)
- (sometimes) the work conditions/context which might affect the required activities, knowledge and skills.

Occupational standards are a key component of an effective VET system. By aligning terminology on occupations, they facilitate public-private dialogue, and improve transparency and communication among all stakeholders. They also facilitate supply and demand analysis and maintenance of statistics due to streamlined terminology. They optimise the responsiveness of education programmes to business demands. Occupational standards have been linked to improved human capital development and productivity increases.

Occupational standards offer additional benefits for the private sector and for education institutions. They assist employers in identifying employee competency gaps to improve in-company training, in developing job descriptions, recognising competencies and qualifications, transferring foreign technologies and organising work processes. Development of occupational standards often also involves closely associated activities, especially functional analysis, which enables industry to identify in a strategic and forward-looking way the optimal mix of occupations needed in the short, medium and long term. Educational institutions and employers then use occupational standards for developing standard-based qualifications and curricula, and skills assessment and certification instruments.

Source: OECD analysis; (OECD, 2010[2])

Challenges: The development of occupational standards

The OECD has identified three main challenges to the development of occupational standards and their integration in the VET system in the sector, with relevance for other sectors of Kazakhstan's economy.

The institutional framework is weak

The domestic structure for creating, monitoring and updating occupational standards is sub-optimal, and there is no body responsible for developing occupational standards in petrochemistry or chemistry.

The Ministry of Healthcare has a small team, fewer than ten people, acting as a secretariat for developing occupational standards in Kazakhstan, with input from other ministries. This is insufficient to deal with all economic sectors. As a comparison, each of the UK sector skills councils, responsible for occupational standards, have about 30-80 people (Cogent Skills, 2015$_{[35]}$). This institutional weakness is especially relevant in view of Kazakhstan's plans to develop occupational standards for all sectors of the economy by 2020 (2015$_{[36]}$). The National Chamber of Entrepreneurs, which is charged with co-ordinating the work on occupational standards from 2016, does not yet have a plan of action for this new role. Additionally, other organisations have tried to establish their own occupational standards – including the Atyrau regional government, the Polytechnic College in Atyrau, the United Chemical Company, KazEnergy association and the Atyrau Chamber of Entrepreneurs. However, none of these were for petrochemistry and very few for chemistry. This multilateral action also leads to incompatible terminology being used to describe occupations, making it difficult for stakeholders to forecast their skills needs or to create study programmes.

The government has taken some initial steps towards improving public-private dialogue, for example by establishing skills councils at national, regional and sector levels. However, employers are not sufficiently involved in the process of developing occupational standards. For instance, Kazakhstan's VET Council on the Petrochemical Industry does not have enough private sector representatives and has no role in developing occupational standards. It is in fact unclear which sector association represents the interests of the petrochemical industry in developing occupational standards. In addition, several petrochemical companies that were interviewed were not aware of the government initiative to develop occupational standards in this sector. Even the state-owned United Chemical Company, which is responsible for developing the chemistry sector, was not involved in developing the occupational standards in this sector. The standards developed for other sectors of the economy by the (then) Ministry of Healthcare and Social Development only involved employers at the review stage, but not in the development process.

Finally, Kazakhstan lacks local experts on occupational standards and on competency-based education, because even though Kazakhstan has contributed to the development of occupational standards, so far their development has taken place within the framework of international projects.

There are no mechanisms for applying occupational standards in the VET system

Occupational standards must form the basis for study programmes and for the assessment of qualifications. The government has recently recognised the importance of the link between professional and educational standards and has expressed the wish that occupational standards form the basis for study programmes and the retraining of specialists (2015$_{[36]}$). However, the current VET system does not have an effective mechanism for translating occupational standards into education curricula, or for the assessment and certification of qualifications. Existing education standards do not specify that they must be based on occupational standards, and Kazakhstan's curricula are not oriented towards learning outcomes. In addition, four independent pilot assessment centres have been established by professional sector associations for six sectors (metallurgy, oil and gas, tourism, machine building, information and communication technologies, and construction and utilities). However, none of these centres conducts assessments based on occupational standards. In the future, the government plans to charge the National Chamber of Entrepreneurs with forming independent assessment centres – it should ensure that their assessments are based on occupational standards.

Awareness of occupational standards is limited

Given their novelty, there is a lack of awareness, especially in the private sector and among regional stakeholders, of the overall concept and the practical application of occupational standards and competency-based education in Kazakhstan, or of the existing government initiatives. This leads to a lack of co-ordination of existing initiatives. This lack of awareness was confirmed in Atyrau region and at national level during meetings with some education institutions and private companies.

Recommendations to improve occupational standards and bridge skills gaps in Kazakhstan

This section recommends several actions, based on international good practice, to address the challenges encountered in developing occupational standards and to integrate them into Kazakhstan's vocational education and training (VET) system for the petrochemical and chemical industry.

Recommendation 1: Put in place a domestic institutional structure to enable OS to support a well-functioning VET system

The government should strengthen the permanent domestic structure for creating, monitoring and updating occupational standards. Implementing this recommendation will involve three actions: 1) strengthening the institution responsible for creating and updating occupational standards, backed up with sufficient, qualified staff and appropriate financing; 2) developing mechanisms for public-private dialogue; and 3) fostering domestic expertise in developing occupational standards.

Action 1: Assign an institution for creating and updating standards

A single institution, such as a skills council, should be responsible for occupational standards in petrochemistry and chemistry, and should act as a secretariat for their development. The institution should ideally be outside government, to avoid it being dominated by civil servants. Having one institution with clear responsibility and powers will be important for streamlining procedures and standards. For example, in the United Kingdom, a skills council called Cogent Skills maintains occupational standards in science-based industries. In Ukraine, the Institute of Professional Qualifications is a non-governmental co-ordinating body aiming to contribute to a commonly recognised system of professional qualifications, including assistance to employers in developing occupational standards (Kolyshko, 2014[37]). In order to prepare for establishing a formal body in charge of developing occupational standards, a working group could be established to launch the process in the petrochemical and chemical industry at the national level. The institution should have access to labour market information to help identify the skills and qualifications that are in demand. It could either gather these data on its own, or commission them from other organisations. Labour market information is also important for career guidance and for accrediting VET programmes based on their correspondence to market needs. To date, career guidance services in Kazakhstan's VET institutions do not seem to have adequate data to undertake their work effectively (Álvarez-Galván, 2014[16]). The institution should also study current national and international trends in sector employment and forecast future trends for the sector to help it decide which qualifications and occupational standards should be introduced. It should then conduct working sessions with employers to define the standards. Once agreed, the standards should be made available on the registry of occupational standards, maintained by the Ministry of Healthcare and Social Development and the Ministry of Justice. The institution should regularly update the standards, either through a formal, timetabled approach or through an informal approach, "on the demand" of employers.

The institution will need sufficient funding – for core staff and infrastructure, as well as for the working sessions with employers. Standards-setting organisations usually rely on a variety of funding sources: from government resources, international resources, grants and levies from stakeholders, product sales and services, etc. In the United Kingdom, Cogent Skills spent on average EUR 61 215 on finalising 30 occupational standards (the range in the United Kingdom is approximately EUR 40 810-122 428), excluding costs to employers for sending their employees to standard-development sessions (Cogent Skills, 2014[38]). On the other hand, it is standard practice for employers to cover their employees' costs in working sessions with employers. In France, a specific tax on salaries is paid by enterprises to fund vocational training. Enterprises can be partially exempted from this tax when their employees take part in vocational training, for example, as members of assessment bodies or bodies in charge of designing qualifications.

Should funding be limited, then generic occupational standards could be adopted from other countries (e.g. financial management or human resource management). Generic occupational standards are non-sector-specific. However, sector-specific occupational standards should be developed by the sector itself. This could possibly be done by adapting overseas occupational standards, but not by adopting external examples unchanged.

Action 2: Develop mechanisms for public-private dialogue

International good practice dictates that occupational standards should be employer-led to ensure that they reflect business needs. To achieve this, Kazakhstan should establish effective mechanisms for public-private dialogue, including:

- **Strategic public-private working sessions**: public-private working sessions are the ideal forum for developing occupational standards. They must bring together a mix of employer and employee representatives. Ideal representatives of the "employer" are actual job holders or first line supervisors. If they are not available, training managers and people responsible for relevant business functions (e.g. managers of departments concerning manufacturing, quality assurance, engineering and technology) could participate. Should human resource managers be involved, it should be mainly to support the process, with the substantive part being developed by the employer representatives. The working groups can be complemented by interviews, company visits, document analysis and surveys (Bosch and Spilioti, 2013[39]). Since private sector participation is not well developed in Kazakhstan, the government could encourage it using a range of tools, such as financial support or memoranda of understanding with employers.
- **Well-structured and strong professional sector associations:** the government of Kazakhstan should ensure that sector associations for petrochemistry and chemistry are well-developed and can voice their concerns to the institution charged with developing occupational standards. However, the petrochemical industry does not have its own sector association. The KazEnergy sector

association currently represents the interests of the oil and gas sector, and the government-run holding United Chemical Company and the chemical industry union represent the interests of several chemical companies. A special effort must be made to include SMEs in the associations, as their needs might be quite different from those of larger companies.

- **Strong links between the industry and the VET system:** the government should explore other means to engage employers in the VET system. This includes strengthening the Kazakhstan VET Council on the Petrochemical Industry by including an adequate number of private sector representatives; increasing transparency in its decisions, meeting dates and outcomes; and ensuring that membership information is made available online. Boards of Trustees in education institutions should also include enough private sector representatives. Work-based training promotes partnership between education providers and employers and should be encouraged (OECD, 2014[12]). This comprises apprenticeships, informal learning on the job, work placements that form part of formal vocational qualifications and internships of various types. In the longer term, Kazakhstan should encourage education institutions to obtain more of their funding from the private sector itself.

It must be kept in mind that in a context in which the private sector is not used to close collaboration with the education sector, the government might need to play a leading role. For example, in most EU partner countries, it has been difficult to involve industry in the development of new occupational standards, therefore public authorities have had to remain the driving force (ETF, 2011[40]). This is due to the lack of representative organisations at national and sectoral levels, as well as the absence of professional capacity among social partners to deal with VET matters in the context of reform.

Action 3: Foster national expertise in developing occupational standards

Domestic expertise is very important for occupational standards, as they are more effective and have more stakeholder buy-in when they are developed domestically. The national structure for occupational standards should ideally be supported by two types of local expertise:

5. Technical experts with knowledge of the industry who can lead the standard-development sessions with employers. The role of these experts would be to moderate working sessions with industry representatives to agree on the content of occupational standards. These experts should ideally be citizens of Kazakhstan with a good knowledge of the industry and of the education sector. They will need to be trained in occupational standards methodology to avoid the risk of over-emphasising the technical side to the detriment of the other aspects of employability.
6. Local experts with knowledge of the local education and VET system. These experts should work in the secretariat for creating and updating occupational standards.

To build national expertise, effective mechanisms should be used to exchange knowledge between international experts and domestic experts. Any local staff participating in international projects should pass on their knowledge to other local stakeholders in the ministries and associations through training sessions. To begin with, a survey of existing experts should be conducted. Lists of local experts with knowledge of developing occupational standards should be maintained and regularly updated to keep track of experts from government agencies and companies.

Recommendation 2: Integrate occupational standards into the VET system

The value of occupational standards lies in their use by the education system and employers to create study programmes, as well as to guide assessments and certification. Occupational standards are part of an integrated VET system, providing the basis for education standards, outcome-based curricula, and assessment of qualifications (Figure 4.3). This second recommendation includes three actions: 1) put in place education standards and curricula based on occupational standards; 2) base assessments and certification on occupational standards; and 3) put in place a monitoring and enforcement mechanism to ensure that occupational standards, education programmes and certifications are aligned.

Figure 4.3. The link between occupational standards, curricula and assessment

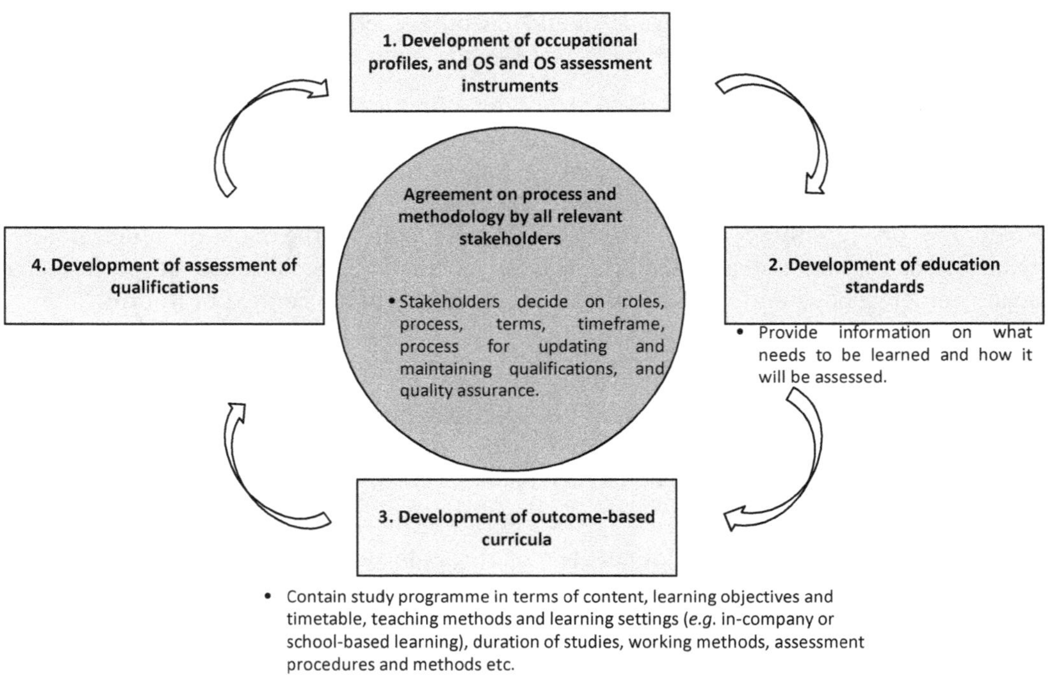

Source: (Bosch and Spilioti, 2013[39]; Fretwell, Morgan and Deij, 2001[41]; Cedefop, 2009[42])

Action 4: Put in place education standards and curricula based on occupational standards

Despite their cost, competency-based curricula, which focus on outputs (what students learn to do) are gaining popularity the world over, because of their greater ability to respond to employer needs. For example, they are used in Australia, New Zealand and most European countries. Kazakhstan should create competency-based curricula based on occupational standards, which it can facilitate through education/training standards.

Education/training standards should contain information on outcomes and processes. For example, they can contain information about:

- learning content (such as the required learning activities)
- teachers (the required teaching methods and teacher qualifications)
- the assessment of achievement (methods to be used and evidence required)
- process (such as the duration of programmes and the desirable learning location or environment).

Even though the required teaching methods are set out, teachers should retain the freedom to implement their own initiatives and to teach additional aspects beyond the standards. It should be kept in mind that students might not be able to learn all competencies in the education institution, therefore education on site in a company or at least in a control room or maintenance shop is very important for teaching the use of work equipment. Kazakhstan is strongly encouraged to include credit-bearing segments of work-based learning in any VET programme to ensure alignment between occupational standards, curricula and industry needs.

The content and format of education standards vary from country to country; Kazakhstan should select a structure that suits its circumstances. The government should develop education/training standards through stakeholder working groups, interviews and questionnaires with employers and employees, and visits to companies.

Employers and education institutions should then create study programmes based on the guidelines provided by such standards and involve awarding bodies (organisations that award qualifications) from the beginning of the process. While some organisations that develop education/training standards also develop curricula, the co-ordinating institution should delegate this time-consuming task to a different organisation or at least a different department. Due note must be given here to the training of teachers, to ensure that they can deliver training programmes of good quality.

Action 5: Base assessments and certification on occupational standards

Kazakhstan should base its assessment tools for graduates on occupational standards (competency-based assessment). This means that in addition to education/ training standards, it should use assessment standards to test what people are able to do in their occupations, including knowledge, skills and performance. In most European countries, for example, qualifications (diplomas) are based on three types of standards: occupational/professional standards, education/training standards and assessment standards.

The assessment of a given occupational standard must clearly test the demand that the occupational standard places on the future employee. The competences that students have gained outside of an academic course should also be assessed. Assessment standards should also be used to recognise competencies gained on the job, to up-skill and re-skill the current workforce. The assessment standards can include knowledge tests in written or oral format, as well as observation of work performance (UNESCO-UNEVOC, 2006[43]).

While assessment standards will usually be written by the same organisation that developed the occupational standards, e.g. a sector skills body, they also require pedagogical and industry input. As a minimum, they should be developed together with the stakeholders who helped to write the initial occupational standards. It is advisable that assessment instruments and bodies be run by private companies. They will need both trained assessors and verification personnel (who verify that assessors themselves are performing well; most of them are former assessors themselves), who could be both internal and external to companies. The government and/or the assessment companies must adequately train staff to conduct assessments properly, and share the assessment requirements with students and trainers. Particular attention should be paid to standardising the assessments across the country, including assessment conditions (e.g. working environment for the practical aspect). Additionally, care must be taken to avoid redundant assessment layers.

Action 6: Put in place a monitoring and enforcement mechanism to ensure that occupational standards, education programmes, assessments and certifications are aligned

Once the framework for qualifications and certification is in place, Kazakhstan should establish a monitoring and enforcement mechanism. It should task qualified inspectors to visit training institutions and evaluate the adherence of study programmes and assessment instruments to the developed occupational standards (see Box 4.3 for an example from France). In Kazakhstan, this could be the role of a skills council.

Box 4.3. France's system for monitoring qualifications

The system of inspection in France consists of two levels:

- Inspectorate General for National Education (IGEN - *Inspection Générale de l'Education Nationale*). This organisation is responsible for monitoring, studying and assessing the education system's operation and effectiveness. Its evaluations focus particularly on the types of training, programmes, teaching content, teaching methods, procedures and resources implemented. It also assesses management, teaching and inspectorate staff, as well as taking part in evaluation missions alongside other departmental, regional education authorities and international bodies. The general inspectorate is also in charge of a specific body called CERPEP, which helps to enhance links between teachers and companies, especially by organising internships for teachers in private or public companies in France and elsewhere in Europe. These internships help teachers to better understand the specific needs of the sector, and to be aware of any changes in technology.
- Regional inspectorates. The regional inspectorates are assigned to specific territories, and the inspectors are state officials. They are under the authority of their area's Chief Education Officer and work in liaison with the Inspectorate General. Among other things, they assess teaching content, teachers and schools. In the specific field of VET, they are also in charge of organising and monitoring examinations, and can lead or participate, at national level, in the groups of experts (from education and sectors) in charge of designing qualifications. They are also in charge of disseminating information about sector needs and changes in the qualifications of their field of expertise.

Source: OECD Analysis.

Recommendation 3: Raise awareness of the value, process and application of occupational standards in a well-functioning VET system

The creation and application of economically effective occupational standards depends heavily on input from key stakeholders. Employers are the main participants in the creation of standards and must be aware of the procedure, as well as their expected role. Similarly, education institutions must be aware of the existing standards and the process for applying them to their education programmes and assessments. Thus, it is recommended that the government regularly conduct training and seminars on the concept, methodology and the role of all stakeholders.

Action 7: Conduct regular training and seminars on the concepts, methodology and the roles of all stakeholders

The institution in charge of occupational standards should conduct regular training in the concepts; the methodology it expects companies to use; their integration into curricula, assessments and certification; and the role of various counterparts in the process. The training should be targeted at government officials, employers and actors in the education sphere who design curricula, assess student performance and award qualifications. The government should intensify its efforts to reach out to the regions and private companies. International experts in the subject should be invited to these seminars, especially at the beginning of the process. Training should include workshops and other participative forums for developing the actual draft occupational standards.

Importantly, the benefits of occupational standards should be clearly communicated to stakeholders to encourage them to participate in creating and applying them. For example, employers should be informed about the occupational standards' positive impact on productivity, the quality of products, cost savings, new work processes, new technology adoption and innovation.

As it can take several years for a national structure of occupational standards to have an impact on education and employment, it is important that a sense of urgency is communicated during the training and seminars.

The government should also conduct similar training on competency-based curricula which are based on occupational standards, because they are likely to involve new ways of teaching and learning.

The way forward

Successful implementation of the policy recommendations will depend on the following factors:

- **Continuous consultation with all relevant VET stakeholders**. The government should consult with the users of occupational standards – employers – in creating the standards. It should also consult with education institutions to determine the applicability of occupational standards in education curricula, assessments and the certification of qualifications. This is crucial for ensuring the relevance and application of the occupational standards. A first helpful step might be to develop a matrix showing the roles of all the actors involved (Bosch and Spilioti, 2013[39]).
- **Policies based on accurate statistics and evidence-based analysis of the VET system**. Any decisions to create or modify occupational standards should be

based on statistics and analysis of the need for qualifications, drawn from labour market analysis and employer feedback.

- **Policy design and implementation that draws from international and existing domestic experience**. The government should follow international good practice in creating and applying occupational standards. While relatively new in the post-Soviet economies, occupational standards have a longer history in European education systems and in other countries such as Australia and Canada. Kazakhstan can also draw from domestic experience in developing occupational standards for other sectors, such as oil and gas, and tourism.
- **Effective monitoring and evaluation.** Kazakhstan should continuously monitor its occupational standards and their use to see if they are easy to understand and apply and if there is a need for additional standards. To be cost effective, only useful occupational standards should be kept; too many standards should be avoided. The government should also keep track of the quality of the entire VET system, including stakeholder involvement, the rate of VET trainee employment after completion of training etc. (Bosch and Spilioti, 2013[39]).
- **Strong leadership**. The development and application of occupational standards requires strong government leadership, as well as leadership of sector associations. It is also useful to have a pioneer company in petrochemistry or chemistry that is firmly committed to the issue to promote occupational standards and rally other companies in the sector.
- **Well-sequenced changes**. It is important to keep in mind that other aspects of the VET system must be improved in order to ensure that occupational standards have a lasting effect. Improvements are needed to the quality of infrastructure, teaching and work-based learning; as well as to forecasting skills needs, independent assessment, statistics on skills, and the assessment of government activity. Additional recommendations for improving the VET system in Kazakhstan can be found in the OECD publication *OECD Reviews of Vocational Education and Training, A Skills beyond School Review of Kazakhstan*.
- **Piloted change**. Kazakhstan is encouraged to run a pilot scheme for developing occupational standards to attempt to satisfy some urgent industry needs before the structures and processes are fully developed. This pilot scheme could focus strategically on the most needed skills and levels. For this, a clear understanding of skills requirements is necessary.

Table 4.2 presents a roadmap for policy implementation, including the expected timeframe for each of the individual policy actions.

Table 4.2. Suggested implementation roadmap for Kazakhstan

Recommendations	Indicative implementation timing		
	Short term < 1 year	Medium term 1-3 years	Long term > 3 years
Recommendation: Put in place a domestic institutional structure to enable OS to support a well-functioning VET system			
Action 1: Assign an institution for creating and updating standards.	■		
Action 2: Develop mechanism for public-private dialogue.	■		
Action 3: Foster national expertise in developing occupational standards.	■	■	
Recommendation: Integrate occupational standards into the VET system			
Action 4: Put in place education standards and curricula based on occupational standards.		■	
Action 5: Base assessments and certification on occupational standards.		■	
Action 6: Put in place a monitoring and enforcement mechanism to ensure that occupational standards, education programmes, assessments and certifications are aligned.		■	■
Recommendation: Raise awareness about the value, process and application of OS to support a well-functioning VET system			
Action 7: Regularly conduct training and seminars on the concepts, methodology and the role of all involved stakeholders.	■	■	■

Kyrgyzstan: Implementing workplace training

Skills gaps are a major concern for firms in Kyrgyzstan. In 2013, the OECD designed recommendations to improve human capital for businesses in the country, focusing on the development of workplace training activities. Three years later, the OECD monitored the implementation of these recommendations, and provided new insights into how to further support the use of workplace training in Kyrgyzstan, such as creating formal requirements for internship agreements, further expanding career centres in vocational education and training (VET) institutions, and establishing online job platforms.

Context: Skills gaps in Kyrgyzstan's workforce

In 2013, limited human capital development was identified as an important constraint on Kyrgyzstan's competitiveness, especially in agribusiness. Skills gaps – disparities between the skills of the existing workforce and the needs of employers – were negatively affecting labour productivity. For example, labour productivity in agriculture was the second lowest in the region, at USD 1 414 per worker in 2013, equivalent to only 8% of the average for OECD countries due to several factors, including limited skills and lack of machinery (World Bank, 2016[44]). Agricultural sector employers surveyed by the OECD mentioned employees' lack of skills and training as one of the top barriers to their activities (OECD, 2014[45]).

Skills gaps were widened by the limited involvement of private companies in human capital development, in particular in workplace training. Partnership agreements signed between educational institutions and private companies appeared to be limited to a few cases – such as several Bishkek vocational schools in the fields of transportation, telecommunications, and garment manufacture. The 2013 OECD survey showed that less than one-quarter of employers in agribusiness processing were working with educational institutions, and only 24% were providing students with workplace training, apprenticeships, internships and mentoring (OECD, 2014[45]).

Policy recommendations were prepared in 2013 and are outlined below.

This note was developed in consultation with the Government of Kyrgyzstan, private sector companies, business associations, and development partners during the monitoring process. It assesses the implementation progress made in the last three years, and makes recommendations for further progress.

Overview of 2013 recommendations

The 2013 review concluded that the government could bridge the skills gap through workplace training and raising the overall involvement of the private sector in vocational education and training (VET). Workplace training, such as internships and apprenticeships, teaches students the practical skills demanded by the labour market. It can "help close the skill gap by facilitating students' access to modern technology and to the latest innovations in the industry and accelerating the transfer of knowledge between the educational system and firms" (OECD, 2014[45]). It can also provide employers with a properly trained labour force, help them promote employment in the sector and improve their interactions with educational institutions. Workplace training programmes build tripartite relationships among the employer, the student and the education institution, based on formal and contractual links (Figure 4.4).

Figure 4.4. Workplace training programmes

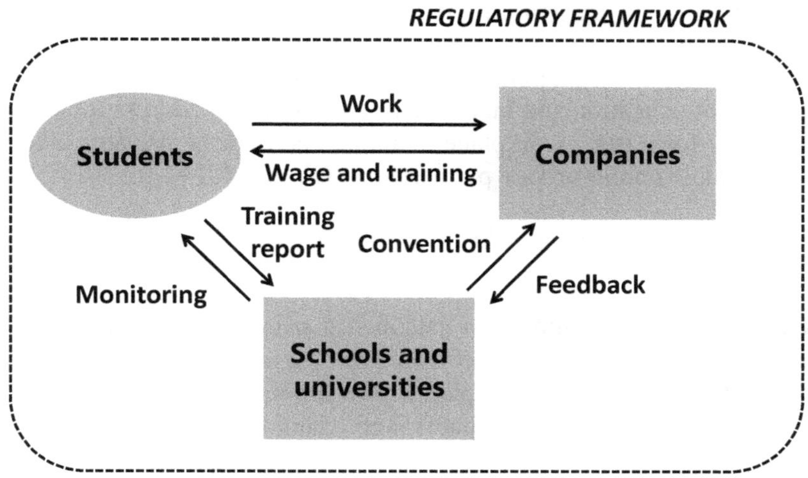

Source: Adapted from (OECD, 2012b[46])

Recommendation 1: Put in place a regulatory and incentives framework for workplace training

The Labour Code regulates training and retraining of staff, including workplace training. The 2013 review recommended measures to enhance the regulatory framework and define the legal boundaries for all parties involved, in particular by setting up a minimum wage for interns and apprentices, establishing duration requirements of training, and considering the inclusion of financial incentives to encourage employers to offer workplace training, such as tax incentives and exemptions from contributions to the social fund.

It also suggested that the government could further strengthen the legal framework by establishing formal tripartite conventions that define the responsibilities and duties among the employer, the student and the education institution. These conventions could include information on the duration of the internship, missions assigned to the intern, competences to be developed through the internship, compensation, code of conduct, insurance and termination of the internship.

Recommendation 2: Increase private sector involvement in workplace training

Co-operation between employers and educational institutions on workplace training programmes is crucial for their success. However, the 2013 review concluded that this co-operation could be expanded beyond the limited bilateral partnerships common at the time by engaging students, companies, and educational institutions alike. This would create a greater sense of ownership of the programmes by engaging all parties in sustainable and formal co-operation. Business associations could also play a key role in collecting business needs, structuring the activities and contributions of business, and mobilising them.

Employers' involvement could be stimulated by providing internships on a competitive basis to ensure that the most motivated and qualified students are selected.

Kyrgyzstan had established public-private skills councils at the national level through the National Council for Professional Skills Development, and at sector level through sector sub-councils, including in agriculture. However, the review recommended that these exchange platforms be revitalised to ensure an on-going dialogue on public-private co-operation in education among employers, business associations, education institutions, and the ministries of education and labour. Discussions could address topics such as skill requirements and forecasts, workplace training activities, private involvement in education and possible public-private partnerships (OECD, 2014[45]).

Recommendation 3: Improve matching of students with training places, including in agribusiness

The review advised the government to establish a national job portal that would help match students and companies, and promote the image of specific sectors and career paths (OECD, 2014[45]).This electronic platform would bring together available job offers, and provide information on career paths and training opportunities in educational institutions.

To strengthen and formalise co-operation with employers, the review suggested that education institutions could also establish career centres as points of contact between students and employers. They could be in charge of reaching out to businesses and co-ordinating activities with them, including creating and following up on workplace training programmes. For example, the education institutions could implement a monitoring system for internships by occasionally visiting and interviewing employers during the internship period. At the end of a workplace training programme, firms could prepare a feedback report for the student and the education institution. This would not only act as a formal certificate, but would also outline the competencies developed by the student and how his/her skills match the companies' needs. This feedback would guide schools on adjusting curricula, while helping the student upgrade skills to match work opportunities.

In 2013, companies were paying income tax and social contributions on the wages of interns and vocational trainees. The review recommended that the government consider exempting internships and apprenticeships from tax and social charges to give them additional incentives to take on interns (OECD, 2014[45]).

2016 monitoring assessment

The government has conducted a number of important reforms in line with the 2013 policy recommendations, particularly to the regulatory framework. These reforms have been implemented with the involvement of business associations through the Chamber of Commerce and Industry.

Monitoring of Recommendation 1 underscores new draft regulations for workplace training

Recommendation 1: Put in place a regulatory and incentives framework for workplace training

The Government of Kyrgyzstan has drafted amendments to the Labour Code to develop workplace training activities. The policy process has been broadly consultative, involving private companies through the Chamber of Commerce and Industry, and the public by posting the draft law on the Internet for comments.

The amendments emphasise the principle of promoting both the interests of students and companies. Their objectives are to improve skills matches for the benefit of employees and employers; to encourage companies to use workplace training activities; and ultimately to provide jobs and employment. Another objective is to reduce the high rate of emigration driven by high unemployment, although other factors – such as low salaries – are also to blame (Government of Kyrgyzstan, 2016[47]).

The draft amendments make a clearer distinction between vocational training contracts (on-the-job and formal training for current employees) and student internships/apprenticeships that was not explicit in the previous version of the Labour Code's articles. They define the expected content of student contracts (for internships and apprenticeships) and introduce training contracts (including retraining for existing employees). These will help to facilitate arrangements between employers, employees and students, and to standardise contractual practices. The contract should include the names of the parties, the student's/employee's specialities, the employer's and the student's/employee's obligations, and the training period. The training contract should specify the employee's conditions and pay during the training. Changes to the contract can only be made with the agreement of both parties (Government of Kyrgyzstan, 2016[47]).

However, the amendments to the Labour Code do not establish a mechanism governing the relations among the employer, the student and the education institution during an internship. Many details are left out of the contract, and are subject to an agreement between the parties, including financial matters, such as payment or reimbursement of expenses, and the detailed organisation of the training period.

The draft amendments set an upper limit of 12 months for the duration of internships and apprenticeships. This can help avoid the abuse of internships as positions of permanent employment by employers. This upper limit is in line with laws in France (6 months), Germany and Italy (12 months), which include restrictions on renewing the internship contract (OECD, 2014[45]).

The updated Labour Code also proposes introducing mandatory compensation and a salary cap for interns. Mandatory compensation is a welcome addition, as it avoids companies benefiting from unpaid labour. Such measures are in line with several OECD countries, such as France and Germany, although legislation in OECD countries typically provides for a minimum compensation level instead of a maximum (OECD, 2014[45]).This salary cap might help contain the tax exemptions and insurance premiums stipulated in the draft Tax Code (see below). In Switzerland, the average salary of an apprentice is around 25% to 30% of a permanent employee's salary according to the Swiss Federal Institute for Vocational Education and Training (SFIVET).

The drafting process has now been transferred from the Ministry of Economy to the Parliament's Commission on Social Issues. Although this might lead to substantial revisions to the next versions of the draft amendments, it shows that the process is moving forward.

Monitoring of Recommendation 2 highlights greater private stakeholder participation

Recommendation 2: Increase private sector involvement in workplace training

The engagement of stakeholders in VET reforms and workplace training activities has increased since 2013, for instance with the development of several career centres. The strong involvement of the Chamber of Commerce and Industry in preparing the amendments to the Labour Code is a positive sign in this regard. Some higher education and VET institutions have also developed action plans for increasing business involvement and establishing boards of trustees, which aim to involve companies in the governance of educational institutions. However, these still need to be implemented in most educational institutions. A first step would be to assess these initial initiatives and to launch additional ones with government support. This could lay the foundations for a strong co-operation model in education in Kyrgyzstan.

The governance of the Kyrgyz education system involves meetings between educational institutions and companies through the National Business Council and sub-sector councils. The frequency of these meetings has increased in recent years, especially in the agribusiness sector according to interviews carried out by the OECD with the Agency of Vocational and Educational Training of Kyrgyzstan and local experts on education as part of the horizontal policy assessment (ADB, 2013[48]; OECD, 2016[49]). The Agency of VET of Kyrgyzstan also conducts regular consultations with employers. These efforts need to be sustained to improve the consultation with and involvement of the private sector in education when designing and implementing policy reforms to the education system.

However, a vibrant internship market has still not developed. Competitive recruitment processes for interns and apprenticeships remain rare and have only been reported in selected sectors, such as banking. This may reflect the lack of employers' interest and engagement in conducting proper recruitment processes and might foster adverse selection of students. Employers report that they lack incentives to hire interns, and need too much time to retrain them on the job. Agribusiness companies also point to the limited attractiveness of their sector to students and the small number of available qualified applicants as interns (OECD, 2016[49]).

Monitoring of Recommendation 3 finds that finding placements for students is being held back by insufficient instruments and incentives

Recommendation 3: Improve matching of students with training places, including in agribusiness

Kyrgyzstan is drafting amendments to the Tax Code to increase the incentives for companies to recruit interns and apprentices, and to promote the active participation of companies in workplace training. According to the draft amendments, companies would be exempt from paying taxes on income, social contributions, and insurance premiums on wages paid to interns/apprentices and vocational trainees. They could also deduct the cost of the preparation and implementation of training activities (Government of Kyrgyzstan, 2016[50]).

Instruments to match supply and demand among the private sector, students and education institutions are still insufficiently developed, including in agriculture. In OECD countries, career centres within educational institutions are useful contact points to build sustainable operational relations between students and companies, share internship opportunities, and seek more involvement from companies in teaching and training activities (OECD, 2016[49]). Although there have been some initiatives to set up career centres within educational institutions, job portals and fairs, for instance in the agricultural sector, these are fragmented and of limited scale and impact (Box 4.4).

Box 4.4. Matching of students with training centres in Kyrgyzstan

Several tertiary schools in Kyrgyzstan have established career centres to improve connections with companies. These include the Bishkek Academy of Finance and Economics, Talas State University, and the Academy of Public Administration under the President of the Kyrgyz Republic in Bishkek (OECD, 2016[51]).

Several job internship platforms have also been established, but with limited scope and number of applicants. These platforms aim to help match internship demand with offers by public and private stakeholders. For instance, the national internship programme organised by the Youth Foundation, Instream, in partnership with the Ministry of Education, has set up an electronic platform where applicants can submit internship requests (Instream, 2016[52]).

Fairs are organised periodically in Kyrgyzstan to promote markets and products in selected sectors, including agro-processing. Job fairs are also regularly held to promote training and retraining opportunities in the sector and involving education institutions. Their impact on hiring and on raising the interest of students in careers in sectors such as agriculture remains limited.

Source: (OECD, 2016[51]; Instream, 2016[52])

The way forward

The government needs to enact, implement and monitor the amendments to the labour and tax codes: this is a prerequisite for the development of workplace training activities in Kyrgyzstan. Further improvements can also be made to foster relations between all parties, including the introduction of an internship contract/agreement (see Box 4.5), the expansion of existing career centres, the enhancement of existing VET and skills councils, and the establishment of online job platforms.

Box 4.5. The *Convention de stage* in France

France established the *Convention de stage* to simplify and formalise internship relationships among students, companies and educational institutions. The *Convention de stage* is regulated by law, but remains flexible enough to be adapted to the various needs and conditions of internships. It governs the relations, rights and duties of students and companies during the course of the internship. It helps better define roles and responsibilities for all parties and enshrines them in a legal document to ensure that each party fulfils its obligations.

The French Ministry of Labour has published a template on its website to simplify procedures and minimise the administrative workload for businesses, while adequately protecting students. A typical *Convention de stage* includes information on registration at a university or school; signatories (the intern, a representative of the university and a representative of the firm); objectives (acquisition of competencies); activities of the intern; duration; compensation; management; accident labour protection; termination of the contract; code of conduct; and the requirement for an internship report. Three copies of the document are signed, one for each party.

Source: (Ministry of Labour, Employment, Vocational Training and Social Dialogue, 2016[53])

The government will submit the amendments to Parliament in 2016. Effective implementation will require careful monitoring of the impact on business and educational institutions' practices, and adjustments may be needed. Among the OECD countries, France has passed several amendments to its provisions for internships and professional training in the labour and education codes over recent years to avoid abuse by the parties involved. In the latest version (2014), the maximum duration of internships was reduced from 12 months to 6 months, the number of interns has been limited within each company, and students have been granted new rights concerning leave and expenses (Ministry of Labour, 2014[54]). Switzerland also has lessons to share on the duration and organisation of workplace training (Box 4.6).

Box 4.6. Public-private collaboration in education in Switzerland

In Switzerland, vocational education and training are based on the dual track system involving education institutions and employers, which is the country's central concept. "Dual" means part-time: 3.5-4 working days are spent by the apprentice at a host company, combined with 1-1.5 working days of classes at a public vocational school. Switzerland has also defined a template for apprenticeship contracts to ensure these contracts cover all the required conditions; they are signed by the three parties.

Employers and professional associations are engaged with and actively contribute to professional education. The Swiss Vocational and Professional Education and Training (FPVET) system is collectively managed as a public-private partnership. It works efficiently because on the one hand it is close to the needs of the economy and market-driven, and on the other it is given state recognition and quality control.

Three main partners play a specific role in the management and implementation of the VPET system (based on the Federal Act on Vocational and Professional Education and Training of 2002):

- The Confederation (federal government) is responsible for strategic planning and development of the entire system. It seeks to achieve comparability and transparency as well as national recognition of qualifications and encourages innovation.
- The cantons (state government) are mainly responsible for the overall supervision of VET programmes. They ensure the quality of work-based training and of classroom instruction, monitor examinations and ensure that apprenticeship contracts are in line with statutory provisions. Furthermore the cantons are responsible for general implementation. They run vocational schools, issue VET accreditation to host companies, provide young people and adults with vocational and career guidance counselling, and take responsibility for the training of instructors.
- The private sector is represented by trade and branch associations as well as their member companies and social partners (employer's unions and trade unions). These associations are mainly responsible for defining and continuously updating training content, with the involvement of representatives of the VET schools and cantons. Individual companies create apprenticeship positions and pay a salary to the apprentices. Companies need to have at least one professional instructor who meets the required professional skills and personal characteristics. Host companies must also obtain a permit from the local cantonal authority.

Building on a long tradition of vocational education and training, Swiss companies consider apprenticeships as beneficial for several reasons. First, the net profit generated by an apprentice exceeds the net expenditures in most professional branches due to the productive work of apprentices. Second, apprenticeships help companies make sure that they have the necessary number of employees with the required competencies, and reduce recruitment costs if the apprentice stays in the company. Third, they boost the reputation of the company, as Switzerland has implemented a specific and prestigious label for companies training apprentices. Finally, professional organisations have the possibility to create their own VPET fund to support workplace training.

Sources: (Strahm et al., 2016[55]; Fazekas and Field,(n.d.)[56])

A formal requirement for internship agreements could be introduced: this could further formalise internship relations, and build trust among companies, students and education institutions by strengthening mutual rights and obligations. The government could prepare a draft document to be discussed with employers, including the Chamber of Commerce and Industry, and publish it as a template for internships on the website of the Ministry of Labour and Social Protection (MLSP), mirroring practices in France, which has amended its Labour Code to introduce mandatory internship agreements (Box 4.5). The *Convention de stage* is a simple, flexible contract signed by the parties that regulates their relationships and specifies the objectives and the conditions of the internship. A formal requirement could also be applied for the interns' report after completing workplace training.

Beyond the establishment of internships, education institutions could prepare companies better: education institutions should conduct preparatory sessions for companies to explain the requirements, conditions and benefits of the internship as well as the expected role of the supervisor. This preparation could raise companies' awareness, increase the quality of the workplace training, and minimise bureaucracy for businesses. They should also provide support during the internship. In Switzerland, each company must have one employee trained in managing an internship/apprenticeship process and supervising interns before hiring an apprentice.

Promotional websites and events could be part of the education promotion and communications strategy in specific sectors, in addition to existing career fairs. The Ministry of Agriculture, in particular, could consider revitalising the sector's image by promoting career paths and opportunities in the sector in association with educational institutions and companies. This could include the creation of a dedicated website for agricultural education promotion and information (or at least a dedicated space on the ministry's existing website), presentations of and training by companies in VET institutions and schools, and active involvement of agricultural schools in education promotion and fairs.

Career centres in educational institutions need to be further expanded to become key contact points between businesses and the education system. Existing career centres should be assessed for the number of internships and jobs found by students and the number of companies met and partnerships signed. They should share good practices with similar teams in other education institutions and follow the principles described below for creating new ones. Where career centres do not exist, they could be created in most tertiary education institutions, replicating the example of several OECD countries. The assessment and adjustment of existing career centres would help build a model to be rolled out in education institutions. These centres could proactively investigate labour market opportunities and administer workplace training offers by liaising with companies, making these offers available to students, and monitoring the internship/apprenticeship period on behalf of the educational institution. Business and engineering schools in France have created career centres that are very active in matching students and training places through a wide range of activities, including online job and internship platforms, managing students' professional curricula, following-up on legal provisions, mentorship, communicating with companies, and organising career fairs.

Public-private dialogue on VET could be further supported through the National Council and the sub-sector councils: this will involve more regular meetings with precise agenda and the inclusive involvement of stakeholders. For example, in the United Kingdom, the UK Commission for Employment and Skills and Sector Skills Councils helps ministries identify skills needs and solutions, create the conditions for increased investment in skills, and raise skill levels across the economy. These councils are industry-led and gather a limited number of members, including business leaders from large firms, SMEs, trade unions, central and local government representatives, non-governmental organisation, and education institutions (UK Commission for Employment and Skills, 2012[57]). Switzerland also offers a good example of close public-private collaboration in education. Education institutions, the government, and companies partner to run the VET system, including workplace-training activities (Box 4.6).

Online job platforms are useful tools to match students and employers. Existing platforms could be further supported by the MLSP. In addition, dedicated sections on existing websites, such as the official sites of the Agency of Primary and Secondary Vocational Education and the MSLP, could be used to display job offers. This would be cheaper than creating and maintaining new job platforms. Until these platforms are implemented, educational institutions need to use pin-boards and so on to display offers for students. They could also use youth centres and other local information centres to disseminate job and internship offers. A good model is the platform established by the French Ministry of Agriculture (Box 4.7).

Box 4.7. Promoting agricultural education in France

The French Ministry of Agriculture promotes and provides information on agricultural education on a dedicated platform (www.educagri.fr). Students and young workers can find all information on education institutions, training paths, degrees, certification and internships on the website.

The ministry also organises career fairs to bring together companies and job seekers as well as educational institutions, who can promote their training and retraining offers to employers and job seekers). This includes annual "open door" days in all agricultural education institutions in France.

Source: (Ministry of Agriculture, Food and Forests of France, 2016[58])

Since the 2013 recommendations, it has appeared that incentives and promotion actions for employers need to be increased. Companies cited the insufficient initial, formal training of students as the main reason for their limited interest in internships and apprenticeships. Awareness could be raised on the new amendments and incentives: informing companies of the new tax and financial incentives for their hiring of interns and apprentices might promote greater uptake of this effective m150eans to train this upcoming branch of the labour force. This may also call for increasing companies' involvement in educational institutions, for instance, by inviting them to schools to give lectures, training, company presentations and regular meetings with directors, teaching staff and career advisers of the institution. Kyrgyzstan could also study Switzerland's instruments (Box 4.6) and consider implementing some of them to promote the use and benefits of workplace training to employers.

Notes

[1] The percentage of firms identifying an inadequately educated workforce as a major constraint is described as the percentage of firms identifying labour skill level as a major constraint to the current operations of the establishment in the World Bank's *Enterprise Surveys Indicator Descriptions*.

[2] This chapter will not assess the VET system as a whole, but focuses on the key instruments that involve SMEs and the private sector at large, and examines selected VET instruments useful for SMEs. Assessing and redesigning the whole VET system would also involve examining additional characteristics and instruments that are beyond the scope of this report, such as decision-making mechanisms on provision and meeting needs, avenues of progression from initial VET to both higher-level vocational and academic programmes, the vocational teaching workforce, and funding arrangements.

References

ADB (2013), *Private sector assessment update - The Kyrgyz Republic, Country Sector and Thematic Assessments*, http://www.adb.org/documents/private-sector-assessment-update-kyrgyz-republic. [48]

ADB (2016), *Strengthening the Labor Market in Mongolia: Skills for Employment Project in Mongolia.* [15]

Álvarez-Galván, . (2014), *A Skills beyond School Review of Kazakhstan*, http://dx.doi.org/10.1787/9789264221826-en. [16]

American Chemistry Council (2015), *Chemical Industry profile*, http://www.americanchemistry.com/Jobs/EconomicStatistics/Industry-Profile. [29]

Ashurov (2015), *The main challenges and trends in VET system of Tajikistan, Presentation to Istanbul University, 10-11 March 2015.* [17]

Bosch, P. and C. Spilioti (2013), *OPEP: From Occupational Profiles to Educational Standards and Programmes: A Roadmap Based on Practical Experiences*, European Vocational Training Association. [39]

Business Monitor Kazakhstan (2013), *"Oil and Gas Report Q2".* [33]

Cedefop (2009), *Dynamics of Qualifications: Defining and Renewing Occupational and Educational Standards..* [42]

CEFIC (2013), *Competitiveness of the EU Chemical Industry, a Key Sector in the Refining Value Chain.* [26]

Central Communications Service under the President, O. (2015), *Central Communications Service under the President of the Republic of Kazakhstan*, http://ortcom.kz/en/briefing/the-ministry-of-health-and-social-development-developed-more-than-900-new-professional-standards-until-2020.6619. [36]

Cogent Skills (2014), *Sector Skills Councils, Rationale and Roles*, Cogent. [38]

Cogent Skills (2015), *About Cogent Skills*, http://www.cogentskills.com/about-cogent-skills/. [35]

Dzekunov, V. and et al. (n.d.), *Нефтехимическая промышленность: мировой опыт развития и казахстанский потенциал (Petrochemical Industry: Global Experience in Developing it* [30] *and Kazakhstan's Potential)*, Centre for physical and chemical methods of study and analysis of the Kazakh National Al-Farabi Institute.

EBRD (2015), *Strategy for the Kyrgyz Republic*, http://www.ebrd.com/documents/osg/kyrgyz-republic-country-strategy.pdf. [25]

EBRD (2017), *Business Environment and Enterprise Performance Survey (BEEPS) data base*, http://ebrd-beeps.com (accessed on 15 March 2017). [8]

ETF (2011), *Developing Qualification Frameworks in EU Partner Countries*, Anthem Press. [40]

ETF (2014), *Torino Process 2014: Tajikistan*, European Training Foundation. [14]

ETF (2014), *Torino Process 2014: Uzbekistan.* [18]

ETF (2015), *Torino Process 2014: Central Asia.* [19]

ETF (2015), *Turkmenistan Overview of Vocational Education and Training and the Labour Market, Update 2015.* [20]

ETF (2016), *Central Asia: Regional Strategy Paper 2017-2020.* [21]

European Union and GOPA (2016), *National Qualifications Framework (NQF) in Central Asia, Stock-tacking report.* [13]

Fazekas, M. and S. Field((n.d.)), *A Skills beyond School Review of Switzerland*, http://dx.doi.org/10.1787/9789264062665-en. [56]

Fretwell, D., V. Morgan and A. Deij (2001), *A Framework for Defining and Assessing Occupational Standards in Developing Countries.* [41]

G20/OECD (2015), *High-level Principles on SME Financing*, https://www.oecd.org/finance/G20-OECD-High-Level-%20Principles-on-SME-Financing.pdf. [4]

G20/OECD (2015), *The G20 Skills Strategy for Developing and Using Skills for the 21st Century*, Prepared for the third G20 Employment Working Group Meeting. [5]

Government of Kyrgyzstan (2016), *Draft Law of the Kyrgyz Republic "On Amendments to the Labor Code of the Kyrgyz Republic"*, Government of Kyrgyzstan. [47]

Government of Kyrgyzstan (2016), *Draft Law of the Kyrgyz Republic "On Amendments to Certain Legislative Acts of the Kyrgyz Republic"*, Government of Kyrgyzstan. [50]

ILO (2011), *Restructuring, employment and social dialogue in the chemicals and pharmaceutical industries.* [28]

Instream (2016), http://instream.kg. [52]

KazMunaiGas (2015), *Modernisation of Refineries*, http://www.thkmg.kz/en/modernization. [34]

Kolyshko, R. (2014), *Legal and Institutional Aspects for Developing Occupational Standards in Ukraine*, Institute of Professional Qualifications. [37]

KPI Inc. (2015), *Atyrau Petrochemical Complex.* [31]

Ministry of Agriculture, Food and Forests of France (2016), *"Enseignement agricole", website (in French)*, http://www.educagri.fr (accessed on 3 June 2016). [58]

Ministry of Labour and Social Protection of Mongolia (2016), *ICT for Skills Development in Mongolia, Presentation to the CASIE 2016, Astana 2016.* [22]

Ministry of Labour, Employment, Vocational Training and Social Dialogue (2016), *Template* [53]

Convention de Stage (in French)., http://travail-emploi.gouv.fr/IMG/pdf/convention_stage_tripartite.pdf (accessed on 3 June 2016).

Ministry of Labour (2014), *Law n° 2014-788 of 18 July 2014 related to the development , the management of internships and the improvement of the status of interns*, http://www.legifrance.gouv.fr/affichTexte.do?cidTexte=JORFTEXT000029223331&categorieLien=id. [54]

OECD (2009), *Clusters, Innovation and Entrepreneurship, Local Economic and Employment Development (LEED)*, http://dx.doi.org/10.1787/9789264044326-en. [23]

OECD (2010), *Learning for Jobs, OECD Reviews of Vocational Education and Training*, OECD Publishing, http://dx.doi.org/10.1787/9789264087460-en. [2]

OECD (2012b), *"Enhancing skills through public-private partnerships in education in Ukraine, the case of agribusiness", Private Sector Development Policy Handbook*, https://www.oecd.org/countries/ukraine/UkrainePPPEducation.pdf. [46]

OECD (2013), *Skills Development and Training in SMEs, Local Economic and Employment Development (LEED)*, OECD Publishing, http://dx.doi.org/10.1787/9789264169425-en. [9]

OECD (2013), *Developing Skills In Central Asia Through Better Vocational Education And Training Systems.* [10]

OECD (2014), *Improving skills through public-private partnerships: The case of agribusiness, Private Sector Development Policy Handbook.* [7]

OECD (2014), *Skills Beyond School: Synthesis Report, OECD Reviews of Vocational Education and Training*, OECD Publishing. [11]

OECD (2014), *Skills beyond School Synthesis Report*, http://dx.doi.org/10.1787/9789264214682-en. [12]

OECD (2014), *Improving skills through public-private partnerships in the Kyrgyz Republic: the case of agribusiness*, http://www.oecd.org/globalrelations/ImprovingSkills%20(3).pdf. [45]

OECD (2015), *Strengthening Kazakhstan's Skills in Petrochemistry and Chemistry through Occupational Standards*, unpublished. [1]

OECD (2016), *Monitoring Competitiveness Reforms in Kyrgyzstan. Draft Peer Review Note*, unpublished. [3]

OECD (2016), *Horizontal policy assessment of Kyrgyzstan*, unpublished, OECD. [49]

OECD (2016), *Anti-corruption reforms in Eastern Europea and Central Asia - Progress and Challenges 2013-2015*, OECD Publishing. [51]

Polytechnic College (2015), *VET Experience of Atyrau Polytechnic College.* [32]

Strahm, R. et al. (2016), *Vocational and Professional Education and Training in Switzerland: Success factors and challenges for sustainable implementation abroad*, http://www.hep-verlag.ch/media/import/preview/vocationaleducation.pdf. [55]

UK Commission for Employment and Skills (2012), *Annual Report and Accounts 2012*, http://www.gov.uk/government/uploads/system/uploads/attachment_data/file/247007/0281.pdf
. [57]

UNESCO (2017), *Using ICTs and Blended Learning in Transforming TVET.* [6]

UNESCO-UNEVOC (2006), *The development of a national system of vocational qualifications*, [43]

Discussion Paper Series, No. 2, UNESCO-UNEVOC International Centre for Technical and Vocational Education and Training.

Union of Chemical Industries of Lyon (2015), *Chemistry in Rhone-Alpes*. [27]

United Chemical Company (2015), *Programme concept for the professional preparation of staff for chemical companies*, United Chemical Company. [24]

World Bank (2016), *World Development Indicators, database*, http://data.worldbank.org/indicator. [44]

Annex A. Country factsheets

Annex Table 1. Key indicators: Kazakhstan

Country profile	
Population, 2016	17.8 mn
Surface area, 2016	2724.9 thsd. km^2
GDP (USD, current price), 2016	133.66 bn
GDP per capita (USD, current price), 2016	7,510
Real GDP growth (y-o-y change), 2016	1%
Inflation (average consumer price, y-o-y change), 2016	14.6%
Exports of goods and services (% of GDP), 2016	32.6%
Imports of goods and services (% of GDP), 2016	29.2%
FDI, net inflows (% of GDP), 2015	3.6%
General government net lending/borrowing (% of GDP), 2016	-4.37%
Unemployment (% of total labour force), 2016	5.04%
Remittances (% of GDP), 2016	0.2 %

Source: World Bank (2017), World Development Indicators, database, http://data.worldbank.org/indicator, (accessed 14 August 2017); IMF (2017), World Economic Outlook Database https://www.imf.org/external/pubs/ft/weo/2017/01/weodata/index.aspx (accessed 14 August 2017).

Annex Table 2. Key indicators: Kyrgyzstan

Country profile	
Population, 2016	6.08 million
Surface area, 2016	199 949 km^2
GDP (USD, current prices), 2016	6.55 billion
GDP per capita, (USD, current prices), 2016	1 077
Real GDP growth (y-o-y change), 2016	3.8%
Inflation (average consumer prices, y-o-y change), 2016	0.4%
Exports of goods and services (% of GDP), 2015	37.3%
Imports of goods and services (% of GDP), 2015	73.5%
FDI, net inflows (% of GDP), 2015	17.1%
General government net lending/borrowing (% of GDP), 2016	-4.5%
Unemployment (% of total labour force), 2015	7.6%
Remittances (% of GDP), 2016	30.5%

Source: World Bank (2017), World Development Indicators, database, http://data.worldbank.org/indicator, (accessed 14 August 2017); IMF (2017), World Economic Outlook Database https://www.imf.org/external/pubs/ft/weo/2017/01/weodata/index.aspx (accessed 14 August 2017).

Annex Table 3. Key indicators: Mongolia

Country profile	
Population, 2016	3.03 million
Surface area, 2016	1,564.1 thsd. km^2
GDP (USD, current prices) 2016	11.16 billion
GDP per capita (USD, current price), 2016	3,856.8
Real GDP growth (y-o-y change), 2016	+1.0%
Inflation (average consumer prices, y-o-y change), 2016	0.6%
Exports of goods and services (% of GDP), 2016	50.8%
Imports of goods and services (% of GDP), 2016	46.8%
FDI, net inflows (% of GDP), 2015	0.8%
General government net lending/borrowing, percentage of GDP, 2016	-17.05%
Unemployment (% of total labour force), 2016	10%
Remittances (% of GDP), 2016	2.4%

Source National Statistical Institute of Mongolia official website, www.1212.mn (accessed 14 August 2017); World Economic Indicators, World Bank, http://data.worldbank.org/indicator (accessed 14 August 2017); IMF (2017), World Economic Outlook Database https://www.imf.org/external/pubs/ft/weo/2017/01/weodata/index.aspx (accessed 14 August 2017).

Annex Table 4. Key indicators: Tajikistan

Country profile	
Population, 2016	8.7 mn
Surface area, 2016	142 550 km^2
GDP (USD, current price), 2016	6.9 bn
GDP per capita (USD, current price), 2016	804
Real GDP growth (y-o-y change), 2016	6.9%
Inflation (average consumer price, y-o-y change), 2016	6.1%
Exports of goods and services (USD), 2016	961 mn
Imports of goods and services (USD), 2016	4 bn
FDI, net inflows (% of GDP), 2016	5.4%
General government net lending/borrowing (% of GDP), 2015	-1.87%
Unemployment (% of total labour force) 2017	10.8%
Remittances (% of GDP), 2016	26.9%

Source: ADB (2017), Asian Development Outlook 2017; NBT (2017), Survey on Saving Behaviour; IMF (2017), World Economic Outlook, April 2017; United Nations (2017), International Migrant Stock 2015; (Federal Migration Service of the Russian Federation, 2016).

Annex Table 5. Key indicators: Turkmenistan

Country profile	
Population, 2016	5.7 mn
Surface area, 2016	488,100 km^2
GDP (USD, current price), 2016	36.2 bn
GDP per capita (USD, current price), 2016	6,389.3
Real GDP growth (y-o-y change), 2016	6.2%
Inflation (average consumer price, y-o-y change), 2015	7.4%
Exports of goods and services (% of GDP), 2012	73.3%
Imports of goods and services (% of GDP), 2012	44.4%
FDI, net inflows (% of GDP), 2015	11.9%
General government net lending/borrowing (% of GDP), 2015	-0.693%
Unemployment (% of total labour force), 2015	8.6%

Note: The Economist Intelligence Unit's estimation of the inflation rate in Turkmenistan is 16% in 2015 and 11% in 2016, while the IMF indicates a price increase of 7.4% in 2015 and 3.5% in 2016.
Source: World Economic Indicators, World Bank, http://data.worldbank.org/indicator (accessed 14 August 2017); IMF (2017), World Economic Outlook Database https://www.imf.org/external/pubs/ft/weo/2017/01/weodata/index.aspx (accessed 14 August 2017). The Economist Intelligence Unit, Country Report, Turkmenistan (accessed 7 August 2017).

Annex Table 6. Key indicators: Uzbekistan

Country profile	
Population, 2016	31.8 million
Surface area	447 400 km^2
GDP (USD, current prices), 2016	67.2 billion
GDP per capita, (USD, current prices), 2015	2 132
Real GDP growth (y-o-y change), 2016	7.8%
Inflation (average consumer prices, y-o-y change), 2016	8.4%
Exports of goods and services (% of GDP), 2015	20.7%
Imports of goods and services (% of GDP), 2015	22.2%
FDI, net inflows (% of GDP), 2015	1.6%
General government net lending/borrowing (% of GDP), 2014	2.2%
Unemployment (% of total labour force), 2016	8.9%
Remittances (% of GDP), 2016	3.4%

Source: World Bank (2017), World Development Indicators, http://data.worldbank.org/indicator; IMF (2016a), World Economic Outlook, April 2016, www.imf.org/external/pubs/ft/weo/2016/01/; ADB (2017), Asian Development Outlook 2017, http://www.adb.org/publications/asian-development-outlook-2017-middle-income-challenge.

Annex B. Details of country projects

The report covers the work and analysis of the OECD Eurasia team on Central Asia from 2015 to 2017, as part of the "Central Asia – Investment and Competitiveness" project, co-funded by the EU.

The first chapter - "A regional agenda for economic diversification in central Asia" – and the "Setting the stage" parts of Chapters 2, 3 and 4 are the results of desk research and consultations with Governments and other stakeholders from the region, from the OECD and from partner organisations.

The country studies presented in Chapter 2, 3 and 4 are the results of country-specific projects on competitiveness carried out by the OECD in close collaboration with the governments of each country that were discussed and peer-reviewed at the OECD Eurasia Competitiveness Roundtable. The OECD Eurasia Competitiveness Roundtable is a policy network that brings together high-level representatives and technical experts from Eurasia countries, OECD members and partner organisations. It meets annually and serves as a platform for peer review and knowledge sharing on the implementation of competitiveness reforms in the Eurasia region.

For Kazakhstan, Mongolia and Uzbekistan, the study includes the output in-country projects carried out in 2015, 2016 and 2017. In all three, the OECD and the government established Public-Private Working Groups that met two to three times a year, and conducted fact-finding missions. The aim of these groups was to strengthen the analysis and develop policy recommendations through a structured dialogue with all relevant stakeholders in the country and the support of international experts and peer reviewers from OECD member economies. The policy recommendations were endorsed by the respective governments during the OECD Eurasia Competitiveness Roundtable, respectively in its 2015, 2016 and 2017 editions.

For Kyrgyzstan and Tajikistan, two in-country projects were carried out in 2013 and 2014 in an earlier phase of the project. The report includes the monitoring of the implementation of the policy recommendations endorsed during this previous phase. The monitoring followed a similar structure, with Public-Private Working Groups gathered by the OECD and the government to discuss advancement and issues on the single policy recommendations. The monitoring took place respectively in 2016 and 2017, three years after the first endorsement of the recommendations. The monitoring has been approved, respectively, by the OECD Eurasia Competitiveness Roundtable 2016 and 2017.

ORGANISATION FOR ECONOMIC CO-OPERATION AND DEVELOPMENT

The OECD is a unique forum where governments work together to address the economic, social and environmental challenges of globalisation. The OECD is also at the forefront of efforts to understand and to help governments respond to new developments and concerns, such as corporate governance, the information economy and the challenges of an ageing population. The Organisation provides a setting where governments can compare policy experiences, seek answers to common problems, identify good practice and work to co-ordinate domestic and international policies.

The OECD member countries are: Australia, Austria, Belgium, Canada, Chile, the Czech Republic, Denmark, Estonia, Finland, France, Germany, Greece, Hungary, Iceland, Ireland, Israel, Italy, Japan, Korea, Latvia, Luxembourg, Mexico, the Netherlands, New Zealand, Norway, Poland, Portugal, the Slovak Republic, Slovenia, Spain, Sweden, Switzerland, Turkey, the United Kingdom and the United States. The European Union takes part in the work of the OECD.

OECD Publishing disseminates widely the results of the Organisation's statistics gathering and research on economic, social and environmental issues, as well as the conventions, guidelines and standards agreed by its members.

OECD PUBLISHING, 2, rue André-Pascal, 75775 PARIS CEDEX 16
(03 2017 11 1 P) ISBN 978-92-64-28812-6 – 2018

www.ingramcontent.com/pod-product-compliance
Lightning Source LLC
Chambersburg PA
CBHW061211240926
51846CB00006B/1185
* 9 7 8 9 2 6 4 2 8 8 1 2 6 *